crave

ED SMITH

Photography by Sam A Harris

Hardie Grant

QUADRILLE

This is for anyone who is currently thinking about their next meal, but can't decide in which direction to turn.

Contents

Introduction

What am I going to eat next?

I spend most of my waking hours thinking, *"what am I going to eat next?"* Probably some of my sleeping hours too. You?

Until recently, I thought a successful answer to this never-ending question was typically inspired by what lies in my fridge, or what seasonal ingredient is currently at its peak, or what condiment or carbohydrate has most recently caught my eye. But, on reflection, I realize that ingredients are the building blocks, not the answer, nor the strategy.

And so it continues: *"What am I going to eat next?"*

Much of the messaging in food media seems to take a *"this is what you *should* be cooking right now"* approach: *"try this cuisine"*; *"use your leftovers"*; *"cook like this chef"*; *"eat seasonally"*.

Yes, to all of these things. But also, how mind boggling. It's probably counterproductive to a (still relatively fresh) cookery writer's career to state it, but there's too much choice. Or, more specifically, recipes are rarely organized in a way that means we efficiently find something that'll hit the spot.

Indeed, at the genesis of this book it struck me that we've found ourselves looking at things the wrong way round. Aspiring to master new (to us) cuisines, to use up our leftovers, to cook like a pro, and to eat ingredients at their peak are relevant. But these are relatively minor and distracting sub-themes when there's something more visceral that sits above them all: most of the time we simply cook the things we do so that we can eat what we fancy. It's no more complicated than that.

With that realization in mind, I set about writing a cookbook that would provide a bit of clarity, order and direction when we respond to our rumblings. In doing so, I concluded that the solution to *"What am I going to eat next?"* is actually best found by asking another question: *"What flavours am I craving right now?"*

On that note, I believe that we can most successfully choose what to cook by organizing recipes into six different flavour profiles.

These are:

– Fresh and fragrant
– Tart and sour
– Chilli and heat
– Spiced and curried
– Rich and savoury
– Cheesy and creamy

So that's what this book offers: six sections based on those flavour profiles, each ready and waiting to answer the call, depending on whichever you are craving.

Of course it's a simplistic approach, not least because many of the best cuisines and recipes balance the full range of tastes and multiple flavours. However, more often than not, dishes have a key characteristic or an edge that can be categorized under one of these six flavour profiles, and that might well be the key reason to cook the dish, or reflect the urge that you need to sate. Thinking along these lines is a starting point. It's a new, if ultimately obvious, framework.

Why we crave what we crave when we do

This cookbook is not about pseudo-scientifically analyzing your physical and mental state and then dictatorially prescribing recipes. It's just me suggesting a way to respond to your hunger. I should probably just stop writing at this point and let you turn to the recipes...

... However, it seems worth noting that each section does begin with a little discourse as to the what, and a little on the why and when. I also thought that I should, at the outset, at least briefly cover a few of the reasons why I think we crave what we crave when we do. Something to maybe reflect on once you're sitting down with food in front of you, or at another time when you're not yet hungry (if such a time exists).

To crave

The verb 'to crave' is often used in the context of unstoppable urges for sweet and fatty decadence; for giving in to so-called 'guilty pleasures' so we can drown our sorrows.

This is reductive. We get 'cravings' for all sorts of foods and in response to a wide range of triggers. I know that, for every time I feel an urge to buy a buttery treat or to wolf down a tub of ice cream, there are tens of times when I've craved a plate of fresh mango seasoned with chilli and lime, a green salad dressed in little more than good olive oil and lemon juice, or some grilled fish and a simple (but spot on) tomato salad. I crave things that are healthy and light, mellow or savoury, fiery and punchy, more often than I do something saccharine or fatty. I'll wager it's the same for you too.

If cravings don't only arise so that you can apply a sugary, sticky (yet not particularly long-lasting) bandage to a broken heart, what other triggers are there?

Weather

We frequently talk and read about how important and beneficial it is to cook and eat seasonally. Mostly that's in the context of ingredients tasting better when they're at their peak, and/or with food miles in mind.

But eating seasonally also means to eat food that feels appropriate to whatever is going on outside: food that feels right for the moment, both in terms of how it is prepared, and the effect that it has. A creamy, cheesy, rich and heavy dish rarely appeals to either the cook or the eater during a summer heatwave, but on a wet Sunday in winter, few things are more satisfying.

The seasons are shifting, though, aren't they? Here in the UK (a once temperate nation) it often feels like we meet peak summer for a week in April then intersperse mini-heatwaves with dark skies and autumnal winds through June and July; there are blue-sky days in December, and today (in late October), we've had a little bit of everything, each time prompting me to want something different for dinner. So, in terms of cravings, it's actually probably more useful to talk about how weather affects what we want to eat on a day-to-day (or hour-to-hour), rather than quarterly, basis.

There's no doubt in my mind that weather is one of the biggest (if not *the* biggest) drivers of food cravings. Step back next time there's a slight change in the meteorological norm and notice how the food you put on your own plate changes, not to mention what you'll see across whichever social media channels you tune in to. Hot days mean light-touch cooking, fresh ingredients and flavours, often something sharp or a hint of chilli to enliven us. Colder days are more likely to prompt braises, stews, bowl food, pastry, dairy and carbs, this time with heat and spice to warm us up. It's instinctive, and I think you know this already.

To compound its importance, weather also really, really affects our mood. Which is another theme that shapes what we crave.

Mood

Happy food = fresh, zippy and zesty.
Sad food = muted, plain, maybe creamy.

There's truth in all of that and I mention similar motivations throughout this book. But these things are never black and white, are they?

There are many articles exploring 'comfort eating' – a concept so frequently anecdotally linked to so-called 'guilty pleasures'. Most tend to assume universal experience of those moments when boredom, stress, hangovers and sadness apparently push us to overeat fats and sugars.

Research indicates, however, that comfort food is diverse, generally tends to be food that is familiar and, in particular, relates to a memory of protective and/or happier times. For many that means the food of their childhood. As a result, we're often pointed towards roast chicken, chicken soup, beans on toast. True for many, I'm sure. But, also, largely blind to the fact that home cooking can also mean spice, heat and flavour. Moreover, that many people's happy reference might be much later on in life, when their exposure to different cuisines results in a sweet spot far removed from bland offerings (indeed, on a personal note, I find spiced foods to be one of the first places to which I retreat).

Much of what I've read also points to research that suggests many crave 'healthy' rather than 'guilty' food when they need comfort, and that actually the effect of gorging on grains and vegetables tends to lead to a quicker bounce back, both physically and emotionally. It's not a particularly controversial topic, but it is emotive and the discourse is wide-ranging. Ultimately, though, it mostly affirms two of my key instincts: that mood does indeed affect what we want to eat; and the reasons for a flavour craving are personal and varied. That is why I leave those to you and just offer six flavour profiles to aim at, whatever your mood.

Green eyes

I'm writing this book with the assumption that it'll generally be used when you're thinking rationally about food. That is to say, neither starving, nor gluttonous. Still, there is something known as 'hedonic hunger', which essentially relates to thinking about and anticipating the reward of eating for the sake of pleasure, and in the absence of calorific need. And I suppose this will often at least partially apply.

It has been suggested that thinking of and/or seeing tasty food is one of the most common motivations for food cravings. Whether it's the case that you find yourself wanting certain foods as you browse a cookbook, watch adverts, television or film, or while you scroll social media, I'm sure this one makes sense to you. The impact of an image can be instant, though for me more often than not certain images just seem to stick in my mind, gradually becoming more prominent until they can't be ignored. I have the same thing with memories of food that I've actually experienced – in a restaurant or on holiday – which snowball to the point of obsession.

In these instances, it tends to be a specific dish that's making us salivate. Which I suppose could undermine the whole premise of this book, save I'd argue that the dominant sensation you crave is the anticipated flavour of that dish: the salt and savoury umami in a burger, the cheesy creaminess of cacio e pepe, the sparky, life-affirming freshness of a salad bowl.

Hedonic hunger exists. Don't feel bad about it. Just be aware, and rationalize your cravings back to those flavour profiles...

Biology

To paraphrase a school of noble philosophers, you can't escape your biology.

There's no doubt that cravings are often a response to things going on within your body. Beyond the largely hedonic hunger-style triggers already mentioned, there are undoubtedly times when the flavours you seek relate to things your body needs. You recall those times when only verdant vegetables and salads will suit? They probably all relate to deficiencies in iron, magnesium and the various vitamins you'd become deprived of.

—

Those are some of the factors that affect your appetite. I imagine they resonate, and there are many, many scientific papers on all of them if you want to go beyond my very light-touch approach.

But I also want to stress again that *Crave* is not a cookbook that claims to match a specific dish to whichever influence has the strongest pull. I don't believe that's truly possible, nor would it be helpful. Rather, it approaches the issue from the other direction, with the six flavour profiles there to help you home in on what it is that you're after, regardless of why it is that you need it. Your cravings – the motivation for browsing a specific chapter on a particular day – will be instinctive and personal, and your memories and moods are different from mine. Sometimes you'll simply crave a particular flavour, and you don't need to think about or justify that. I just want to facilitate the intuitive pleasure of cooking and eating what you fancy, whatever the reason you fancy it.

Scratching the itch

Certain cravings need instant sating. There are recipes in here for that: noodles that are combined with store-cupboard ingredients for a meal within minutes; spiced nuts to have on hand; relatively speedy salads and assemblies; wilted greens on toast.

However, not all cravings arrive kicking and screaming at the last minute, nor is a quick fix the best way to respond. In fact, most of the time our cravings will be gently nudging us when we're only just beginning to contemplate the next meal, or when planning meals to be eaten in a few days' time. That's also reflected in many of the recipes, all of which are things that are cooked from scratch. You might need to buy an unusual ingredient or two (though you'll then have those on hand for the next time). You might need to do a bit of prep and wait a while for the result. I'm not going to apologize for that. Sometimes it takes a few grunts and awkward postures to scratch an itch. Sometimes delicious food takes a bit of effort and/or time.

My 'style' of cooking is not unique. It's just about coercing decent ingredients into a pleasurable meal. I've got a fair amount of experience and my intuition for flavour combinations seems good, but I like to think that what I really offer is an organized mind and a refreshing approach to planning your meals. So, as with my first cookbook, *On the Side*, my intention is for *Crave* to be a true resource: a place to come for an easy answer, because I've done half the thinking for you.

Undermining everything I've said so far, I do of course recognize that flavour might not be the first thing that comes to mind when you're staring at the fridge, nor is it necessarily the only sensation that will provide gratification. As such, and consistent with my first book, there's also a directory of alternative cravings (page 242) at the back of *Crave*, which provides another way in to the recipes. Here you'll find recipes organized according to other urges: what to cook when you want something soft or crunchy, if you're on your own or to share, and what's best when the weather is really, really hot (or freezing cold).

Finally, I view my recipes and cookbooks as a starting point. By all means be pragmatic and tweak the recipes to suit your own ideas and experience. In particular, please do use the concept of choosing from six flavour profiles to refine where and how you look for ways to sate your cravings. There are answers here, but there are also so many other good places and people to look and learn from. Check out the further reading on page 246.

—

What's the weather like? How was your day? Have you been dreaming about your last trip abroad? And are you now hungry? Before you stare into your fridge, flick desperately through cookbooks, mindlessly browse the internet, or simply throw the first thing you can at your rumblings, just focus in on the key question: *"What flavours am I craving right now?"*

Ed Smith
London, October 2020

Cooking with me

So that we are on the same page:

For best results — Sorry to 'splain, but do always read the ingredients and method to the end, and decide what to assemble and prepare before you begin to cook.

Oven temperature — Conventional oven temperatures are included, but I always use the fan oven setting.

Teaspoons and tablespoons — are technically measurements of volume: meaning 5ml and 15ml, respectively. When specified, measuring spoons will give best results (though it won't be the end of the world if you pick a spoon from the drawer and guesstimate).

'Unusual' ingredients — None of the store-cupboard ingredients are actually that unusual and all are used at least twice through the book (for example 'nduja, tamarind, dried shrimps, the various spices, leaves and specialist chillies). Hopefully you can find other recipes, too, to help make use of them, and so they'll become staples for you as well. Suppliers suggested on page 247.

Oils — Neutral cooking oil means sunflower or vegetable (rapeseed/canola) oil. I tend to use the latter. Cold-pressed rapeseed oil is the extra virgin equivalent of that oil; when I use it, it's largely because of the nutty taste, though it also has a high smoke point. Olive oil is always extra virgin if used to dress and virtually always the rest of the time; although light olive oil is fine if large quantities are required.

Dairy — Butter is salted. Cream is double (approximately 48% fat – heavy is the closest US equivalent). Milk is always whole (3.5%). Crème fraîche and cream cheese are also always full fat (in part because of flavour, but also because half-/low-fat versions contain stabilizers, which don't behave well when heated).

Eggs — are large unless stated otherwise. In the US and Australia this is extra-large and jumbo, respectively.

Fresh herbs — Depending on the kind of dish or cooking style, I specify either the leaves picked from a weight or number of sprigs, or from the dreaded 'handful' if a precise quantity seems over the top. If that seems a little prescriptive, please note it's just a guide. If ever in doubt, use loads.

Salt — is almost always flaky sea salt. This is particularly relevant where there is a measure (rather than simply a pinch). I use Halen Môn, Maldon or Cornish sea salt.

Spices and condiments — vary in aroma and quality. The chances are that mine will be different to yours. Have a play and season to taste.

Rice — When it's a key element of a recipe, a specific variety and cooking method is set out. When it's just a serving suggestion, rice is whatever variety you prefer and however you like to cook it.

Tamarind — means tamarind pulp (which is sold in blocks). Each recipe using tamarind describes the method of extracting the flavour from the pulp. You can also buy tamarind paste and concentrate, but they vary wildly in strength (and quality) and the recipes do not account for them.

Garlic — Where the preparation is "minced", that means the garlic has been puréed. I use the back of a knife, you might prefer to use a micro-grater, garlic crusher or pestle and mortar.

Ginger — Where the preparation is "minced", that means the ginger has been puréed. I use a micro-grater, or roughly chop then bash with a pestle and mortar.

fresh and fragrant

Fresh and fragrant means salads full of herbs with crisp lettuce leaves cupping and clinging to droplets of perky dressings. It means cold noodles, crunchy raw vegetables, the lactic tang of cheeses like feta, ricotta and burrata, plus ingredients that pop when chewed, inevitably drawing an involuntary smile – peas, sweetcorn, radishes. Fresh and fragrant feels good.

There's rarely much cooking involved (the clue's in the 'fresh') and dishes that fit this theme are as much assemblies of good things as they are 'recipes': chopped salads; cold soups; citrus segments turned savoury through antipasti from the deli counter; lavish plates of pure-white burrata cut open and oozing between perfumed peaches and torn basil; and dippy things such as unapologetically garlicky aioli surrounded by wedges of fennel, blanched and shocked asparagus spears and cauliflower florets. Some of the components might normally be destined for grazing or side dishes. But when fresh and fragrant – and light – is called for, they transform into something more essential and fortifying, and they absolutely hit the spot.

When cooking is required it's a quick steam or stir fry, or it's otherwise gentle and pretty much hands-free. Moreover, the warm (or, once warm) elements are often a support act. For example, later on you'll hopefully find blushing flakes of poached salmon appealing, yet that fish plays second fiddle to the green goddess-dressed salad it sits with. In another gathering of ingredients, warm baby potatoes and shreds of ham hock gratify, but in part that's because their mellow taste, temperature and texture counter the peppery bite of fridge-cold radishes and sweet, grassy asparagus, and otherwise because they soak up the sharp, cooling menthol and anise of a tarragon dressing.

On which note, fresh herbs always bring vitality. So it's no surprise that in this section things like parsley and mint stand out, appearing as they do across multiple dishes. Tarragon, dill, coriander (cilantro) and Thai holy basil do too. Crucially, all of them are used in abundance. Indeed, my general rule of thumb is to think of fresh herbs as an ingredient, not a delicate sprinkle or miserly garnish. If in doubt about quantities, always err on the over-generous: using more of the bunch than you might be conditioned to will be far more gratifying than letting that same bunch wilt and fade in the fridge.

Many of the recipes that follow are inspired by and approximated from dishes typical to warm climates. That's not a strange coincidence: one significant reason to want fresh and fragrant food is because it's hot outside. Whether consciously or subconsciously, balmy days and nights make us want meals redolent of sun-soaked trips abroad. These dishes, the ingredients involved, the low-effort preparation: they're a natural response to sweltering blue skies or muggy, soporific conditions. In such instances we need food that just quietens hunger rather than stuffs us, that leaves us sprightly, not leaden. I also find the moments we associate with this flavour profile are better suited to steamed, baked or poached fish, rather than big hunks of roast or fried meats. Perhaps that reflects a yearning for a coastal holiday. Regardless, you'll note that this chapter is more measured pescatarian than ravenous carnivore.

There are other, non-weather-driven reasons for wanting fresh and fragrant food. I know that when I'm sad or slovenly I'll sometimes crave food that doesn't drag me further down – ingredients that are naturally sweet and light – perhaps because I know it'll bring cheer and energy. Yes, in sullen moments rich and savoury or cheesy and creamy tend to appeal. But science also tells us that if we're dehydrated or our blood sugar levels are low, our bodies desire fresh fruits and vegetables that are relatively high in fructose. So if you're instinctively reaching for some ice cream to slump into, don't ignore a secondary, unexpected pull towards fruits like papaya and melons in perfumed syrups, or apricots and tomatoes paired with salty-sweet honeyed halloumi (plus more of those herbs). Naturally sweet (but not saccharine) ingredients awaken the tongue, make eyes light up and cut through salty and fatty ingredients; just as the sensation of consuming them cuts through heat-induced sloth, bad-news melancholy, self-inflicted dehydration or sugar low, or whatever caused a craving for fragrance in the first place. More often than not you'll feel better for having plumped for the fresh green pill.

Fresh and fragrant might just be the flavour profile I crave most often; and not only prior to, but also at the end of a meal. There are a couple of easy and quick dessert suggestions here, but you might also find satisfaction by simply picking something from the fruit bowl or fridge, and eating the ripest, juiciest samples while standing over the sink, or otherwise roasting or poaching them to soften and draw out flavour, to be served with cold yoghurt. Think also of fruit salads and pastry tarts packed with fruit or citrus-fuelled custards – sweet things that are energizing, spiriting and colourful in every sense.

Burrata with burnt peaches and basil

This mix of burnt peach, basil, pistachio and burrata feels like peak summer on a plate; the perfumed fruit and herbs relax so effortlessly into cold, creamy fresh cheese. Indeed it is something you'll most likely want to eat if the weather matches, or your mind is in holiday mode. A low-effort high-reward assembly, this works well as a starter or a meze-style dish to lazily graze on. The peaches need to be ripe enough to be flavourful, but not so ripe that they're mushy and can't be grilled.

Serves 2 (scales well to serve 4, 6 or more)
—

2 flat peaches or 1 large white peach, pitted and quartered
4–5 tbsp extra virgin olive oil
6–8 basil leaves, largest leaves roughly torn
20g (¾oz) shelled pistachios, roughly chopped
Juice ¼ lemon
125g (4½oz) burrata
Flaky sea salt and ground black pepper

Place a griddle pan or heavy-bottomed frying pan (skillet) over a high heat and allow it to warm for 3–4 minutes.

Brush the peach flesh with a little oil, then place on the (near-smoking) pan and leave to colour for 2–3 minutes. Use tongs to turn the peach segments and char any other cut surfaces, then transfer them to a chopping board. Chop into 1–2cm (½–¾in) dice.

Put the diced peach into a mixing bowl. Sprinkle the basil leaves over the peach, then add three tablespoons of the olive oil along with the pistachios, lemon juice a pinch of sea salt and a couple of grinds of black pepper. Mix well.

Place the burrata in the centre of a plate, using a sharp knife or scissors to open it up, then spread it out a little so the middle oozes out. Spoon the peach mixture over the top, and drizzle with the remaining olive oil.

Chilled cucumber and melon soup

"*Gazpacho*" is always in the top three responses to the question *"What to eat in a heatwave?"* Rightly so: the Andalusian chilled soup is the liquid embodiment of refreshing and you should consume it whenever you feel as though it is too hot to cook. But there are so many very good (or perfectly adequate) versions already out there and I'm not going to add another minor tweak on the ratio of tomato–cucumber–pepper to the mix.

Instead, if the heatwave is ongoing but you can't stomach any more of the red stuff, try this chilled melon and cucumber alternative. To my palate it's at least as tasty and just as revitalizing.

Every soup needs textural contrast in order that it is interesting beyond the third spoonful. In this case, the chopped salad that sits in the middle, seasoned with lemon and mint, seems to double-up the cooling properties of the dish. Crisp, salty, fried coppa adds balance (if you can't find this, use prosciutto or any other cured air-dried ham).

Serves 4

—

1 cantaloupe melon, quartered,
  seeds scooped out and skin cut away
3 large cucumbers, peeled
1 small clove garlic
12 yellow cherry tomatoes
100g (3½oz) ice
1 small banana shallot
2 tbsp extra virgin olive oil, plus extra for drizzling
Juice 1 lemon
8–10 small radishes, quartered
Leaves picked from 2–3 sprigs mint,
  finely chopped
1 tbsp neutral cooking oil
50g (2oz) sliced coppa (or other cured
  air-dried ham)
Flaky sea salt

Serve with crusty bread.

Very roughly chop half the melon and two of the cucumbers, and transfer to a blender jug. Add the garlic, tomatoes, ice, half the shallot, the olive oil, one teaspoon of salt and half the lemon juice, then pulse and blitz for 2 minutes until completely smooth (pass through a sieve/strainer if any flakes or seeds remain). Refrigerate until you've finished the next stage.

Chop the remaining shallot as finely as you can and dice the leftover melon and cucumber into 1–2cm (½–¾in) pieces. Combine them in a bowl, adding the radishes, mint, a good pinch of salt and the remaining lemon juice.

When ready to eat, warm the neutral cooking oil in a frying pan (skillet) over a medium heat. Fry the ham until crisp, flipping just once. Meanwhile, give the chilled soup a good stir (it may have separated a little) and divide between four bowls. Pile the chopped salad in the middle of each bowl, add the crisp ham, and season the soups with a few flakes of salt, a decent glug of extra virgin olive oil, and additional lemon juice if you think it needs it.

Three citrus salads

Current availability of produce means you could make each of these salads, or a variation of them, all year round. Technically, however, European citrus is in season and at its best in winter. Which is a neat coincidence as the vibrant colours and sharp, bracing flavours are a particularly good way to pierce gloomy days and reinvigorate tired minds.

I'd serve them as sharing platters at the start of a meal, with some good bread to mop up juices or oils. Alternatively, assemble as a side salad to go with roast leg or rump of lamb, crisp, golden chicken thighs, feta or burrata, poached salmon or trout, or tuna steaks; or make a real meal of those pairings by adding herb-heavy grains such as bulgur wheat, freekeh or pearl barley.

Each serves 4 as a starter or 4–6 as a side dish

Parsley, orange and grapefruit salad with artichoke hearts and olives

2 oranges
1 grapefruit
200–250g (7–9oz) artichoke hearts
  (in brine or oil), cut into bite-size chunks
120g (4¼oz) plump green olives, halved
  and pitted
Leaves picked from 50g (1¾oz) flat-leaf parsley

For the dressing
1 tsp sherry vinegar
3 tbsp extra virgin olive oil
1 tsp golden caster (superfine) sugar
Juices from the citrus fruits and any oils from
  the olives or artichokes
Flaky sea salt

—

Use a sharp knife to trim the peel from the fruit (slice off the top and bottom first to provide a flat base then work methodically cutting vertical strips down the sides). Chop the fruit into bite-size chunks and transfer to a large mixing bowl. Scrape any juices from the chopping board to a separate bowl and squeeze any juice from the peelings into that too.

Add the artichokes and olives to the fruit. Chop any really large parsley leaves, but keep most whole, like salad leaves, and add to the mixing bowl.

Make the dressing in the bowl containing the reserved juices by combining them with the vinegar, olive oil, sugar and any oils from the artichokes and olives (these might include other herbs and aromatics… which will be lovely!) and a pinch of salt. Beat with a small whisk or fork until emulsified, then pour over the salad, gently tumble and toss, and transfer to a platter.

Ribboned carrot salad with lemon, mint and a honey and orange blossom dressing

2 plump unwaxed lemons
  (or 1 Bergamot lemon, if in season)
2 large carrots, peeled
Leaves picked from 3–4 sprigs mint,
  finely chopped
1 tbsp toasted sesame seeds
Flaky sea salt

For the dressing
2 tsp runny honey
1 tbsp orange blossom
1 tbsp extra virgin olive oil
½ tsp ground ginger
Juice ½ lemon (included above)

—

Squeeze the juice from half a lemon into a bowl for the dressing. Use a sharp knife to cut the peel away from the remaining 1½ lemons, then cut the flesh into 2–3mm (⅛in) discs, and those discs into quarters. Put these in a large mixing bowl and scrape any juices left into the dressing bowl.

Use a vegetable peeler or mandoline to turn the carrots into a tangle of ribbons. Add those to the chopped lemon, along with the mint and sesame seeds and a good pinch of salt. Mix and leave for 5 minutes.

Add the honey, orange blossom, olive oil and ginger to the lemon juice. Beat with a small whisk or fork until emulsified, then pour over the salad, mix again and serve.

Blood orange, ricotta and watercress platter

3 blood oranges (or another variety if blood
  oranges aren't available)
2 tsp moscatel vinegar
  (or other white wine vinegar)
3 tbsp extra virgin olive oil
1 tsp golden caster (superfine) sugar
1 tsp warm water
100g (3½oz) watercress
60g (2¼oz) ricotta
Flaky sea salt and ground black pepper

—

Use a sharp knife to cut away the skin from the oranges, then slice into 2–3mm (⅛in) discs. Lay these on a serving plate, squeezing any flesh left on the skin and scraping any juices into a mixing bowl for the dressing. Into that bowl add the vinegar, oil, sugar, warm water and plenty of salt and pepper, and whisk to combine. Pick the watercress apart so that there's a good balance of leaf and stem to each mouthful, then add to the dressing and toss well.

Sprinkle a few flakes of salt onto each piece of orange, then tip the excess dressing from the mixing bowl over, before dotting the ricotta around the oranges. Finish by placing the dressed watercress on top.

Bún chả

I don't actively seek 'wellness' or a diet of denial in January, yet I do always find myself drawn to this Vietnamese-style pork patty and rice noodle salad at the turn of every calendar year. And it feels kind of healthy... the cold noodles, crunchy and invigorating lettuce and carrots, the aromatic patties, and, crucially, an abundance of fragrant herbs seem to be what my 'new year, new me' cravings require, while a salty, sweet, sour and spicy sauce pulls all of that together in bracing fashion.

There are a few elements, but it's ultimately very easy to put together – something to return to whenever your body is telling you it needs to start over (whether at the beginning of the year, or after a heavy night).

Serves 4

–

For the pork patties
500g (1lb 2oz) pork mince (ground pork)
1 clove garlic, minced
1 small banana shallot, very finely chopped
1 stick lemongrass, very finely chopped
3 tsp golden caster (superfine) sugar
3 tbsp fish sauce
2 tbsp cold water
1 lime, zest finely grated, remainder quartered
1 tbsp neutral cooking oil, for frying

For the sauce
3 tbsp fish sauce
3 tbsp rice vinegar
1 tbsp golden caster (superfine) sugar
1 clove garlic, minced
1 red bird's eye chilli, finely chopped
150ml (scant ⅔ cup) water

For the noodle salad
2 large carrots, peeled
25g (1oz) mint
25g (1oz) coriander (cilantro)
25g (1oz) Thai holy basil
400g (14oz) dried rice vermicelli noodles
1 butterhead lettuce, torn
2–3 tbsp roasted, salted peanuts, crushed
2 tbsp crisp fried shallots or onions
1 lime, zested and quartered (included above)

Combine all the ingredients for the patties into a bowl (except the oil, which is used for frying), mix well, then use wet hands to shape into eight balls, approximately 80g (2¾oz) each. Set on a plate, lightly press into patty shapes and refrigerate until required.

Combine the sauce ingredients in a small bowl.

Cut the carrots into thin matchstick-like strips, ideally using a julienne peeler if you have one, or with a sharp knife and a bit of patience. Cut away the thickest stems from the herbs but otherwise leave as intact sprigs.

Cook the noodles following the packet instructions (usually around 3–4 minutes), drain and either plunge into iced water or cool under a running tap, then drain again, shuffling them with clean fingers to ensure they don't clump together.

To cook the patties, place a large, heavy-bottomed frying pan (skillet) or griddle pan over a medium heat. Add a tablespoon of neutral cooking oil and, once hot, add the patties. Fry for 90 seconds before flipping them and cooking for the same amount of time, then repeat on both sides. Sear the edges too, then remove from the heat.

While the pork patties are cooking, assemble four separate bowls of noodles, adding the carrots, lettuce and fresh herbs. Add the patties and a good sprinkling of peanuts, shallots or onions, and a lime quarter to each bowl, before pouring the sauce over the top.

Not Caesar salad

This is not a Caesar salad, though there are shades of that often loosely interpreted dish here: in the anchovy, Parmesan and egg-yolk dressing; the crouton-like crunch of the smashed, roasted potatoes; and, err, the chicken. But it's fresher than a proper Caesar, too, thanks to the lemon juice and zest plus the copious amounts of mint and parsley, which work in tandem with the cold, crunchy and cooling romaine lettuce and raw courgette, to ensure this is light and invigorating. I eat it often: when I'm after something that mixes an initial blast of raw, herbal salad, and the kind of ballast and comfort that roast potatoes, succulent chicken and a salty, umami-rich dressing can provide.

This is not a Caesar salad but it is the kind of salad that should be in everyone's regularly repeated repertoire.

Serves 2 (doubles well)
–

500g (1lb 2oz) small, waxy new potatoes
2 chicken breasts, skin removed
1 lemon, zest finely grated and juiced
3 tbsp cold-pressed rapeseed (canola) oil
1 romaine lettuce, roughly chopped
1 medium courgette (zucchini),
  cut into 2mm (⅛in) discs
Leaves picked from 25g (1oz) mint,
  finely shredded
Leaves picked from 25g (1oz) flat-leaf parsley
Flaky sea salt and ground black pepper

For the dressing
4 salted anchovies in oil, roughly chopped
1 small clove garlic, roughly chopped
1 egg yolk
½ tsp golden caster (superfine) sugar
⅓ tsp ground black pepper
20g (¾oz) Parmesan, finely grated,
  plus extra to garnish
1 tbsp cold-pressed rapeseed (canola) oil
Juice ½ lemon (from lemon above)

Put the potatoes in a pan of cold water, add half a teaspoon of salt, bring to the boil and simmer for 15–20 minutes, until just cooked through.

Meanwhile, use a heavy object like a rolling pin to bash and flatten the chicken breasts so that they are an even thickness of about 2cm (¾in). In a bowl combine the lemon zest, half the lemon juice, one tablespoon of the cold-pressed rapeseed oil, half a teaspoon of salt and a few grinds of a pepper mill. Roll the chicken in this marinade and set to one side.

Heat the oven to 220°C/200°C fan/425°F. Once the potatoes are just tender, drain and leave to cool (or speed things up under a cold-running tap). Spread the potatoes over a baking sheet and then squash them flat, while still keeping them intact – you could use a fish slice or similar, but I find the palm of my hand the best way. Drizzle with the remaining two tablespoons of cold-pressed rapeseed oil, then roast for a total of 35–40 minutes.

After 15 minutes, make space on the baking sheet and add the chicken breasts. Return to the oven for 15 minutes, then remove the meat and leave to rest on a warm plate, pouring any residual juices over the top. Increase the oven temperature to 240°C/220°C fan/475°F to cook the potatoes for 5–10 minutes more, so their skins are crisp and golden.

While the chicken is cooking, make the dressing: put the anchovies and garlic in a pestle and mortar and pound to a paste. Add the egg yolk, sugar and black pepper and stir vigorously, then add the Parmesan. Stir until well mixed, then drizzle in the rapeseed oil while stirring continuously. Once fully combined, add the lemon juice and stir again. Decant into a large mixing bowl, add the lettuce, courgette and herbs and toss through so everything is coated.

Once crisp, generously salt the potatoes. Chop the chicken into strips, add them and their juices to the salad and mix. Then transfer to shallow bowls, scattering the potatoes among the salad as you do so. Grate a little Parmesan over the top and serve.

Slow-cooked, minted courgettes with white beans and fresh cheese

As you will see in later chapters, I often seek bean-based dishes when either I am, or the weather is, grey and subdued. The act of simmering beans is somehow restorative, and their temperate nature pairs well with other comforting tastes and textures. But to eat beans only in these circumstances would be limiting. Whether swimming in a light broth or tumbled through salad, beans also satisfy when something refreshing is required; they are superb carriers of all things bright, zippy, zesty and herbal.

This gentle assembly conveys the point well: there's a luscious but invigorating gloop of jammy, slow-cooked courgettes, primed with fresh mint and peppery olive oil, some of which is dragged through beans and broth, the rest dropped on top, to be enjoyed alongside a shock of fresh cheese, be that soft chèvre, labneh (strained yoghurt, page 200), ricotta or feta, plus preserved and fresh lemon and more mint. Bowl-and-spoon food to suit hot and lazy days.

By all means soak and simmer the beans yourself. However, I suspect the convenience of pre-cooked beans will suit your likely mood when preparing this dish.

Serves 4

–

20g (¾oz) butter
6–7 tbsp extra virgin olive oil
700–800g (1lb 9oz–1lb 12oz) courgettes (zucchini), sliced into 5mm (¼in) discs
3 cloves garlic, finely sliced
1 lemon, zest finely grated and juiced
Leaves picked from 7–8 mint sprigs, finely chopped
2 x 400g (14oz) cans white beans – butter (lima), haricot (navy) or cannellini beans all work well, drained and liquid set aside
500ml (2 cups) residual bean liquid, water or any stock
200–250g (7–9oz) soft chèvre, labneh, ricotta or feta
1 small preserved lemon, flesh and seeds scraped out, skin finely diced
Flaky sea salt and ground black pepper

Warm a heavy-bottomed lidded casserole or sauté pan over the lowest heat possible. Add the butter and three tablespoons of the olive oil. When the butter has melted, add the courgettes and a generous pinch of salt, toss so the courgettes glisten, then place the lid on top and cook very gently for 45 minutes. The courgettes shouldn't fry and brown, rather they'll mostly steam.

Check the pan from time to time, shuffling the courgettes to swap those on top with those at the bottom. After 45 minutes gently fold the garlic slices into the courgettes, then cook for 15–30 minutes more, or until around three-quarters of the courgettes have fully collapsed. Remove from the heat, season with a little more salt, lots of black pepper and half of the lemon zest, then leave to cool for 15 minutes.

When the courgettes are at a 'just above room temperature' kind of vibe, add half the lemon juice, three to four more tablespoons of olive oil and three-quarters of the mint.

In a large pan, gently heat the beans in the liquid – either from the cans, water or stock. After 5–8 minutes, stir a third of the courgettes through the beans and divide the beans and broth between four bowls.

Spoon the rest of the courgettes into the bowls, add a few scooped teaspoons of fresh cheese to each, then sprinkle over the preserved lemon and the remaining mint and lemon zest. Finish with any oils from the courgette pan, a final glug of olive oil and a little more lemon juice to taste.

Poached salmon
green goddess salad

Succulent, blushing flakes of poached pink fish are among my favourite things to eat when after something revitalizing. Not because the fish cures my itch; more because of the things that tend to go with it. Meaning a salad. Or an assembly involving something like couscous or quinoa. Or something involving both of those things. Which this dish is.

The bright and sharp, tarragon-loaded green goddess-style dressing is what pulls everything together, though there are fresh and cooling ingredients at every turn. You can cook and cool the fregola (or alternatively giant couscous, moghrabieh or maftoul) in advance if 'cooling' is what you're after. Or just cook it to order alongside the fish. Either way, make sure the lettuce, cucumber and avocado are fridge-cold.

Serves 4

—

150g (5½oz) fregola
500g (1lb 2oz) middle section salmon
   or sea trout, skin on
2 ripe medium-large avocados
   (less the quantity used in the dressing)
1 cucumber, peeled, halved lengthways,
   seeds scooped out and discarded, flesh cut
   into 1cm (½in) crescents
1 round or butterhead lettuce, leaves separated
4 tbsp nori and sesame sprinkle
   (see recipe opposite)

For the dressing
60g (2¼oz) ripe avocado
10g (¼oz) tarragon, leaves stripped and
   stalks reserved
15g (½oz) flat-leaf parsley, leaves picked
   and stalks reserved
150g (5½oz) cultured buttermilk or plain yoghurt
2 tsp moscatel vinegar (or white wine vinegar)
Pinch flaky sea salt

Cook the fregola in salted boiling water for the time specified on its packet (usually 10 minutes). Drain through a sieve (strainer) and cool under cold-running water.

Make the dressing by filling a blender with 60g (2¼oz) avocado, the fresh herb leaves, buttermilk or yoghurt and vinegar, and blitz until silky smooth. Taste and add salt, a drop more vinegar and/or loosen with extra buttermilk or yoghurt as you see fit. Decant into a bowl or jug.

To poach the fish, scatter the reserved herb stalks over the base of a saucepan wide enough to comfortably fit the fish. Place the fish on top, skin-side down and fill the pan with cold water. Put the saucepan on a medium-high heat, bring to the point just beyond energetic simmer when it looks like it's about to boil (probably 6–8 minutes) then remove from the heat, place a lid on top and leave it to sit for 8 minutes more.

Cut the remaining avocado into chunks or slices (as you prefer), and arrange with the cucumber and lettuce in a bowl or on a platter. Dollop the dressing generously on and around the salad.

Use a fish slice or similar to lift the fish onto a plate and carefully flip it so the skin faces upwards. The skin should peel off relatively easily (if not it may need a little more time in the poaching water). Use your hands to push the salmon into large, chunky flakes. Sprinkle two to three teaspoons of the nori and sesame mixture over each portion of fish and encourage everyone to help themselves to salad and fregola.

Nori and sesame sprinkle

Nori forms the crisp, edible seaweed sheets used for wrapping sushi rolls and onigiri. Shredded finely, it becomes an incredibly flavourful, savoury seasoning. Combine it with sesame seeds and salt to make a very basic version of the Japanese condiment nori furikake, which you can add to multiple dishes as a no-effort flavour-booster (for example the rice bowls on page 71, soba noodles on page 178 and miso-braised duck on page 195). You could, of course, use store-bought nori furikake instead (often these seasoning mixes will include spices, bonito or dried roe).

Makes a small pot to cover a few 4-person meals
—

3 sheets roasted nori
3 tbsp sesame seeds
Generous pinch flaky sea salt
—

Use scissors to cut the nori into six or eight pieces. Put these into a spice grinder, along with one tablespoon of the sesame seeds and the salt, then pulse about ten times until the seaweed is in small flakes but not yet dusty. Mix with the remaining sesame seeds and store in an airtight container until required.

If you don't have a food processor, fold the nori sheets tightly and cut into tiny flakes with a pair of scissors (this doesn't actually take that long). Use a pestle and mortar to grind the salt and one tablespoon of sesame seeds into a powder, then mix with the remaining seeds and the nori flakes. Store in an airtight container.

Chopped kale, dill and chickpea salad with smoked trout

The herbs, cucumber and yoghurt in this chopped kale salad are a notably cooling combination, and one that's a particularly good foil for hot-smoked river trout – with its subtle whiff of charred woodchips, and flaky but still succulent flesh. It's a cheering, fresh dish that's robust enough to fill you up, but not so heavy that it weighs you down. You'll know best the moments when that kind of thing is needed.

If you can't find or don't fancy hot-smoked trout, try smoked mackerel, or grilled fresh mackerel or trout.

Serves 4

—

2 x 400g (14oz) cans chickpeas (garbanzos), drained
1 tablespoon olive oil
250g (9oz) kale (not the pre-prepared kind), leaves shredded (stems discarded)
1 lemon, zest finely grated and the juice of ½
1½ large cucumbers, peeled, halved lengthways, seeds scooped out and discarded, flesh cut into 1cm (½in) crescents
10 dill sprigs, ½ fronds finely chopped and ½ left whole
Leaves picked from 10 sprigs mint, finely chopped
100g (3½oz) Greek yoghurt
4 fillets hot-smoked trout
Flaky sea salt and ground black pepper

Heat the oven to 220°C/200°C fan/425°F.

Spread half the chickpeas over a small baking sheet. Add the oil, roll the chickpeas in it until glossy, and cook at the top of the oven for 30 minutes until golden (they become crunchier as they cool). Season immediately with lots of flaky salt then set to one side.

Transfer the shredded kale leaves to a mixing bowl, add half a teaspoon of flaky sea salt, then use one hand to squeeze or 'massage' the kale for a minute or so, until wet and reduced in volume. Add the lemon zest and juice along with the non-roasted chickpeas, mix and fluff with a fork.

Put the cucumber crescents into a separate bowl, add a pinch of salt and stir. Add to the cucumbers the chopped herbs and the yoghurt before transferring two thirds from that bowl to the kale. Mix again with a fork, then pick and add most of the remaining dill fronds (saving a few for the garnish) along with lots of black pepper, and mix again.

Decant onto a large platter or individual plates. Top with the remaining cucumbers and yoghurt, the crisp chickpeas, then the smoked fish in large flakes, and finish with a final flourish of dill fronds.

Ham hock, spring greens and radish salad

You can buy pre-cooked ham hock, or actually use pretty much any type of pork product in this salad (including sausages stripped from their casings, torn up and gently fried). But if you've a butcher nearby, do get hold of a ham hock from time to time (either smoked or unsmoked). They're inexpensive and require little effort to cook – just time. From one you should get enough hammy meat for this recipe, plus a few weekday sandwiches or the gumbo on page 118.

This salad is a go-to for me on those blue-sky days that call for food that's light and uplifting yet still satiating. It's about the crunch and pepperiness of radishes, the sweet and verdant pop of asparagus and sugar snaps, the crisp lettuce... all pulled together by the cooling anise qualities of tarragon. My urge for this is strongest from spring to mid-summer. If you find it grabs you outside those months, then swap the asparagus for green beans, Tenderstem or purple sprouting broccoli.

Serves 2 as a substantial salad

—

250–300g (9–10½oz) cooked, flaked ham hock, at room temperature

400g (14oz) baby potatoes
250g (9oz) asparagus
150g (5½oz) sugar snap peas
Handful sorrel leaves (optional)
150–200g (5½–7oz) breakfast radishes, leaves reserved
Leaves stripped from 6 sprigs tarragon
1 baby gem lettuce, leaves separated

For the dressing
4 tbsp extra virgin olive oil
2 tbsp apple cider vinegar
2 tsp golden caster (superfine) sugar
½ tsp flaky sea salt and a generous grind of black pepper
Leaves stripped from 5 sprigs tarragon, roughly chopped
1 heaped tbsp Lilliput (petite) capers

To cook a ham hock

Place a ham hock (around 1–1.3kg/2lb 4oz–3lb) in a large saucepan. Cover by 3–4cm (1¼–1½in) with cold water, place over a high heat and bring to the boil, then reduce the temperature to simmer very gently with lid ajar for 2 hours. Take off the heat but leave in the water to fully cool down. After that time, remove from the water and pull apart the meat into slightly bigger than bite-size chunks. Use 250–300g (9–10½oz) for this salad and save the rest for other meals.

For the salad

Put the potatoes in a saucepan with a teaspoon of salt. Cover with cold water, bring to the boil then simmer until tender, about 20–25 minutes. Drain.

Meanwhile, bring a separate saucepan of salted water to the boil. Snap the bottom woody part of the asparagus spears away, then cut into two to three pieces, each about 4cm (1½in) long. When the water is boiling, drop these into the pan, and add the sugar snaps after 60 seconds. Count to ten, then drain everything through a colander, and cool under a cold-running tap or in a bowl of ice-cold water.

If using sorrel, refresh it in cold water too, then pat dry with a cloth.

Make the dressing in a large mixing bowl by whisking together the oil, vinegar, sugar, salt and pepper until emulsified. Add the chopped tarragon and capers.

Add the drained, warm potatoes to the bowl of dressing along with the meat and tumble them around. Leave this to sit for a few minutes so the two warm ingredients get to know the dressing. Then, when you are ready to eat, add the radishes, radish leaves, asparagus, sugar snaps, tarragon, lettuce leaves and sorrel (if using). Toss so every element is glossy, and then serve before any leaves wilt.

Honeyed halloumi with apricot fregola

This dish is best assembled when apricots are at their sweet, perfumed, flavourful peak. Fortunately, that will most likely coincide with a craving for fresh and fragrant – a late spring, early summer's day, when the sky is blue and an al fresco lunch or dinner is calling.

At this time of year, larger tomatoes will provide more in texture than they do flavour, but there's plenty going on elsewhere, not least the fennel seeds and Kalamata olives that punctuate each bite, plus copious amounts of my go-to fresh herbs, parsley and mint. On which note, feel free to be even more free-flowing with them than I have suggested, or even add tarragon and/or dill to the mix as well.

Even with all this going on, the star is the halloumi, which you should cook, glaze and serve at the very last minute.

Serves 4 (or more as part of a bigger spread)
–

300g (10½oz) fregola (alternatively, giant couscous, moghrabieh or maftoul)
300g (10½oz) large, fleshy tomatoes, cut into rough chunks
75g (2½oz) Kalamata olives, pit in
300g (10½oz) apricots, pitted and quartered
Leaves picked from 30g (1oz) mint, finely chopped
Leaves picked from 30g (1oz) flat-leaf parsley, roughly chopped
1 tbsp fennel seeds
5 tbsp extra virgin olive oil
2 tbsp red wine vinegar
1–2 tbsp light olive oil
2 x 200–250g (7–9oz) blocks halloumi, cut into 1–1.5cm (½in) strips
1 tbsp honey
Juice ½ lemon
Flaky sea salt

Bring a large pan of well-salted water to the boil and cook the fregola according to the packet instructions (usually around 10 minutes). When al dente, drain through a sieve (strainer) and leave briefly under cold-running water to wash away some starch, and to cool to slightly above room temperature.

Add the tomato chunks to a mixing bowl and season with lots of flaky salt. Bash the olives with the base of a mug, remove the pits, roughly chop the flesh and add to the bowl. Add the apricots along with the fresh herbs. Lightly toast the fennel seeds in a dry pan until aromatic, grind to a rough powder (i.e. not quite a dust) and sprinkle three-quarters of it over the bowl. Add the extra virgin olive oil and vinegar, and mix well before folding in the fregola. Taste and add more extra virgin olive oil, vinegar, salt or herbs if needed.

Warm one to two tablespoons of light olive oil in a large heavy-bottomed frying pan (skillet) over a medium heat (if necessary, use two pans or cook in two batches, rather than overcrowd the pan), then fry the halloumi pieces for around 2 minutes without touching them, flipping only when a golden crust has formed. Colour on this side for 1 minute, then dot the honey in the gaps between the pieces and let that bubble in the pan and caramelize under the cheese for 30 seconds. Remove the pan from the heat, squeeze the lemon juice in, then transfer the halloumi to a warm plate, crustiest side up, scraping all the pan juices on top and sprinkling the remaining fennel seeds over too. Eat immediately alongside generous servings of the apricot fregola.

Celery, fennel and egg salad with rye croutons

This crunchy salad is something I turn to when I need a reboot; it's a crisp, punctuating dish that seems to reset palate and mind, thanks to the texture and temperature of the core ingredients working in tandem with their fresh flavour. Chopped egg and malty rye croutons add balance and ensure that this is perfectly good as a meal on its own, probably serving two people with reasonable appetite. That said, it's also excellent alongside platters of cured meats, smoked fish, or cooked white fish too (lose the eggs if the latter). For best results ensure the fennel and celery are fridge-cold and use a mandoline to finely shave them (or do what you can with a very sharp knife).

Pictured on pages 38–39.

Serves 2 as a meal, 4–6 as a side
—

2 eggs, at room temperature
160g (5¾oz) 100% rye bread
5 tbsp extra virgin olive oil
1 lemon, zested and juiced
1 tbsp moscatel vinegar (or white wine vinegar)
½ tbsp tepid water
Leaves stripped from 5 sprigs tarragon, roughly chopped
1 tsp caster (superfine) sugar
1 tsp Dijon mustard
1 small–medium fennel bulb, sliced wafer-thin to 1mm (½₀in), fronds reserved
4 celery sticks, very thinly sliced to 2–3mm (¹⁄₁₆–⅛in), handful leaves reserved
Leaves picked from 15g (½oz) flat-leaf parsley, roughly chopped
Flaky sea salt and ground black pepper

Heat the oven to 240°C/220°C fan/475°F.

Put a small saucepan of water on a high heat. When it's boiling, lower the eggs in and cook at an energetic simmer for 9 minutes. Remove the eggs and immediately plunge into a bowl of iced water or leave to chill under a cold-running tap. Peel and roughly chop.

Meanwhile, cut the rye bread into 1–2cm (½–¾in) slices, then tear those into fingernail-size crumbs. Measure two tablespoons of the olive oil into a small baking tray. Roll the rye crumbs in the oil until glossy, then bake at the top of the oven for 7–10 minutes, removing when the edges of the bread are just charred, but the insides are still chewy.

Measure the remaining olive oil, all the lemon zest and half the juice, the vinegar, water, tarragon, sugar and mustard, and whisk together to make a vinaigrette. Taste, season with salt and pepper, and taste again (and add more of whichever component you see fit).

Combine the fennel and celery in a large bowl with the vinaigrette, mix well then leave for 4–5 minutes to soften a little. Add the parsley, celery leaves and rye croutons, mix again, then tumble the salad onto a platter. Top with the egg and fennel fronds.

Bream with whipped tahini and glazed green beans

This is crunchy and creamy – but never heavy – with invigorating and varied tastes and textures to every forkful. Which is, I think, what you're after when seeking something 'healthy-ish'.

It's centred around a side of Middle Eastern vibe that'd go well with many things – blanched and still squeaky beans that sit on zingy whipped tahini and underneath a crunchy dusting of spiced dukkah. The simple and pure white fish, baked whole on the bone, holds its own, but knows the side is the star.

I tend to keep this carb-free. For additional ballast, add boiled baby potatoes.

Serves 4
–

2 whole bream (approx. 600g/1lb 5oz each), gutted and scaled
1 lemon, ½ sliced, ½ juiced
1 tbsp extra virgin olive oil, plus a little extra
300g (10½oz) green beans
60g (2¼oz) tahini
4 tbsp fridge-cold water
2 tsp runny honey
1 tsp tepid water
Flaky sea salt and ground black pepper

For the dukkah
2 tsp coriander seeds
2 tsp cumin
20g (¾oz) blanched almonds, roughly chopped
1 tbsp toasted sesame seeds
½ tsp flaky sea salt

–

Heat the oven to 200°C/180°C fan/400°F.

Season the inside of the fish with salt and pepper and stuff with lemon slices. Place on a baking sheet, rub a little oil on both outer sides of each fish, and sprinkle with more salt. Bake on an upper shelf for 18–20 minutes, removing when the skin begins to split a little and the flesh feels firm. If you have a temperature probe, push to the bone at the thickest part of the fish, removing once somewhere between 56–60°C (132–140°F).

If you don't have one, try poking in the same place with a metal skewer, then touch the tip of that to your lips. If it's hot (rather than warm), take the fish out. Leave to rest for a couple of minutes while bringing the rest of the meal together.

Meanwhile, put a saucepan of salted water on to boil (for the green beans).

Make a dukkah by toasting the coriander and cumin seeds in a dry pan over a warm heat for about 2 minutes. Remove when they are fragrant and transfer immediately to a pestle and mortar to bash and split without completely grinding to a powder. Toast the chopped almonds in the same pan until tinged with a golden colour, add to the spices and pound to a coarse grit. Add half the sesame seeds, pound a bit more, then add and mix with the remaining seeds and salt. Set to one side until needed.

Put the tahini, cold water and the lemon juice into a small bowl and whisk until thickened, then spoon it onto a serving platter or wide bowl.

In a different bowl (big enough to hold the green beans) combine the honey, one tablespoon of extra virgin olive oil, the tepid water and a pinch of salt and pepper. When the fish has been cooking for around 15 minutes, drop the green beans into the now boiling water and cook for 3–4 minutes, so that they're tender but still bright green and a bit squeaky if bitten. Drain and transfer to the bowl with the honey dressing. Mix well. Then pile the dressed beans onto the tahini, and sprinkle all of the dukkah on top (it might seem a lot, but it will all go).

Serve together with the fish, as soon as that is cooked and rested. The top fillet should come away easily with the prod of a fork and fish knife, and then the bone can be pulled away from the flesh underneath.

Poussin, artichoke and pea traybake

The 'freshness' in this comes via lemony peas and potatoes, a minted-yoghurt dressing, and cute poussin (spring chicken), which hits the spot without weighing you down. This suits those times when you'd rather be outside than in the kitchen – happily, everything sits within the same roasting tin, with no more exertion than remembering to put things in at the right time. So it's a good one for a low-effort, high-reward meal with friends.

Serves 4

–

2 poussin
1 garlic bulb, cloves separated and peeled
4 tbsp extra virgin olive oil
2 lemons, zest finely grated then quartered
800g (1lb 12oz) baby potatoes
120g (4½oz) Greek yoghurt
Leaves picked from 4 sprigs mint, finely chopped
150g (5½oz) artichoke hearts, halved
400g (14oz) frozen peas
100ml (scant ½ cup) water
Flaky sea salt and ground black pepper

–

Heat the oven to 200°C/180°C fan/400°F.

Split the poussin in half down the middle along their back bones, using a heavy knife or sturdy pair of scissors.

Mince two of the garlic cloves. Then combine half of that with one tablespoon of the olive oil, all the lemon zest, and squeeze over the juice from one of the lemon quarters. Sprinkle the bird portions generously with salt and pepper then rub the flavoured oil all over. Set to one side.

Measure the rest of the oil into a 20 x 30cm (8 x 12in) baking or roasting tin. Add the potatoes and the remaining whole garlic cloves and roll everything around until glossy. Dot all but one of the remaining lemon wedges among the potatoes, then roast in the oven for 40 minutes until golden, shuffling after 20 minutes or so to ensure an even roast.

While waiting, combine the yoghurt, mint, the remaining minced garlic and juice from the last lemon quarter. Season to taste with salt and pepper then refrigerate.

Once the potatoes have had 40 minutes and are nicely tinged, remove the tray from the oven and use the back of a spoon to squash the lemon wedges to release their jammy juice. Squash any garlic cloves you see too, then pick out the lemons (which will add too much of a bitter edge if left in). Pop the artichokes and the still frozen peas onto and around the potatoes, add the water, then put the marinated poussin on top, breast side up.

Roast for 35 minutes, by which time the birds should be bronzed but still succulent, and everything below will be tender, with a gravy emerging from the peas and chicken juices. Once you've transferred the poussin to plates, give the contents of the tray a good stir before serving, then complete the scene with a hefty dollop of the minted yoghurt.

Grand aioli

A fair few weekends during my late 20s and early 30s were spent in Tuscany or Provence celebrating friends getting married. Always lovely... but also always a little bit too hot and sweaty. (No offence, friends.)

The parties were well catered; however, I now only really remember the lunches either side of the events – because the Tuscans and Provençals really know how to eat when it's hot and you just want to graze: fresh seasonal produce, simply prepared, generally served at ambient temperature. Best of all the options is a Provençal grand aioli, which somehow sits astride both 'humble' and 'flash'. It's wholesome and convivial, and just the thing for when weather and mood are, too.

In mid–late spring or early summer, you'll be able to serve this with English asparagus. Or, rather, the appearance of those sticks of 'gras ought to be a good prompt to prepare this dish. Should you get the urge to make aioli later on in the year (a balmy weekend in August, for example), swap the asparagus for green beans and the cherry tomatoes for larger versions that by now actually taste of tomatoes. In fact the whole thing is a moveable feast: there are a few other vegetable suggestions listed opposite; you might add mussels or octopus too, if you're feeling fancy.

Serves 4–6 (scale up or down as you see fit)
—

The aioli
2 cloves garlic, minced
3 egg yolks
80ml (⅓ cup) vegetable oil
1 lemon, juiced
150–200ml (scant ⅔ cup–scant 1 cup) extra virgin olive oil
4 tbsp cold water
Flaky sea salt

The trimmings

Warm
4 medium-size waxy potatoes, peeled (or 8–12 baby potatoes)
2 x 150g (5½oz) fillets cod or pollack
2 small courgettes (zucchini), halved lengthways

Cold
250–300g (9–10½oz) asparagus, blanched and shocked under cold-running water
250–300g cauliflower florets, blanched and shocked under cold-running water
8 small carrots, boiled
4 eggs, hard boiled
225g (8oz) cherry tomatoes, halved

Alternatives
(Quantities depend on what or how many things these are substituting)
Green beans, blanched and shocked under cold-running water
Breakfast radishes, leaves intact
Fennel, segmented
Late summer tomatoes, quartered
Globe artichokes, trimmed and boiled
Romanesco broccoli florets, raw

To make the aioli add the garlic and half a teaspoon of flaky salt to a medium–large mixing bowl. Add the egg yolks and beat vigorously using a balloon whisk for more than a minute until light in colour and texture. Set the bowl on a folded dish towel (which will help to hold it steady) and begin to pour the vegetable oil in a very fine, slow stream, whisking all the while. Once that has been incorporated, add just a teaspoon of lemon juice, stir, then a teaspoon of water, stir again.

Now begin incorporating the olive oil, still using a balloon whisk. At this stage you can go for an oil in one hand, whisk in the other approach. Or, if less confident, just alternate whisking and drizzling, adding one to two tablespoons of oil each time. Roughly every three tablespoons of olive oil, add another teaspoon of water, a teaspoon of lemon juice and a little pinch of salt until the aioli is thick and clingy but not bouncy. Taste. Add additional salt and a final squeeze of lemon if you think it needs it, plus another teaspoon or two of water if you think it should be thinned a little.

Decant the aioli into a serving bowl – wide enough for the table to use as a communal dip (alternatively they can take a large spoonful to their plate, returning for seconds and thirds as they pick away).

Prepare the trimmings and lay them on a platter with the aioli in the middle.

Anything filed under 'cold' can be cooked in advance: asparagus and cauliflower florets cooked in already boiling water for 3–4 minutes, then 'shocked' under a cold-running tap; small carrots (or larger, peeled and split down the middle) and eggs also plunged into boiling water for 8 minutes, then 'shocked' (and the eggs peeled).

Those items labelled as 'warm' are best cooked just as you're about to eat. I put the potatoes in a medium-size saucepan that fits a steamer basket, filling the saucepan with cold water, bringing to the boil before simmering with a steamer basket on top for 15–20 minutes until the potatoes are tender. For the last 10 minutes I add the courgette halves and fish to the basket, and let them cook away until the flesh of the fish feels plump and the skin peels away easily. The courgettes will be soft and glassy at this point, which works well here.

Cantonese-style steamed white fish with pea shoot and garlic asparagus

Cantonese-style steamed fish – topped with coriander and oil-scorched spring onions and ginger and swimming in (mostly) soy sauce – is hardly a novel suggestion, but there are few fresher-feeling or more fragrant dishes around. Often, this is presented as a meal involving on-the-bone whole sea bass or bream. But as it happens, it's also a good way to prepare and enjoy any of the flat fish – plaice, dab, dover sole (or lemon sole and turbot if you're feeling flush). Moreover, you can use the steaming, garnishing and saucing with off-the-bone fillets of the same fish (or indeed cod, haddock and pollack), so I have included cooking instructions for that too. Take whichever approach suits you.

There's a green side dish here too for added vibrancy. Use Tenderstem broccoli or green beans if asparagus is out of season.

Serves 2

–

650–800g (1lb 7oz–1lb 12oz) whole flat fish (e.g. plaice, dover sole, dab, lemon sole or turbot), skin on, gutted and wings trimmed
Or
350–400g (12–14oz) filleted fish (e.g. plaice, dover sole, dab or any white fish such as turbot, haddock, cod or pollack)
30g (1oz) fresh ginger, peeled, sliced into thin matchsticks
4 tbsp light soy sauce
2 tsp sesame oil
½ tsp caster (superfine) sugar
3 spring onions (scallions), thinly sliced vertically
2 tbsp neutral cooking oil
Leaves and thin stems picked from 10–15g (¼–½oz) coriander (cilantro)

For the greens
2 tbsp neutral cooking oil
2 cloves garlic, minced
250g (9oz) asparagus, trimmed and cut into 4cm (1½in) pieces
100g (3½oz) pea shoots
2 tbsp Shaoxing wine
1 tsp caster (superfine) sugar

Serve with plain rice.

There are three things to do: cook rice, cook fish, cook greens.

Prepare your rice according to the packet instructions (or to your preferred method).

While the rice is cooking, pat the fish dry and season with salt on both sides. Prepare a wide steamer over a saucepan or on a rack in a wok. Scatter half the ginger underneath the fish, lay the fish on top, then add the remaining ginger. Steam with a lid on for 8–12 minutes, until the flesh is firm (56–60°C/132–140°F at the thickest part is ideal). If you are using fillets the steaming will likely take less time, more like 5–6 minutes. The fish should be just firm and will flake fairly easily if squeezed/pushed.

Meanwhile, mix the soy sauce, sesame oil and sugar together.

Remove the fish from the steamer and place on a warm platter. Pour the sauce over the fish and scatter over the cooked ginger followed by the spring onions. Heat the cooking oil in a small saucepan until near smoking hot and pour this in a measured drizzle over the spring onions and fish. Garnish with coriander.

The asparagus and pea shoots side is quick to cook and can be made while the fish is resting. Empty your wok of water (assuming you used it to steam the fish), or find a high-sided frying pan, add the neutral cooking oil and garlic and place over a hot heat. Once the oil is hot and garlic is bubbling (not yet burning), add the asparagus and cook for 60 seconds, then the pea shoots and stir fry for 40–60 seconds more, until half to two-thirds of the pea shoots have wilted. Add the Shaoxing wine and sugar, stir very quickly, and serve alongside the fish.

Papaya, lychee and Thai basil fruit salad with anise syrup

I used to summarize and link to the recipes in the papers over on my blog *Rocket & Squash*. That meant reading around 70–100 recipes every weekend. Each time a score of them would really resonate, perhaps subconsciously depending on what I was craving at the time. Five or six years later, I still recall a handful of the standout ideas, often because I've been prompted by a relevant urge. One – a plate of berries soaked and interrupted by an aromatic anise syrup – recurs to this day thanks to Mark Hix, then the *Independent*'s recipe columnist).

This assembly is adapted from his, with syrup tweaked and spooned over papaya and lychee instead of strawberries. I recommend serving with a dollop of cold coconut yoghurt. The combination will reinvigorate your palate and transport you, momentarily, to somewhere sun-drenched.

Serves 4
—

½ large papaya, peeled, seeds scooped out
12 fresh lychee, peeled
About 15 leaves Thai holy basil

For the syrup
2 sticks lemongrass, chopped
50g (1¾oz) fresh ginger, thinly sliced (skin on)
1 star anise
120g (4¼oz) caster (superfine) sugar
120ml (½ cup) water

Serve with thick-set coconut yoghurt.

Combine the syrup ingredients in a pan. Bring to the boil and simmer for around 8 minutes, so the liquid is glossy and fragrant. Remove from the heat and leave to cool for an hour. Strain through a sieve (strainer) into a bowl, discard the aromatics and chill the syrup until required.

Cutting across the width of the papaya, slice it into 2cm (¾in) crescents. Arrange them on a platter and scatter the lychee into the gaps, then spoon the syrup over the top (by the way, people can remove the lychee seeds themselves as they eat). Drag the basil leaves through any residual syrup, add as a garnish, and serve with a heavy dollop or two of coconut yoghurt.

Orange blossom melon with frozen raspberries

This is low effort, a little old school, but ultimately a very pleasing end to a meal; particularly suited to a slow, hot lunch or balmy evening. Cantaloupe melons are already fragrant, but the orange blossom and honey syrup accentuate that nectared quality. The crumbled raspberries are like little balls of sorbet, and bring a necessary sharpness that cuts through the perfume.

As a side note, any in-season cantaloupe is good, but if you come across the sub-varieties sun sweet or charentais, then they are (and this will be) even better.

Serves 4

–

1 ripe cantaloupe melon (approximately
　750g–1kg/1lb 10oz–2lb 4oz), quartered,
　seeds scooped out
1 tsp ground ginger
2 tsp orange blossom water
2 tsp runny honey
2–3 tbsp frozen raspberries

With each quarter of the melon, cut the flesh away from the skin in one boat-like piece, using a sharp knife with a little flex to it. Return to the skin and cut vertically into the flesh to create five pieces sitting in a retro melon boat.

Sprinkle a pinch of ginger over the top of each serving of melon.

Add the orange blossom water and runny honey into a bowl, stirring until fully combined. Drizzle a teaspoon of the syrup over each of the melon portions. (If you would like to prepare this in advance, the melon slices can happily sit in the fridge for a few hours but bring them out an hour before eating and re-baste with the perfumed syrup before serving.)

Finally, just before eating, gently squeeze and roll the frozen raspberries between your fingers; they should crumble into tiny sorbet-like segments. Spoon these over the melons and enjoy.

tart and
sour

If the tart and sour flavour profile was a punctuation mark it would be an exclamation. It's a flash of acidity that, even when relatively subtle, provokes an instinctive pucker of the lips, draw of cheeks, smack of tongue and furrow of brow. These are actions of recoil, and yet tart and sour foods are actually fiendishly moreish. Watch a toddler pile into salt and vinegar crisps, the spoils of a redcurrant bush or a wedge of lemon and tell me we're not programmed to crave acidity.

That acidity arrives on our plates through the addition of ferments, vinegars and sharpened syrups. It's also inherent in certain ingredients such as citrus fruits, berries, pomegranate, tomatoes and tamarind, and is cultivated in others like buttermilk and soured cream. In this section, some dishes are permeated with sourness because components have been steeped in pickling liquor or braised in vinegar; some celebrate naturally sour ingredients in relatively unadulterated state – for example, the tamarind paste and blood oranges that are paired with brown-sugar meringues and cream; while others have sourness thrust upon them, such as lightly salted cod doused in quick-pickled celery and fizzing fermented tomatoes that are squashed so their juices acidulate the cured fish.

Sure, sounds nice. But when and why might we feel drawn to tart and sour flavours? I suppose the easy answer is that tart and sour foods provide a jolt. They're sparky, perky and invigorating, whether you need a pick-me-up or want to keep an already positive moment going.

Applying a little more consideration, though, I wonder whether we feel the need for the kind of recipes that follow in order to achieve balance. Dishes bursting with acidity can bring a grey day to life, cutting through turgid moments in the same way they cut through and enliven fatty or bland foods. They're equally good at applying that aforementioned punctuation mark to sunny days and moods – an abrupt but uplifting rather than deadening pause.

Then again, is it even necessary to analyze or justify this craving? I personally find there are times when I simply find myself pulled towards a little something that will briefly make my gums recede, for no discernible reason beyond a base urge. As with the chilli and heat chapter, I think that once you become accustomed to and appreciative of this flavour profile, you find yourself needing a regular fix. It's addictive. It's a craving...

Aside from naturally acidic ingredients, sourness arrived in our diets as a by-product of preservation: techniques like Filipino adobo and Central American escabeche, which (in the absence of refrigeration) ensured precious proteins lasted longer; the souring and fermentation of milk to make cheese; also the fermentation of fruits, vegetables and cured meats. These traditions and the foods created by them are wonderful. Magical, really. But for the most part they're also technically unnecessary now we've freezers and freight. That they endure and spread is in part because of emotional bonds, and also (or, crucially) because they're delicious.

Returning to that point about balance, as a general rule of thumb pretty much any dish or meal you will ever eat will be better off for having a little acidity in it. Most of the time that's achieved via a sprinkle, splash or splodge of a piquant condiment, tangy dressing or sharp sauce. But simply seasoning with sour is not really what I'm talking about here. These recipes go beyond that, as they are ones in which the balance has tipped firmly towards tart – the sharpness is the reason for the dish. For example, see (or better still, taste) the fermented and fresh tomato salad with feta, which has layers and layers of the stuff; also an assembly of whole-roast squash, mozzarella and bitter leaves, which is fine on its own but transformational when swimming in an agrodolce dressing. Even those recipes where the tart and sour element is technically a mere condiment (fridge-drawer pickles; Thai dipping sauces; mackerel rice bowls with ginger-pickled rhubarb), that condiment is the thing that pulls you in, and which will provide the most satisfaction during and beyond your meal.

There's a negative connotation to the word sour: sour face; sour grapes; events turning sour. Presumably that derives from spoiled meats, underripe fruit and milk that's on the turn. To me, though, when I experience sour, tart, sharp and tangy in food and drink the feeling I get is quite the opposite: it's the key quality I look for in coffee and chocolate, and in other sweets, snacks and fruits.

If you've been on a wine-tasting course you might recall being told that you can gauge levels of acidity according to how much saliva is generated to the sides of the tongue – in other words, sourness is quite literally mouthwatering. Please do get stuck into these recipes and let me convince you to become a fan of it too.

Fridge-drawer pickles

It is good foresight always to have a jar of zingy preserved vegetables to hand – to go with cold meats, cheeses, pork pies, in sandwiches or simply to be eaten as you stand staring into the fridge contemplating its contents/your life.

While fermentation has become a bit of *A Thing* in recent years (or at least that's the case in my echo chamber), I am an infrequent briner of anything other than cherry tomatoes, so it would be misleading of me to write that homemade kimchi, fermented chard stalks or some other fizzing vegetable scrap regularly satiates my cravings. I do, however, often yearn for and occasionally make basic garden pickles. Well, less 'garden', more often just 'fridge-drawer' regulars. Courgettes and red peppers are essential, texturally, taste-wise and also emotively (Mum makes something similar, albeit actually from her veg patch). Since yellow peppers so often come with red, they go in too, plus red onions and a mild red chilli or three. All are best when softened a touch by the pickling process, yet still retain a snap.

Fills 1 x 2 litre (70fl oz) jar or equivalent volume of small jars

—

250ml (generous 1 cup) red wine vinegar
200ml (scant 1 cup) extra virgin olive oil
3 tbsp water
50g (1¾oz) golden caster (superfine) sugar
20g (¾oz) flaky sea salt
1 clove garlic, finely sliced
1 red (bell) pepper, cut into 1–2cm
    (½–¾in) squares
1 yellow (bell) pepper, cut into 1–2cm
    (½–¾in) squares
2 courgettes (zucchini), cut into 1–2cm
    (½–¾in) dice
1 small red onion, cut into 6 wedges,
    petals separated
2 mild red chillies, deseeded, roughly chopped

Combine the vinegar, oil and water in a saucepan. Measure in the sugar and salt, set over a medium heat and stir until both are dissolved. Add all the vegetables, increase the temperature to bring the pickling liquid to a boil, then immediately remove the pan from the heat and leave to cool for 10 minutes.

Transfer the still-warm contents of the pan to a sterilized jar, seal and keep in a cool, dark place for up to 6 months, rotating occasionally to mix oil and vinegar (or move straight to the fridge – just wait for a week or so before cracking the seal).

Once opened, store in the fridge and use within a month.

Pickled mussels

Pickled mussels aren't particularly common in the UK. Which *adopts Rick Stein voice* is a real shame because our mussels are both fantastic and inexpensive, and we could really learn something from the people of northern Spain, Portugal and Central America, who know very well that mussels 'in escabeche' are very good indeed.

Quickly steamed mussels readily take on an aromatic, tangy marinade, while keeping their own character, and so become pleasing little eyebrow-raisers, and not chewy as you might expect. Superb on toast (make sure it's properly 'browned' and a little crusty so as to not get soggy), or alternatively picked at with thick chunks of charred bread nearby to dip in the pickling liquor.

Serves 4 on toast, more as a snack

—

1kg (2lb 4oz) mussels
4 tbsp extra virgin olive oil
1 medium–large carrot, peeled, cut into fine discs
4 cloves garlic, thinly sliced
1 small echalion shallot, sliced into thin rings
100ml (scant ½ cup) rice vinegar
2½ tbsp sherry vinegar
2 tsp caster (superfine) sugar
½ tsp flaky sea salt
½ tsp whole peppercorns
3 or 4 sprigs thyme
½ tsp sweet paprika

Serve with well-toasted sourdough bread.

Purge the mussels in a bowl of cold water for 5 minutes. Lift out the mussels into a temporary container, discard the water, then return the mussels to the bowl and repeat – the second time round pulling away any stringy beards while the mussels are still underwater, and subsequently lifting the cleaned mussels out again, and discarding the water and grit. Discard any mussels that remain open when tapped. This can be done in advance, though you must store the mussels in the fridge until needed.

Put 200ml (scant 1 cup) of water in a wide saucepan, bring to the boil, add the mussels, shuffle the pan and place a lid on top. Cook for 3 minutes and remove from the heat. Remove the lid – if all the mussels are open, you're done. If not, use a large spoon to quickly move the mussels at the bottom of the pan to the top, put the lid back and wait for 1 minute more for them to steam open. While they're hot, use an empty shell to pick the rest of the mussels out of their shells and transfer them to a bowl, dish or Tupperware that will fit them in one or two snug layers. Discard any that refuse to open.

Measure two teaspoons of the oil into a small saucepan and place over a low heat. Add the sliced carrot and garlic and cook very gently for 2 minutes, to soften a little. Now add the rest of the ingredients (including the remaining oil), bring to the boil and simmer for 3 minutes, ensuring all the sugar and salt is dissolved. Leave to cool for 7–8 minutes, then pour over the mussels and leave to cool completely before refrigerating.

Transfer to the fridge for at least an hour or two, although they're best left overnight. They're good for up to 3 days like this, though the vinaigrette will eventually overpower.

Serve on what some would call burnt but I call perfectly browned sourdough toast. Alternatively, they could just be picked at until all gone, with chunky, charred bread to mop up the juices. Use any remaining pickle juice as a vinaigrette for things like bitter leaves and blanched greens.

Fermented cherry tomatoes

Fermented cherry tomatoes are intense little flavour bombs that fizz and pop with lactic sourness. They're something I first came across thanks to the Ukrainian food writer Olia Hercules, and now make them often, nearly always having a jar to hand, and probably another batch on the go. Originally, this method was going to be included within one of the next two recipes (in which you'll see they are key). But on reflection, fermented cherry tomatoes deserve a page of their own – add them to or serve with a cheese toastie, enjoy cold next to omelettes, gently warmed to go with scrambled eggs, or fully cooked-down into a layered and umami-rich pasta sauce.

Fills 1 x 2–3 litre (70–100fl oz) jar

–

1 litre (4⅓ cups) water
30g (1oz) flaky sea salt
20g (¾oz) caster (superfine) sugar
600g (1lb 5oz) cherry tomatoes
   (a mix of colours is nice but not essential)
1 mild red chilli (optional)

Measure the water, salt and sugar into a saucepan. Bring to the boil, stir to dissolve the grains, then leave to cool completely.

Sterilize a Kilner jar (or similar). Wash the tomatoes and chilli (if using), add to the jar and pour over the cooled brine. You may not need it all, though the tomatoes do need to be completely submerged to prevent spoiling – this is easily achieved by partially filling a clean, sealable sandwich bag with water and placing it above the tomatoes before sealing the jar.

Leave in a warm place for 10–14 days, until the water is cloudy and the tomatoes sour, blistered and fizzing. Unless using within a day or so of being 'ready', transfer to the fridge (if necessary, decanting the tomatoes with enough brine to cover them into smaller containers to suit your fridge) where they will last for 3–4 months.

Fermented tomato, pickled celery and salted cod crudo

'Raw' fish dishes are such a pleasing thing to assemble at home as they feel very restaurant, but rarely involve any skill nor too much organization. They also seem to span the seasons weather-wise; obviously suiting balmy days and nights when something light is required, though apt at cutting through and lifting gloomier moments too.

Most versions require an acid to both 'cook' the fish, and to wake and refresh the palate. So often that comes from citrus – lime, various shades of lemon, grapefruit and pomelo too. I love them all... although an overenthusiastic squeeze can overwhelm. This recipe takes a slightly different approach. There's still sharpness – from the fizzing, fermented tomatoes (page 60) and the relatively subtle moscatel vinegar-dressed celery – but it's layered and supportive, so the fish should still shine. On which note, salted cod works a treat, but if the recipe catches your eye too late to salt and soak, then bream is so often one of the freshest items on a fishmonger's slab, with a clean, sweet, slightly creamy taste that stands up well to the dressing.

Serves 4 as a starter or sharing plate

—

200–250g (7–9oz) cod fillet, pin-boned, skin on
30g (1oz) fine table salt
Or
200–250g (7–9oz) bream fillet, pin-boned, skinned

2 celery sticks
½ tsp golden caster (superfine) sugar
3 tsp moscatel vinegar (or white wine vinegar)
16 fermented cherry tomatoes (page 60)
2 tbsp brine from the fermented tomatoes
3 tbsp extra virgin olive oil
8 fresh cherry tomatoes, sliced thinly
A dozen young celery leaves, picked from the middle of the bulb

If using cod, on the evening before you plan to eat measure the salt into the base of a small bowl or Tupperware. Roll the fish in the salt, ensuring all sides are well dusted. Cover the container and refrigerate for 8–12 hours. Brush the salt away. Wash the container, return the cod to it, fill with cold water, refrigerate again and leave to soak for 3 hours. The flesh will still be taut but won't now be overly salty. Pat dry and refrigerate uncovered for another hour or more.

Use a sharp, flexible knife to cut the skin away from the fish. Then slice vertically down in wafer-thin pieces – about 2mm (¹⁄₁₆in) thick. Arrange over a platter or four individual plates, in not too regimented a fashion, and with a little space around each.

If using bream, ask the fishmonger to skin and fillet the fish for you. When home and ready to eat, use your sharpest knife almost at a horizontal angle to slice wafer-thin pieces from the fillet – as if it was a piece of smoked salmon. Arrange on a platter or plates as described above.

Cut the celery lengthways into very thin strips, 1–2mm (¹⁄₁₆in), then cut across those so you have tiny dice. Transfer to a bowl, add the sugar and vinegar, mix and set to one side for 5 minutes (or longer).

Put the fermented tomatoes in a bowl and squash and burst them with the back of a fork. Leave the juices in the bowl but distribute the skin and flesh around the fish. Whisk the brine and oil into the remaining tomato juices, then spoon over the fish.

Spoon the celery over the plates, plus a few drops of the vinegar. Garnish with the sliced cherry tomatoes and celery leaves and a little more extra virgin olive oil if it feels appropriate (you can't really have too much). Eat immediately.

Fermented and fresh tomato salad with feta

I couldn't not have a tomato salad in this book. In part because I'm very partial to them. But also because with the right tomatoes, and an appropriate dressing, they really hit the 'tart and sour' sweet spot.

This one hints at Middle Eastern fattoush – the pita, the sumac – but also nods towards eastern Europe thanks to the fermented cherry tomatoes (page 60), which pop as you stumble across them amid the milder, softer, fleshier beef heart tomatoes.

Ordinarily I'd say that one or other of the herbs mentioned here are optional, but the differing menthol qualities of both mint and tarragon are particularly important as they seem to both deflect and enhance the various sour elements at the same time, while the parsley grounds the dish.

Finally, you do technically need to have fermented cherry tomatoes on tap for this (they take 7–10 days to be ready). But if you've read to this point, haven't yet started fermenting, and want to make the salad right now, then (whisper it) you could substitute them with the same quantity of cherry tomatoes roasted in one tablespoon of olive oil for the same time as the bread (10–12 minutes). They should be shrivelling but still definitely tomatoes after this time. Drizzle with two teaspoons of red wine vinegar, a pinch or two of sugar and salt, allow to cool just for a moment then fold them and any juices from the tray through the salad at the last minute, after the toasted pita.

Serves 2 as a generous salad, 4–6 as a side dish

—

500g (1lb 2oz) large beef heart tomatoes or similar, cut into chunks of varying shapes
300g (10½oz) fermented cherry tomatoes (page 60) and 2 tbsp of their brine
2 pita breads
6 tbsp extra virgin olive oil
Leaves picked from 7–8 sprigs tarragon, finely chopped
Leaves picked from 4–5 sprigs mint, finely chopped
Leaves picked from 7–8 sprigs flat-leaf parsley
2 tsp red wine vinegar
1 tsp golden caster (superfine) sugar
2–3 tsp sumac
200g (7oz) sheep's feta
Flaky sea salt and ground black pepper

—

Heat the oven to 220°C/200°C fan/425°F.

Put the tomato chunks along with any juices into a mixing bowl, add just a little salt (a pinch or two). Spoon the fermented tomatoes and two tablespoons of brine on top, but don't mix just yet. Set to one side.

Open the pita up with a sharp knife to create two thin halves, then tear each of those into thumb-size shards. Place the pita on a baking sheet, tumble in two tablespoons of the oil, then bake for 10–12 minutes until golden and crisp.

Prepare the herbs, add to the tomatoes, along with the still-warm pieces of pita, red wine vinegar, sugar and half the sumac. Gently tumble the salad so as to avoid popping too many of the cherry tomatoes. Check for seasoning and add black pepper and more salt and vinegar if needed.

Decant the salad onto a platter or individual plates. Scrape any juices over, crumble the feta on top, and finish with the rest of the olive oil plus a dusting of sumac.

Chicken, sour cream and dill pickle soup

My wife's grandmother – a Second World War refugee from an area of Poland annexed by Russia and now part of Belarus – used to cook an extremely restorative chicken soup. Not an unusual grandmotherly habit, I know. And in fact, this is not even her recipe.* I mention mostly because when I was trying to reconstruct her soup from both flavour recollection and Polish cookbooks, I came across a chicken soup that's lifted by brined dill pickles and soured cream (zupa ogórkowa). There's a pleasing semi-sour background note that lifts and lightens, and pushes you back to your better self, rather than letting you passively sink into a healed state in the way so many other bowls of chicken soup do.

Because the vital ingredient in any chicken soup is 'soul', the base of this should not be a store-bought stock, but one made from the leftover carcass of a roast chicken. Also, the recipe uses brined not vinegar-pickled gherkins. If you can only find the latter, use about a third of the amount and then add more to taste – their sourness is much more aggressive, and you don't want it to dominate.

* The only dish I extracted from Babcia before she passed was for golabki, which after the lesson she confided wasn't a centuries-old family secret, but a recipe she'd found in the *FT Weekend*...

Serves 4–6

—

For the stock
1 roast chicken carcass, with any excess of leftover meat picked and reserved
1 onion, peeled, halved
2–3 cherry tomatoes or 1 small tomato, halved
1 carrot, peeled and roughly chopped
2 celery sticks and their leaves
5 cloves garlic, halved
3 or 4 sprigs thyme

For the soup
30g (1oz) salted butter
200g (7oz) carrots, peeled, finely diced
250g (9oz) parsnip, peeled, finely diced
2 celery sticks, finely diced

1 leek, shredded
1.2 litres (5 cups) chicken stock
½ tsp ground allspice
200g (7oz) (drained weight) brined dill pickle cucumbers
4–7 tbsp brine from the pickle jar
200g (7oz) sour cream
Fronds picked from 4 sprigs dill, finely chopped
1 tsp lemon juice (optional)
Flaky sea salt and ground black pepper

Serve with rye or soda bread alongside.

—

To make the stock, pick any meat from the chicken carcass and set to one side. Place the carcass in a large saucepan and cover with cold water, so the surface of the water is three or four fingers clear of the bird. Add the remaining stock ingredients, bring to the boil then simmer uncovered for an hour. Strain though a fine sieve and transfer the stock back to a saucepan. Boil and reduce to around 1.2 litres (5 cups). This can be done well in advance (freeze the stock if you don't intend to make the soup within a couple of days).

To make the soup, melt the butter in a large saucepan over a medium heat. Add the vegetables and a pinch of salt, and sweat for 10 minutes, stirring occasionally to ensure none stick or burn. Add the stock and allspice, bring to the boil then reduce to a simmer for 10 minutes.

Meanwhile, use a coarse box grater to grate the pickled cucumbers. Add these along with four tablespoons of brine from the jar, plus any scraps of leftover chicken you have, then simmer for 5–10 minutes more. Remove from the heat and wait 5 minutes to cool a little.

Place the sour cream in a bowl and add a ladle of hot soup, whisk and add another, then pour into the soup and stir. (This is to 'temper' the cream and avoid it splitting.) Add the dill. Taste and season with more pickle brine, black pepper, sour cream or dill as required, plus the tiniest squeeze of lemon juice if you have it, then serve.

Pomegranate and sumac roast courgettes

This is a sparky little side dish that's good when fresh out the oven, but also enjoyable at room temperature (so good mass feasting/ buffet material). There's a sweet tang from the pomegranate molasses, the fresh pop of pomegranate seeds and also a sharp-sherbet zing of sumac.

The aubergines are deliberately cooked nearly to a purée and sit in the background, whereas the courgettes are (ideally) charred but with a little bite remaining. Both take on the sour Middle Eastern seasonings extremely well, and the whole thing is a perfect foil for things like slow-cooked lamb, roast squash, and roast or traybaked chicken. You could make a bigger thing of it by tumbling through some cooked grains – freekeh, pearl barley, bulgur wheat – and topping with feta or labneh, each of which would raise the tang further still.

Serves 4

—

2 large aubergines (eggplants), cut into
   1–2cm (½–¾in) dice
4 tbsp sunflower or vegetable oil
3 medium courgettes (zucchini), cut into
   2cm (¾in) discs on a slight angle
2–3 tbsp pomegranate molasses
1–2 tbsp extra virgin olive oil
2–3 tbsp mixed seeds (e.g. sunflower,
   pumpkin, sesame)
Leaves picked from 4–5 sprigs mint,
   finely shredded
120–150g (4¼–5½oz) pomegranate seeds
   (from 1 small or ½ large pomegranate)
2–3 tsp sumac
Flaky sea salt and ground black pepper

Heat the oven to 200°C/180°C fan/400°F.

Put the aubergines in a medium-size roasting tin – they can be close together but ideally not in more than two layers. Add two tablespoons of the sunflower or vegetable oil to the tin and roll the aubergines around until glossy. Place in the middle of the oven for a total of 50 minutes, shuffling occasionally so that by the end they're evenly bronzed and softened.

Put the courgettes in another roasting tin or baking sheet, this time one that's big enough to leave a little space between courgette pieces. Add the remaining two tablespoons of oil, jumble the courgettes until they're all glossy then set each piece flat on a fleshy side. After the aubergines have been cooking for 25 minutes, turn the oven up to 220°C/200°C fan/425°F and slide the courgettes above the aubergines. After 15 minutes bring the courgettes out and flip each piece so that both sides get a chance to colour, then cook for 10 minutes more, bringing the courgettes and aubergines out of the oven at the same time.

Combine the vegetables in one tray. Be deliberate but gentle as you do this – the aubergines will be soft and will inevitably squish, but try to keep the courgettes relatively intact. While still hot, season very generously with salt and pepper, drizzle over two tablespoons of pomegranate molasses and the olive oil, and turn the vegetables over in the tray (again, gently), before letting them cool a little while preparing whatever else you're having.

Finally, when cooled a little, add two thirds of each of the mixed seeds, mint and pomegranate seeds, then transfer everything to a large serving platter (so the vegetables sit in one or two layers). Drizzle with more pomegranate molasses, a touch more olive oil, add a thick dusting of sumac, finally scattering over the rest of the mixed seeds, mint and pomegranate.

Agrodolce squash platter

An Italian classic, this sweet and sour platter of colourful and flavourful ingredients is something that will be particularly enjoyable in late winter/early spring, as you start the mental move from comforting stews and bakes to salads and fresh assemblies. It's a nice lunch on its own, with bread to mop the juices. Alternatively, fit it among a series of other sharing dishes, or omit the cheese and ham and serve the sweet-sour squash and bitter leaves alongside a roast chicken or slow-cooked lamb.

Baking the squash whole has at least two benefits. One is that the result has the intensity of flavour that you get when roasting squash, without the oiliness. I feel this helps the squash to soak up rather than repel the agrodolce dressing and makes for a more texturally pleasing platter. The second is that there's no need to worry about losing your fingers because your knife is too blunt to chop a raw squash. Which I know is a fear a few have.

Serves 4–6

—

1 butternut squash (approximately 1kg/2.2lb)
1 red onion, halved, thinly sliced
5 tbsp light olive oil
1 clove garlic, finely sliced
100ml (scant ½ cup) red wine vinegar
4 tbsp water
2 tbsp golden caster (superfine) sugar
1 heaped tbsp sultanas or golden raisins
2 tbsp extra virgin olive oil
½ small radicchio, leaves separated, cut into palm-size pieces
Handful mint leaves, finely chopped (optional)
250g (9oz) mozzarella
80g (2¾oz) thinly sliced prosciutto
Flaky sea salt and ground black pepper

Heat the oven to 180°C/160°C fan/350°F. Wash the squash, put it on a small baking sheet and into the oven. Let it bake, untouched, for 90 minutes until the skin is blistered and weeping, and the flesh beginning to sink.

Meanwhile make the agrodolce dressing by gently frying the sliced onions, with a pinch of salt, in the light olive oil until they're soft and sticky but not at all brown (adding the salt at the start will help speed things along). Over a low–medium heat this will take around 10 minutes.

When the onions are looking sweet and slippery, add the garlic and cook for 1 minute more, then add the vinegar, three tablespoons of the water and the sugar. Bring this to a boil and cook for 5 minutes, by which time the dressing should look and feel glossy, almost syrupy. Remove from the heat, add the sultanas or raisins and leave to cool.

When the squash is cooked, remove the baking sheet from the oven and roll the squash onto a serving platter. Add the remaining tablespoon of water into the hot baking sheet and stir into the caramelized squash juices to loosen them. Tip these into the dressing.

Use the tip of a sharp knife to cut the squash in half lengthways. Scoop the seeds out (and discard) and slice each half into chunks. Push the chunks apart a little, season generously with salt and pepper, then spoon over the dressing – reserving a tablespoon of it to dress the radicchio. Leave to mingle, ideally for 3–4 hours, though you could tuck in sooner if you wish.

When you're ready to eat, measure a couple of tablespoons of extra virgin olive oil into a mixing bowl, along with the reserved agrodolce dressing and a good pinch of flaky salt and black pepper. Beat with a fork, then toss in the radicchio and the chopped mint, if using. Add the leaves to the squash platter, along with generous tearings of mozzarella. Drape the prosciutto over the top, or serve on the side.

Sweet and sour vegetable puff tart

This is absolutely not the Sicilian god-tier dish caponata on a puff pastry base. Yet it does borrow something of its spirit – not least the pleasingly brutal assault from sweet-sour vinegared summer vegetables (well, botanically they're fruits), and also the fact that those flavours come through best once cooled to ever so slightly above room temperature. It's a level up from a straight tomato tart, and very welcome at a warm summer's lunchtime or early evening meal – with a green salad to pick at and, more importantly, chilled wine.

The multi-staged method is required in order to pull maximum flavour from each element, provide the right balance of sweet and sour, and to ensure the tart has a crisp, not soggy, bottom.

Serves 4
–

2 medium aubergines (eggplants)
   (approximately 500g/1lb 2oz in total)
4 tbsp extra virgin olive oil, plus extra to drizzle
400g (14oz) cherry tomatoes
2 tsp caster (superfine) sugar
1 medium courgette (zucchini), cut into
   1cm (½in) dice
3 tsp red wine vinegar
2 tsp dried oregano
40g (1½oz) Kalamata olives, pits in
1 clove garlic, minced
1 x 320g (11¼oz) sheet pre-rolled all butter
   puff pastry
60g (2¼oz) feta, crumbled
Handful basil leaves (optional)
Balsamic vinegar, to drizzle
Flaky sea salt and ground black pepper

Serve with a green salad.

–

Heat the oven to 220°C/200°C fan/425°F.

Slice the aubergines in half lengthways. Use a knife to cross-hatch their flesh, then put these cut-side up in a roasting tin. Add a sprinkle of salt plus a tablespoon of olive oil to each half, then bake in the oven for 25 minutes. At this point, turn the aubergines over (so now the cut sides face down), and arrange 100g (3½oz) of the tomatoes in any gaps between them. Sprinkle the tomatoes with the sugar and more olive oil, then return to the oven for a further 20 minutes.

Meanwhile, halve the remaining tomatoes and add them, along with the courgettes, to a container that will hold the cut vegetables in two to three layers. Sprinkle with one teaspoon of salt, two teaspoons of the red wine vinegar and the dried oregano. Tap the olives with the base of a mug to split them, remove the pits and roughly chop. Add these and the garlic to the tomatoes and courgettes, mix well and set to one side.

Remove the aubergines from the oven, transfer to a chopping board and set the roasted tomatoes aside. Chop the aubergine thoroughly, including the skin, until you have a speckled paste. Add the final teaspoon of red wine vinegar, a generous pinch of salt and a few grinds of black pepper. Spread the paste out on the board to dry out a little bit while you roll out the pastry (after a few minutes it will darken – this is fine).

Roll the puff pastry sheet out onto a flat baking sheet. Use the blunt back edge of a knife to score a margin 3cm (1¼in) from the edge. Spread the aubergine paste in the middle of the pastry, up to the scored lines. Arrange the pre-roasted tomatoes evenly on top. Strain the courgette, tomato and olive mix through a sieve then arrange around the cooked tomatoes.

For best results chill the tart for 20 minutes or longer, then slide towards the top of the oven (still heated to 220°C/200°C fan/425°F) and bake for 35 minutes until the edges are golden and the underside is fully cooked through. If it's looking a bit too bronzed after 25 minutes, reduce the temperature to 180°C/160°C fan/350°F and cook for a total of 40 minutes. Allow to cool for 5–10 minutes. Just prior to serving, crumble the feta over the top, add the basil leaves, and drizzle with balsamic (the more retro and viscous, the better in this instance) plus a little extra virgin olive oil. A tart that appeared slightly dull and dry when you pulled it from the oven will now be as lively, glistening and sharp to look at as it is to eat.

Charred mackerel rice bowls with ginger-pickled rhubarb

I'm sometimes tempted to treat sushi ginger as a side dish rather than a condiment or palate cleanser (as it's intended to be). I find it zippy, a sweet kind of sour, extremely moreish, and more satisfying when crunched through in copious amounts than in delicate, occasional shreds. That kind of ginger is the inspiration for this rhubarb pickle, which also works so well when served (generously) next to oily mackerel and short-grain rice seasoned with a seaweed (nori) and sesame sprinkle (furikake – page 31).

Though simple, there are a few stages here (making the pickle, curing the mackerel, cooking the rice, cooking the mackerel). It's no great effort, but you could skip the mackerel cure. The pickle does need half a day or so to steep.

Serves 2 (with some pickles left over)
–

For the ginger-pickled rhubarb
1 stick forced rhubarb
   (approximately 160g/5½oz)
50g (1¾oz) fresh ginger, peeled
½ tsp salt
90ml (6 tbsp) rice vinegar
4 tbsp water
50g (4 tbsp) caster (superfine) sugar
1 tsp fennel seeds
1 tsp coriander seeds

For the mackerel rice bowls
2 mackerel fillets, pin-boned
1 tbsp caster (superfine) sugar
1 tbsp fine table salt
200g (7oz) short-grain sushi rice
2 tsp sushi vinegar
1–2 tsp neutral cooking oil
3 tbsp nori and sesame sprinkle (page 31)

As a dressing
1 tbsp light soy sauce
1 tbsp sesame oil
2 tbsp pickling liquor from the pickled rhubarb

Slice the rhubarb on a 45° angle as finely as you can. Then use a mandoline to slice the ginger paper-thin. Put both in a non-reactive container (Tupperware is ideal), add the salt and mix. In a small saucepan, combine the vinegar, water, sugar and spices. Bring to the boil for 3 minutes then pour over the rhubarb and ginger. Leave to cool then cover and refrigerate until needed.

Set the mackerel fillets skin-side down in a container. Combine the sugar and salt, then sprinkle over the fish flesh. Refrigerate for 45 minutes, during which time the mackerel will firm up. Wash off the curing mix under a trickle of water from the cold tap and pat dry with paper towels. Wash and dry the container previously used for the curing, then return the mackerel to it and refrigerate, uncovered, until required. (Although you can cook it straight away.)

To cook the rice, first measure it into a saucepan and cover with cold water. Stir for 20 seconds, drain through a sieve, return the rice to the pan and repeat the process six times so the water is much less cloudy. Add 300ml (1¼ cups) of cold water and set on a high heat. As soon as the water boils, stir to ensure the rice is not stuck to the bottom of the pan, then reduce to the lowest heat possible, place a lid on top and simmer for 7–8 minutes. Remove from the heat at the point the water has almost all been absorbed, but the rice is still loose. Stir in the sushi vinegar and place a folded dish towel over the top, leaving just a little gap. Leave for 20 minutes for the rice to steam, finish cooking and also dry out a little, stirring three or four times over that period.

Near the end of the rice's resting time, put the grill (broiler) on its highest temperature and place a rack high up. Rub the mackerel with a little cooking oil and place on a baking sheet skin-side up. When the grill is piping hot, place the mackerel underneath and cook for 3 minutes.

Divide the rice between two bowls, add the nori and sesame sprinkle. Combine the soy, sesame oil and pickling juice to make a dressing. Then top the rice with the mackerel fillets, tip the dressing over them, and add a heap of pickles.

Buttermilk chicken with sour watermelon salad

True connoisseurs of fizzing penny sweets will identify sour watermelons as the greatest of them all. The little peach-coloured half crescents are the best version, but those that actually look like slices of watermelon are great too.

I only note this to provide background when I state that this is not a fruit gum salad; however, Haribo and co. were on to something when combining the sweetness of watermelon with seasonings that make your gums recede. In this instance the (actual fresh) fruit does a dance with a lime and honey dressing, quick-pickled cucumbers and also a sumac-laced spice mix. That same spice mix seasons chicken nuggets made from thigh pieces that have been tenderizing in buttermilk overnight. This is best eaten when you have or want a smile on your face, perhaps with a bowl of well-salted fries or other form of crunchy potato nearby. Corn on the cob is an excellent partner too.

Or, if you are just after sour watermelon, you might ignore most of the recipe below, and simply serve very cold slices of watermelon, doused in the sweet-sour dressing, a little chopped mint, then heavy and possibly repeated dustings of the sumac and fennel seasoning.

Serves 4–6

—

For the buttermilk chicken
1kg (2lb 4oz) boneless, skinless chicken thighs
300ml (1¼ cup + 1 tbsp) cultured buttermilk
8g (1½ tsp) flaky sea salt
1 clove garlic, crushed
4 tbsp neutral cooking oil
140g (5oz) panko breadcrumbs

For the sumac and fennel seed seasoning
1 tbsp coriander seeds
1 tbsp fennel seeds
1 tbsp sumac
½ tsp pul biber (Aleppo pepper flakes)
1 tsp flaky sea salt

For the salad and dressings
2 heaped tsp runny honey
2 tsp extra virgin olive oil
1 lime, zest finely grated and juiced
1kg (2lb 4oz) watermelon, flesh cut away
    from the skin, cut into 2cm (¾in) chunks
½ large cucumber, peeled and cut into
    1cm (½in) dice
½ tsp caster (superfine) sugar
1 tbsp moscatel vinegar (or white wine vinegar)
80g (2¾oz) watercress, picked apart into
    mouthful-size pieces of stem and leaf
Leaves picked from 5–6 sprigs mint,
    finely chopped
Flaky sea salt

—

Cut the chicken thigh fillets in half down the middle, so they're like stumpy rectangles a bit bigger than a chicken nugget. Combine with the buttermilk, salt and garlic. Cover and refrigerate for 12–36 hours.

At some point before cooking the chicken, you need to bake the breadcrumbs so that they're golden. To do this, heat the oven to 200°C/ 180°C fan/400°F. Spread the neutral oil over a baking sheet and sprinkle over the breadcrumbs, then shuffle to mix. Bake at the top of the oven for 6–12 minutes, until the crumbs are the golden colour you'd expect on a store-bought fishfinger or chicken kiev. The exact time will depend on the depth of the crumbs in the tray – ideally no more than 5mm (¼in). Check after 6 minutes, shuffle to swap the crumbs at the top with those at the bottom, then check and shuffle every 2 minutes thereafter. Leave to cool – store in an airtight container in a dark cupboard if not using straight away.

To cook the chicken, heat the oven to 200°C/ 180°C fan/400°F and line a baking sheet with baking paper. Dredge the chicken in the golden panko crumbs and lay on the lined sheet, with about 1cm (½in) between each piece (use a second sheet if necessary), then bake for 35 minutes. Once cooked, dust with a tablespoon of the seasoning (see opposite) plus an additional half teaspoon of salt.

Make the seasoning while the chicken cooks (or well in advance), by toasting the coriander and fennel seeds in a dry pan for 2–3 minutes until aromatic. Use a pestle and mortar to pound them to somewhere between a coarse rubble and dust, then combine with the sumac, Aleppo pepper and salt. Store in an airtight container if not using straight away.

For the watermelon salad, loosen the honey by whisking it together with the olive oil and a squeeze of lime. Then mix in the rest of the lime juice and the zest, and roll the watermelon pieces around that. In a separate bowl mix the cucumber, sugar, a pinch of salt and the vinegar

and leave for 5 minutes. After that, add two tablespoons of the sumac seasoning to the melon, add the watercress and mix one more time before transferring to a bowl or platter. Spoon the cucumber pieces and vinegar over the top of the salad and sprinkle with the mint.

Thai-style dipping sauces with sticky rice

Dishes involving dipping sauces from Laos and Thailand are something I find hard to resist if ever I see them on a restaurant menu. Those sauces typically accompany something like grilled fish or smoked and grilled meats, plus a bamboo basket of sticky rice that begs to be eaten with your hands. It's a simple combination but with long-lasting impact; one I found necessary to replicate at home frequently when 2020's pandemic hit and I could no longer get out to those restaurants.

The nam phrik (dried shrimp, lime and fish sauce dip) works best with fish, while the more intense yet also rounder tamarind-spiked nam jim jaew (tamarind and chilli dip) is one for rich, fatty and smoky (if you have an outdoor grill) meats.

Base each dip on the guidelines overleaf, but every fish sauce is different, as are the limes and the tamarind pulp you use, so taste and adjust. Both have a touch of chilli-heat in them, and indeed the sourness should be tempered by salty fish sauce and sugar too, but the balance should edge in favour of mouth-puckering.

The sticky rice and the dipping sauce recipes here are suitable for four people, as an accompaniment to meat, fish or vegetable centrepieces of your choosing. The ground roasted rice is required for the nam jim jaew.

Ground roasted rice

This recipe makes far more than you need for the nam jim jaew (overleaf). However, the excess can be stored in an airtight container for quick use in future meals, including the laab on page 100.

—

100g (3½oz) white rice (glutinous, jasmine or basmati)

—

Heat the oven to 200°C/180°C fan/400°F. Spread the rice over a baking sheet so that it fits in one layer. Bake in the middle of the oven for 35–40 minutes until golden, shuffling the tray after 25 minutes. Grind to a grit (rather than a dusty flour) using a pestle and mortar or by pulsing in a spice grinder. To avoid much of it becoming dust-like you will need to do this in three or four batches, depending on the size of your mortar/grinder.

Sticky rice

250g (9oz) Thai glutinous rice (sometimes labelled 'sticky' or 'sweet' rice)

You will need a steamer and a muslin cloth (cheesecloth) or fine sieve (strainer) that fits within it.

—

Measure the rice into a container and completely cover with just-boiled water. Leave to soak for 1 hour. Drain the water, then either leave the rice in the sieve or decant into a muslin cloth, tie, and place in a steamer basket over a pan of water at a rolling boil. Cover and steam for 30 minutes. Transfer to a serving dish, cover with a clean dish towel and leave to steam, cool and dry out a bit for 10 minutes more – in fact it could sit like this for another half an hour (it will still be warm enough).

Continued overleaf

Green nam phrik

2 tsp dried shrimp
2 cloves garlic, roughly chopped
2 green bird's eye chillies, roughly chopped
1 coriander (cilantro) root or 2–3 coriander
    stalks, roughly chopped
1 tbsp golden caster (superfine) sugar or
    palm sugar
2 tbsp fish sauce
2 tsp water
Juice 2 limes
Flaky sea salt

Serve with butterflied and grilled sardines,
herrings, mackerel, grilled fillets of mullet
or bream, flat fish like plaice or sole, or
crisp-skinned fried trout or salmon.

—

Put the dried shrimp and garlic in a mortar with
a pinch of salt and pound with a pestle until well
bashed (this might seem unlikely to begin with,
but you'll get there). Add the chilli and coriander
and pound again until you have a paste. Add the
sugar and grind that in, then measure in the fish
sauce, water and lime juice and mix well. Divide
between a few saucers for easy dipping.

Nam jim jaew

30g (1oz) tamarind pulp (from a block)
5 generous tbsp just-boiled water
Juice 1 lime
2 tbsp fish sauce
1 spring onion (scallion), very finely chopped
4 tsp golden caster (superfine) or palm sugar
1 tbsp cold water
2 tsp dried chilli flakes
1 tbsp ground roasted rice (page 74)

Serve with barbecued or roast chicken legs,
crisp-skinned duck breasts, pork or lamb chops.

—

Put the tamarind in a small bowl or mug, then
add three tablespoons and an extra splash
of the just-boiled water. Allow it to soak for
30 seconds, then mash the pulp with the back
of a fork, encouraging the tamarind to dissolve
and also thicken a little. Push this through a fine
sieve (capturing the paste), then repeat with an
additional two tablespoons of just-boiled water.
Discard the seeds and woody bits once done.

Combine all the ingredients except the ground
rice in a small bowl. When ready to eat, add half
the rice powder and stir, then divide between a
few saucers for easy dipping and sprinkle the
remaining ground rice on top.

Chicken adobo

The Filipino dish adobo (or perhaps more accurately 'genre of dishes') is a master example of the addictiveness of soured foods. Cloudy white vinegars from the Philippines (distilled from, among other things, sugar cane, coconut and palm tree sap) would originally have been used to prevent spoiling and so extend the life of a meal. Now, it's about the flavour.

There's a relatively significant quantity of vinegar used in this recipe, and the resulting sharp-tasting braising liquid is reduced to an intense glaze. Yet it is very definitely not 'too much'; the acidity seems to mellow through time in the pan, pulling your mouth back towards the food, rather than forcing it to recoil as might be expected.

Many adobo recipes substitute Filipino vinegar with cider, wine and rice vinegars. Tasty, but not quite the same. Given the limited number of ingredients, it is worth trying to get hold of the real thing: the Datu Puti brand is accessible – both in Asian supermarkets and also online – and I am confident the bottle you source won't become store-cupboard clutter. You'll cook this more than once.

Serves 4

—

4–5 tbsp neutral cooking oil
1 bulb garlic, cloves minced
300ml (1¼ cups + 1 tbsp) Filipino white cane vinegar (sukang maasim)
150ml (scant ⅔ cup) Filipino soy sauce (or another light soy sauce)
100ml (scant ½ cup) water
4 bay leaves
1 tsp whole black peppercorns
4 chicken legs (about 1.2kg/2lb 10oz), portioned into thighs and drumsticks
1–2 spring onions (scallions), finely chopped

Serve with jasmine or plain white rice.

Place a large, heavy-bottomed saucepan (for which you have a lid) on a medium heat. Add a tablespoon of the neutral cooking oil and the minced garlic, and sauté for a minute or so to soften. As the garlic begins to turn golden (and before it browns and becomes bitter) pour in the vinegar, soy sauce and water, add the bay leaves and peppercorns, then arrange the chicken thighs and drumsticks so that they fit in one layer, and if not totally, then mostly submerged.

Bring to a light boil, then reduce the heat so that, with the lid on, the contents of the saucepan simmer away for 45 minutes, by which time the leg meat should be coming away from the bone, and the thigh meat pliant and no longer bouncy. Continue simmering for 5 more minutes if not.

At this point, either leave to cool and refrigerate until you're ready to eat or follow the instructions coming up. If you are reheating the chicken from fridge-cold, follow the same processes, it will just take a bit more time.

Remove the chicken from the saucepan and set to one side. Use a spoon to skim off a little of the fat, then bring to the boil, keeping the lid off, until the sauce has reduced by a third to a half and has thickened enough to leave a light sheen on the back of a spoon.

Meanwhile, place a large frying pan over a medium–high heat. Add three to four tablespoons of cooking oil, let this heat up for 45 seconds then arrange the chicken pieces skin-side down. Cook until the skins have browned and crisped. The pan will spit a bit. If you prefer you could line a tray with foil or baking paper, arrange the chicken skin-side up and grill (broil) for 4–5 minutes bronzing (not blackening) them. Serve with rice, lots of sauce and a scattering of sliced spring onions.

Cider vinegar-roasted pork belly and apricots

I find a craving for something sharp often goes hand in hand with a desire for something rich and fatty. It's not obvious which sensation I'm really after, although the former is essential to cut through the latter. Does that make the sour element more or less important? Does it matter?

Pork belly is one example of an ingredient that needs acid to complete it. In cold months it's fine if accompanied by similarly heavy and savoury ingredients and something only slightly sour, like an apple sauce. But come spring and summer, a meal involving pork belly needs a lighter touch. Green salads, grains, baby potatoes are all helpful, yet there needs to be something bright and sharp too. Apricot season often chimes with a desire to edge away from comfort food, and the tart notes that appear when cooked go perfectly here (you could use batons of rhubarb in exactly the same way).

Serves 4–6

–

4 tbsp fennel seeds
10–20g (¼–¾oz) flaky sea salt
1.25–1.75kg (2lb 12oz–3lb 12oz) pork belly
  (bone in, skin scored)
250ml (generous 1 cup) dry (hard) cider
100ml (scant ½ cup) apple cider vinegar
10 baby shallots, peeled and halved
40g (1½oz) fresh ginger, sliced
6–9 apricots (3 halves per serving),
  halved and pitted

Bash the fennel seeds to open them up. Mix half of them with one tablespoon of the salt, then rub that into the flesh of the pork (the base and the sides). Sprinkle the rest of the salt, or as much as you need, to completely cover the skin on top. Refrigerate uncovered for 90 minutes or more (overnight is best).

Heat the oven to 240°C/220°C fan/475°F.

Brush the salt off the top of the pork and discard, but leave any fennel seeds still attached to the flesh. Place in a roasting tin in which the pork fits snugly. Roast in the middle of the oven for 45 minutes, during which time the skin will puff up and harden.

After that time, remove the roasting tin from the oven and reduce the oven temperature to 140°C/120°C fan/275°F. Carefully decant the rendered fat from the base of the tin into a heatproof container, then pour the cider and vinegar into the tin (taking care not to get the crackling wet). Add the shallots, ginger and the remaining fennel seeds, then return the roasting tin to the oven for a further 1¼ hours, adding the apricot halves (cut-side down), to the liquid around the pork when there's 30 minutes to go.

Once cooked, remove the pork from the roasting tin and leave to rest on a board in a warm place for 15 minutes. Meanwhile, transfer the apricots to a plate or container, taking care to keep them intact. Place the roasting tin (with the liquid, shallots and ginger still in) on a high heat and bring to a furious boil for 10 minutes, reducing the liquid by half to two-thirds so it becomes a glossy and viscous sauce. Pick out and discard the ginger. Serve the apricots next to generous slices of pork belly, with the sweet-sour sauce and shallots spooned over both, and a big green salad and bowl of well-salted baby potatoes nearby.

Pickled walnut-braised shallots, steak and rocket salad

The absolute best pickled thing is a pickled walnut (Opies is the brand to look out for). This curiously tender, dark treat is classically matched with blue cheese, cured beef or a venison or pheasant pie. But it cuts through ferrous steak incredibly well, too. So much so that I was tempted to simply provide a recipe stating: *"Cook a bavette or onglet, serve with pickled walnuts"*, but decided to embellish a little.

The various components here could be served in any number of ways, but I choose the kind of sharing platter that works so well as an *"I just threw this together"* thing. Each of the elements are super-punchy but they temper each other and the net result is joyous. You'll want a bottle of something red alongside.

Serves 4

–

500g (1lb 2oz) small shallots
2 tbsp neutral cooking oil
2 tbsp golden caster (superfine) sugar
100ml (scant ½ cup) red wine
100ml (scant ½ cup) liquid from a jar
   of pickled walnuts
5 pickled walnuts, quartered
600g (1lb 5oz) bavette (flank) or onglet
   (hanger) steak
2 tbsp extra virgin olive oil
200g (7oz) rocket (arugula)
200g (7oz) Japanese radish (daikon),
   peeled and cut into 1cm (½in) dice
2 tbsp crispy shallots
Flaky sea salt and ground black pepper

Serve with French fries and a tomato salad.

–

Put the shallots in a bowl, cover with just-boiled water and leave for 10–15 minutes so the skins pull away from the bulbs. Use a small paring knife to trim the bases off each shallot and to peel the skin away, leaving the shallot whole. You can prepare these well in advance (and you might want to watch a boxset while doing so...).

Heat the oven to 200°C/180°C fan/400°F.

Find a skillet or ovenproof sauté pan into which the shallots fit in more or less one layer. Set this over a medium–high heat, add the neutral cooking oil, the peeled shallots, sugar and a generous pinch of salt. Mix, then fry for about 8 minutes, shuffling the pan regularly, until the shallots are burnished and the sugar is caramelizing. Pour in the wine and let that reduce by about half over the course of a minute or so. Add the pickling liquid, shuffle the contents one more time, place a lid (or foil) on top and cook in the oven for a total of 20 minutes – lid or foil on for the first 10 minutes, lid off thereafter. Remove, sprinkle half a teaspoon of flaky salt over the top and leave to cool for up to 10 minutes before adding the pickled walnut quarters and gently mixing them into the shallots.

Shortly before removing the shallots from the oven, begin to cook the bavette or onglet to medium/medium–rare. Cook however you prefer – for what it's worth, I'd cook the steak a couple of minutes per side in a very hot heavy-bottomed pan, in oil to begin with then, after the first two turns, a load of frothing butter for 2–3 minutes more, until the core is a touch over 50°C/122°F (if you're a thermometer person). Rest for 5 minutes, then slice into 1cm (½ in)-wide pieces and season with a lot of flaky salt.

Measure the extra virgin olive oil into a mixing bowl. Add half a teaspoon of flaky salt and lots of black pepper. Toss in the rocket, daikon and crispy shallots and decant onto a platter or individual plates. Use a slotted spoon to distribute the still-warm shallots and pickled walnuts over the rocket, then arrange the sliced steak on and around.

Finally, stir any cooking and resting juices from the steak pan and board into the remaining syrupy sauce in the shallot pan. There'll be four to five tablespoons' worth of liquid – whisk in a tablespoon or two of hot water if necessary. Spoon this over the platter and serve with well-salted fries and a tomato salad.

Brown-sugar meringues, tamarind and blood orange

The sour elements of this dessert make it akin to finishing a meal by inhaling a bag of Tangfastics. Appealing? Read on.

If you can get hold of blood oranges when in season, do (though normal oranges work well enough), as they and the similarly fantastically sour tamarind bounce off the tongue, their effect softened only by a luxurious double-thick crash mat of mellow cream and brown-sugar meringues.

This has all the elements of a pavlova, but I find it's more enjoyable if the cream is whipped at the last minute and the pudding served almost as a DIY assembly.

Serves 4

–

100g (3½oz) golden caster (superfine) sugar
50g (1¾oz) soft light brown sugar
2 large egg whites
Pinch flaky sea salt
50g (1¾oz) tamarind pulp (from a block)
150ml (scant ⅔ cup) just-boiled water
230ml (7¾oz) double (heavy) cream
1 tsp icing (confectioners') sugar
2 blood oranges

–

Heat the oven to 170°C/150°C fan/325°F.

Combine the two sugars in a heatproof bowl. Use the back of a fork to break up any clumps in the brown sugar and stir to ensure the two types are well mixed.

Set up a stand mixer and ensure the bowl and whisk are spotless. Put the egg whites and pinch of salt in the bowl, turn the machine to a medium–fast pace and whisk to stiff-peak stage. At the same time, place the sugar in the oven and allow it to warm for 2–3 minutes (incidentally about the same time it'll take to whisk the eggs...), then increase the speed of the machine and add the sugar to the whites in a slow but steady stream. Once the sugars have been added, whisk at high speed for around 10 minutes longer.

The meringue is ready when you can no longer feel any sugar granules if you take a pinch and rub it between thumb and forefinger.

Line a baking sheet with baking paper or a silicon mat. Use a large metal spoon to heap the mix into four mounds. Then use the back of a clean teaspoon to make a little dent in the middle of each mound (these will become the ponds in which the tamarind will pool). Place in the middle of the oven, close the door and immediately reduce the temperature to 140°C/120°C fan/275°F. Bake for an hour, then turn the oven off, leaving the meringues to cool inside for 30 minutes. Store at room temperature in an airtight container until required.

To make the purée, put the tamarind in a small bowl, then add four tablespoons of the just-boiled water. Allow it to soak for a couple of minutes. Stir vigorously, encouraging the tamarind to dissolve and also thicken a little. Push this through a sieve (capturing the paste), then repeat twice more, and on the third occasion add just two tablespoons of water. Discard the seeds and woody bits once done. Refrigerate the purée until required.

Before assembling, put the cream and icing sugar in a mixing bowl, and find a hand whisk and, ideally, a bag of frozen peas (the cold will help to whip the cream faster and stay lighter). Use a sharp knife to trim the skin from the oranges, then cut those oranges into chunks, slices or segments. Scrape the juice from the board into the cream. Sit the bowl of cream on the bag of frozen peas, whisk until it's thick, ribboning and just about holds itself if you put a dollop on a plate.

Drop a teaspoon or two of tamarind purée into the dents in the meringues, spoon the cream on top, and arrange the oranges on or around. Drizzle the remaining tamarind over the top (and put the peas back in the freezer!).

Cherry and apricot slab pie

I *quite* like a fruit pie; I *really* like a 'slab' fruit pie (because: the corners); and I *love* a slab pie filled with naturally sour fruits. Rhubarb and gooseberries are the obvious choice for fans of seasonal British fruit – and as it happens, 800–900g (1lb 12oz–2lb) of either substitute perfectly in this recipe without any other changes. However, there's something about an apricot pie that sucks me in, largely because of that fruit's transformation from mellow and sometimes dull when raw, to always tart once cooked. Here I've added cherries for their dramatic colour and sweet flavour that pairs neatly with the cooked apricots, without diverting attention from the desired sourness. Serve with crème fraîche for additional tang.

A note on the pastry – they might seem a bit onerous, but each of the three (three!) refrigeration steps prescribed below are important: to create a 'short' not chewy pastry, to ensure the buttery dough is easy to handle, and to make sure that the butter doesn't melt when first placed in the oven. Please do follow them.

Pictured on pages 84–85.

Serves 8

—

430g (15¼oz) plain (all-purpose) flour,
   plus extra for dusting
200g (7oz) unsalted butter, plus extra
   for greasing
100g (3½oz) icing (confectioners') sugar
½ tsp flaky sea salt
1 tbsp apple cider vinegar
3 tbsp cold milk, plus a little extra as a wash
700g (1lb 9oz) apricots, pitted and quartered
250g (9oz) cherries, pitted
100g (3½oz) golden caster (superfine) sugar
120g (4¼oz) ground almonds
2 tbsp demerara (light brown) sugar

Serve with crème fraîche.

This works particularly well in a 30 x 20 x 3cm (12 x 8 x 1¼in) baking tin.

Rub together (or use a food processor to pulse) the flour, butter, icing sugar and salt into a breadcrumb-like consistency. Add the vinegar and cold milk, and press into a ball of dough. Divide the pastry into two not-quite-equal pieces, push into rectangles about 3cm (1¼in) thick, then wrap both and refrigerate for at least an hour, ideally longer.

The pastry is very buttery and can be tricky to handle, so roll out between two sheets of baking paper: the smaller one so that it's the same size as your tin (this will be the lid); the other, big enough to line the base and sides; and both to 2–3mm (1⁄16–1⁄8in) thick. You'll be able to break off bits that are not in the right shape and place them where they should be as you go. Refrigerate for at least an hour (again).

Combine the fruit in a bowl with the caster sugar and leave to macerate. After 20 minutes, add half the ground almonds, stir and set to one side.

Butter the baking tin, dust with flour, then line the tin with the larger pastry sheet. Use a knife to trim the pastry so it's flush with the top of the tin, using the excess to patch up any holes or thinner areas. Sprinkle the base with the remaining ground almonds then tip the filling in, ensuring an even distribution. Brush the edge of the pastry base with milk, then place the lid on top, pressing down firmly to seal the pastry together. Trim any overhang. Brush with milk, then add a liberal sprinkling of demerara sugar. Refrigerate one final time for at least 30 minutes (the pastry needs to be cold and the oven fully to temperature).

Heat the oven to 200°C/180°C fan/400°F. Place the baking tin on a larger sheet (to catch any spilled juices) and bake for 45 minutes, until the pastry is hard and golden, with some of the fruit bubbling through. If after 35–40 minutes the pie is looking very bronzed, turn the oven down to 180°C/160°C fan/350°F but do keep it in for the full amount of time. Leave to cool for 10 minutes before serving with big dollops of crème fraîche.

Buttermilk pudding
with sharp fruits

A cross between a posset, a panna cotta and just a big splodge of dairy, this thickened, wibbling combination of cream and cultured buttermilk boasts a quiet but definite lactic tang. As such it qualifies under the tart and sour category on its own.

The key to the package, however, is the fruit that you serve with it – which should be sweet, but also sharp and lip-puckering. It's a flexible dessert, so please use whatever is in season, to hand and that takes your fancy. Many fruits are naturally tart – I'm thinking rhubarb, gooseberries, apricots, loquats and plums – and all you need to do is bake, roast, poach or stew them until tender, adding just 10–15 per cent of the fruit's weight in sugar (and then adjusting to taste). Alternatively, take sweeter summer berries and currants and macerate them in white balsamic vinegar as below.

The crumbled amaretti biscuits round the flavours a little and provide a necessary crunch.

Serves 6
–

For the buttermilk pudding
1 vanilla pod (bean)
300ml (1¼ cups + 1 tbsp) double (heavy) cream
100g (3½oz) caster (superfine) sugar
3 (4.5g/⅛oz) leaves gelatine
4 tsp lemon juice
300ml (1¼ cups + 1 tbsp) cultured buttermilk

For the fruit
400g (14oz) cooked tart fruit, as described
  above (optional)
Or
For white balsamic macerated strawberries
  (optional)
400g (14oz) strawberries, hulled and halved
  (or other summer berry)
2 tbsp granulated sugar
2 tbsp white balsamic vinegar

To serve
12 amaretti biscuits

Use the tip of a sharp knife to split the vanilla pod in half, then use the blunt edge of the knife to scrape the seeds out. Combine the seeds, pod, cream and sugar in a medium–large saucepan with tall sides (as the cream is about to expand significantly).

Prepare a small bowl of cold water for the gelatine leaves to 'bloom' in.

Place the saucepan over a medium–high heat and boil for exactly 2 minutes. Start the timer when the cream in the middle of the pan is beginning to bubble and threatens to rise up (not when it's simply bubbling around the edge). Leave the gelatine to soak in the bowl of water for the same amount of time.

Remove the pan from the heat immediately once the time is up. Add the lemon juice to the hot cream, then squeeze the water from the gelatine leaves and add those too, whisking until dissolved. Leave to cool for 30 minutes.

Decant the buttermilk into a medium-size mixing bowl or Tupperware. Strain the cooled cream through a sieve (strainer) into the buttermilk, using the back of a spatula to push the cream and vanilla seeds through. Using the same spatula, fold and stir the two liquids together until they are one. Cover and refrigerate for at least 6 hours.

Prepare your choice of sharp seasonal fruits as you wish, or, if serving with strawberries: put the halved strawberries in a bowl 30–60 minutes before serving, sprinkle with the granulated sugar, mix and add the white balsamic vinegar. Leave to macerate, tasting just before you serve in case more sugar and/or vinegar is required.

Use the biggest spoon you have to scoop a portion of set(ish) buttermilk cream per person, alongside a serving of tart fruits. Crumble the amaretti biscuits and pile near the cream (or leave for others to do so).

chilli and
heat

The dominant characteristic of a craving for this flavour profile is the weirdly masochistic desire to feel as though you've burnt yourself. As such, this section provides the best illustration of how 'flavour' is a combination of taste, smell and physical sensation.

Capsaicin, which is the key heat-generating element in chilli peppers, stimulates the same receptors in your mouth that respond to increases in temperature. So the sensation of eating food laced with chillies is exactly the same as if you had consumed something actually burning hot. Ordinarily such a signal means *Danger! Stop! Don't do that!* Yet for many the experience is pleasurable. Objectively that's odd. But it's also undeniably thrilling, addictive and, because it's a characteristic of many cuisines around the world, triggering of fond memories of travel and/or heritage. I frequently have a strong urge to seek out this flavour, this experience, and suspect many of you do, too.

That said, a desire for chilli-fuelled foods is more nuanced than wanting to compete in a horrifically machismo 'how hot can you go' competition. There are scores of different chilli peppers, presenting in multiple shapes and sizes, with varying levels of heat, and made available to us in fresh, smoked, dried and bottled form. Some are mild and gentle, some have an immediate but ephemeral effect, others build slowly to a fierce crescendo. The place of impact can differ too, with some tickling your lips and tongue, others landing at the back of the throat. Moreover, chillies taste different, displaying qualities including fruity, sweet, vegetal, dusky and smoky. This last point is overlooked but crucial: I find the style of a dish (via the taste of the chillies used) just as relevant in sating a craving for chilli as the level of heat.

Accordingly, choice of chilli is important when writing and following recipes – both in terms of simple enjoyment of a dish, but also in accurately representing the story and history behind it. While it's not realistic to be unforgivingly prescriptive, we should also do more than suggest or use a generic red chilli when another would be better. So the dishes in this book make use of a short but not unvaried selection of chillies and chilli-infused products, which I hope hit the right combination of distinctiveness, respect for global cuisine and practicality. It's worth noting that fresh chillies freeze really well – so any you don't use should be stored in the freezer (then chopped and cooked from frozen). Also, although I use a handful of specialist chilli powders and flakes – Kashmiri and Korean (gochugaru) chilli powders, and Calabrian, Aleppo (pul biber) chilli pepper flakes – it's still a relatively small selection, which you can hopefully rotate and use before their potency fades.

As an aside, although chilli peppers are very much the focus here, the physical sensation of heat in food is relevant to other ingredients too: wasabi, horseradish, mustard and even olive oil all trigger similar experiences in the mouth (and nose!). To my mind, the heat elements of each of those is most pleasurable when deployed as a complementary condiment rather than the main draw, so none of the recipes that follow focuses on them. However, if you have a craving for heat, but are not near to or in the mood for chilli, then a smudge of one of these on the side of your plate could well be the answer.

One other heat-like sensation is catered for, though, and that is the lip-buzzing characteristic found in Sichuan cooking, known as ma la. The la is the spice (heat) that comes from chillies. The ma is the tingling sensation provided by Sichuan peppercorns. Their combined effect is unique and long-lasting, not dissimilar to putting your tongue on a battery. Which again sounds weird. But a couple of recipes here utilize ma la, and if you don't love it already, I'd be delighted if these proved to be a gateway to this cuisine (if so, see the further reading on page 246).

Food writers tend to wheel out dishes on hot days that are heavy with chilli, the logic being that the heat (from the chilli) can cause us to perspire, and so help to cool us down. Also: hey, chillies are often eaten in hot countries! There's something to that rationale, of course. But chilli's warming effect is undeniably welcome on cold days too. So while season and weather are not irrelevant, neither can they be the dominant cause. Indeed, the style of dish in which the chilli features is more relevant to the nudge that comes from external temperatures. For example, I reckon the incendiary northern Thai-style chicken laab is a helpful fire-cracker in summertime, whereas other dishes like smoky chipotle tomatoes and sardines on toast and the throaty kick of cayenne and Tabasco in a quail gumbo probably sit better on colder days.

What other factors might prompt a desire for chilli and heat? Given the stimulating effect capsaicin has, it follows that this flavour provides relief on monotonous days; a fix for thrill seekers and addictive personalities if feeling drowsy or generally down. The instant-ish geki kara ramen, rainbow root som tam, 'nduja spatchcock chicken and mango with chilli, lime and salt are all things that frequently provide me with a quick pick-me-up.

Those recipe titles hint at one other broad factor: as already intimated, I'm sure that for many of us a need for a little fiery something is often in response to a recent trip or current desire to get away, a desire to recall a moment in which eyes were opened, taste buds recalibrated. Moving away from an Anglo-centric narrative, we must also recognize that a craving for the deployment of chilli and heat might also be because it provides the same kind of home-cooking 'comfort' that others get from beans on toast or roast chicken. This chapter owes a debt to the food and history of places like Mexico, Korea, West Africa, the Deep South of America, the Caribbean, Thailand, Calabria in Italy and Sichuan in China.
I think it's also important to note that, beyond the transporting factor, there's also the fact that very often chilli-rich dishes are ones of remarkable depth and complexity, the heat just one element in an intricate dance of spicy, flowery, salty, bitter, sour, smoky and sweet. Put simply, chilli and heat tend to accompany delicious.

A final thought: I'm very aware that we all have differing sensitivity and tolerance to heat. Though I think I've employed decent understanding of the various chillies through these recipes, you may well want more or less of a burn than these recipes provide. I would say I'm an enjoyer of moderate-high heat, rather than a masochist. Make of that what you will but use my suggested quantities as a base – making notes for (hopefully) the next time you cook the recipe, and keeping to hand either a few additional chopped chillies or flakes, or more of your favourite hot sauce. Or a glass of cold milk.

Chipotle tomatoes
and sardines on toast

Canned sardines on toast are a favourite quick-fix of mine. All the better if the sardines in that can are shrouded in a tomato sauce. And better still if that sauce is spiked with the heat of chilli peppers.

This dish runs with the theme of that snack, though not too far or with much more effort, as it relies on another canned wonder – chipotle chillies in adobo sauce – to add fire and smoke to an otherwise minimalist cherry tomato sauce. You will use about half a can in this recipe – decant the rest into a small container, or an ice cube tray, and freeze to use at a later date. If you can't find fresh sardines, then similarly butterflied herrings or fresh anchovies work equally well, or alternatively a fillet of mackerel, per person.

Serves 2

–

½ x 200g (7oz) can chipotle chilli peppers
 in adobo sauce
350–400g (12–14oz) cherry tomatoes
150ml (scant ⅔ cup) water
1 tsp golden caster (superfine) sugar
1 tsp sherry vinegar
6 fresh sardines, butterflied
Knob of butter, for frying
Juice ⅓ lemon
Extra virgin olive oil
Flaky sea salt

Serve on thick-sliced, well-browned toast (ideally sourdough, for the bounce and the holes).

–

Empty the half a can of chipotle in adobo into a blender and blitz until smooth and silky.

Tumble the cherry tomatoes into a saucepan that fits them in mostly one snug layer, add the water and place over a medium–high heat. Bring to the boil and shuffle the pan occasionally as the water bubbles and froths over the tomatoes. After 6 or 7 minutes, the tomatoes should still be spherical, but many will be splitting and shrinking. Sacrifice seven or eight of the most affected by squashing them against the side of the pan with the back of a fork. Leave the remainder, which should still be whole – albeit close to collapse once the sauce is cooked.

Turn the heat right down, add the chipotle purée, sugar, sherry vinegar and a very generous pinch of salt. Stir carefully and then simmer for around 3 minutes longer. Add a touch more water if necessary (the sauce around the tomatoes shouldn't be a paste and should be loose enough that it quickly covers up any gaps caused by dragging a spoon through it, but not as runny or plentiful as a pasta sauce or soup). Set to one side to cool for 2–3 minutes more while you brown some toast and cook the sardines.

Fry the sardines in a little butter skin-side down over a medium heat until two thirds of the flesh has changed colour, remove the pan from the heat and gently flip the fish over, and then almost immediately transfer them to the tomato-topped toast (see below). Alternatively, arrange the fish on a baking sheet skin-side up and grill (broil) directly under the heat element for 2–3 minutes until the skin is charred and the oils are bubbling.

While the sardines are cooking, line-up your toast on two plates and spoon over the tomato sauce so they're set for the fish as soon as it's ready. Once toast, tomato and sardines are plated, add a pinch of salt and a squeeze of lemon, plus a drizzle of extra virgin olive oil if you wish.

Note: instead of being 'on toast' this also works well with the chipotle tomatoes stirred through 200g (7oz) of cooked white beans, with tortillas – or other flatbreads – to mop things up, plus a squeeze of lime, instead of lemon, over the sardines and beans at the end. Just a thought.

Kimchi jeon and Tteokbokki rice cakes

CHILLI AND HEAT

When I changed career from lawyer to cook, I enrolled on a chef's course at Westminster Kingsway. The institution has links with Korean culinary schools, and my particular programme always includes students from Korea keen to skill themselves in the ways of Escoffier. I learnt many things from my extraordinarily precise colleague, Seo Hyung Im, though I remember in particular being struck by how different the calm and intricate traditional royal court Korean food was to the relatively in-your-face 'Korean-style' permeating London's street food and restaurant scene. I was really interested to find that the 'on-trend' genre, typified by bright-red, glistening, taste-bud-stimulating dishes, was a relatively recent invention, and generally regarded as having materialized following the split between the north and south of the country, reflecting both a need and a desire for an instant hit of sweetness and spice in economic and emotionally depressing times.

Writing this book mid-Covid pandemic I wonder what our needs will be when it is published and indeed beyond. These two sparky, relatively frugal and instantly satisfying snacks (the jeon a pancake, the tteokbokki a bowl of moreishly gummy rice-flour lozenges in an umami-chilli rich sauce) will either fit the zeitgeist completely, or (more positively), they'll simply be a tasty and satisfyingly fiery thing to enjoy whenever your mood requires it. Both turn from snack to meal with the addition of a fried egg or two, or if eaten as side dishes to steamed greens, fish or pork belly.

Kimchi jeon

Serves 2

—

Dipping sauce
1 tbsp light soy sauce
1 tsp sesame oil
½ tbsp gochujang
2 tsp rice vinegar
1 tsp sesame seeds

Kimchi jeon
150g (5½oz) mature, hot kimchi, finely chopped
1 spring onion (scallion), finely chopped
125ml (½ cup) fridge-cold water
1 tbsp kimchi brine
75g (2½oz) plain (all-purpose) flour
25g (1oz) cornflour (cornstarch)
1 tbsp gochugaru flakes

1–2 tbsp neutral cooking oil, for frying
1–2 fried eggs per person (optional)

—

Combine the dipping sauce ingredients in a little bowl, stirring until well mixed.

Measure all the jeon (pancake) ingredients into a bowl and mix well to form a batter. Place a roughly 25cm (10in) non-stick frying pan (skillet) over a medium heat. Add a tablespoon of cooking oil, allow to warm for 30–60 seconds, then add the batter and use a fish slice or palette knife to push to the edges and flatten to an even layer. Fry for 3–4 minutes, carefully flipping the pancake when the bottom is relatively crisp and firm. As you turn it over, add a little more oil underneath for lubrication, then fry for 3 minutes more. Serve as small bites with the dipping sauce, or in larger sections if you're also frying eggs.

Tteokbokki rice cakes

Serves 2

—

1 x 10g (¼oz) sachet instant dashi,
  dissolved in 350ml (1½ cups) boiling water
1 tbsp golden caster (superfine) sugar
1–2 tbsp gochujang
1 tbsp gochugaru flakes
1 tbsp light soy sauce
180g (6¼oz) Korean rice cakes
  (the lozenge shape)
¼ Chinese cabbage, roughly chopped
2 cloves garlic, minced
2 spring onions (scallions), roughly chopped,
  greens and whites separated
Sesame seeds, to garnish
1–2 fried eggs per person (optional)

—

Combine the dashi stock, sugar, one tablespoon of gochujang, the gochugaru and soy sauce in a large saucepan, bring to the boil and stir to ensure the paste and granules have dissolved. Add the rice cakes and simmer energetically for 10 minutes, until they have softened and the liquid has reduced by at least a third. Drop in the cabbage, minced garlic, all the white and half of the green parts of the spring onions, and cook for 3–5 minutes more, until the rice cakes are soft and the sauce is glossy – it's not a broth but the sauce should be loose and silky. Add another tablespoon of gochujang if you'd like the extra heat. Garnish with sesame seeds, more gochugaru flakes and the spring onion greens, and devour.

Haggis wontons
with chilli oil

I considered including a recipe for Sichuan chilli oil as it's a condiment I frequently add to rice, noodles and eggs when I crave both chilli heat and the 'ma la' lip-tingling and numbing quality of Sichuan peppercorns (indeed it's called for in the gong bao prawns recipe on page 121). But you can also just buy a jar, and for something like this recipe, convenience seems most appropriate. I love the oils made by the Way-On brand found, for example, on souschef.co.uk, also the oils made by Pippy Eats. In any case, these wontons are not picky and could just as well be drenched in non-numbing chilli oils too; look for a chiu chow or one with crunchy bits.

To the wontons then: a relatively forgiving dumpling to fold and cook and extremely satisfying to eat, the use of haggis means that along with ready-made wrappers there's a ready-made filling that's both flavourful and succulent. This recipe utilizes a pack of wonton wrappers and a small haggis to make 40–50 wontons. Freeze any you don't need, as this will leave you with a willing carrier of chilli oil never more than 5 minutes away.

—

For the wontons (makes 40–50)
1 packet frozen wonton wrappers, defrosted but fridge-cold
500g (1lb 2oz) haggis, uncooked, skin removed
Handful plain (all-purpose) flour

For the dressing and accompaniments (per serving of 8 wontons)
1 tbsp light soy sauce
1 tsp golden caster (superfine) sugar
1 clove garlic, minced
1 tbsp chilli oil
½ spring onion (scallion), chopped

Fill a little bowl with cold water, and line that up next to an open pack of wonton wrappers, the haggis decanted into a bowl, a teaspoon and (ideally) a set of electric scales for portion control. Scatter a handful of flour over a baking sheet and put that nearby too.

Place a wonton wrapper on a clean, dry surface, oriented as a diamond with a point towards your chest. Use a teaspoon to put a small nugget of haggis (10–12g/¼oz) in the centre of the diamond. Wet a finger and use that to dampen the top left and right edges of the diamond, then bring the bottom point (at 6 o'clock) to meet the top (at 12 o'clock), creating a triangle. Press the wet and dry edges together and squeeze out any air around the filling, pressing the edges to seal. Wet a finger again and dampen the plump centre. Fold and press one of the side points (at 3 or 9 o'clock) into it, dampen that and press the other on top. Place on the floured baking sheet and repeat with the remaining ingredients.

If not using straight away, freeze the wontons on the floured sheet (spaced apart so no two are touching), bagging them later once frozen – they will be easy to separate this way.

To cook, bring a saucepan of salted water to the boil. Cook one portion at a time (I find eight wontons about right), for 3 minutes if fresh or 3½ minutes from frozen. Lift the wontons out of the water with a slotted spoon, transfer to a colander set over a bowl (and add another batch of wontons to the saucepan if you're cooking additional portions).

Ready the dressing while the wontons are boiling by combining the soy sauce, sugar and garlic in a serving bowl, then add the drained, cooked wontons. Give the chilli oil a good stir to dredge up any sediment and pour a tablespoon over the wontons (including the sediment), gently rolling them around so they are well-dressed, then garnish with the spring onion. Keep the chilli oil to hand to add more if you desire it.

Fiery chicken laab with extinguishing salad

"Just to warn you, the laab is very hot." If advice like this from a waiter serves as attraction rather than a repellent, then this is for you.

I love a northern Thai or Laos-style laab; the minced meat or fish cooked relatively dry, fragrant with garlic and lemongrass, plus fresh mint and holy basil... and enough chilli to make your eyeballs sweat. This is the addictive kind of heat that can seemingly only be cooled by eating more of the same.

Sticky rice and a glass of milk would be one way of putting out the fire. But a laab is technically a salad, and pairing it with cooling cucumber, more of that Thai basil, and a crunchy lettuce is a good way to temper the heat. Wedges of unfashionable iceberg lettuce are perfect here. Gem, cos or romaine all work too. The ground roasted rice is essential, both texturally and to bind the flavours.

Serves 2

—

400g (14oz) chicken thigh, skin off and boneless
1 clove garlic, chopped
25g (1oz) ginger, peeled and finely chopped
1 coriander (cilantro) root or the bottom
   3cm (1¼in) of 8 coriander stems (optional)
4 bird's eye chillies, finely chopped
1 tbsp golden caster (superfine) sugar
Juice 1½ limes
2 tbsp fish sauce
2 tbsp vegetable or sunflower oil
½ tsp chilli powder
3 tbsp water
1 stick lemongrass, finely chopped
1 small banana shallot or ½ small red onion,
   finely sliced
Leaves from 3–4 sprigs Thai holy basil
Leaves from 1–2 sprigs mint, finely shredded
2 tbsp ground roasted rice (page 74)
Flaky sea salt

To accompany
½ iceberg lettuce, cut into wedges
1 cucumber, peeled, halved lengthways
   and cut at an angle
Handful Thai holy basil sprigs
Handful mint sprigs
½ lime, quartered

—

Use a heavy and sharp knife to first chop and then repeatedly run the knife through the chicken thigh meat so as to mince it.

Put the garlic, ginger, coriander root or stems (if using), two of the chopped bird's eye chillies and a pinch of flaky sea salt in a pestle and mortar. Pound into a smooth paste.

In a cup or small bowl, mix the sugar, lime juice and fish sauce together.

Arrange the accompanying salad items on a platter or plates at this point, as the cooking stage takes no time at all.

Place a wok on a very high heat. Pour in the oil and wait for 30 seconds for that to warm up, before adding the paste. Push that around for 20 seconds, then add the minced chicken and chilli powder and cook for 90 seconds, stirring regularly. Now add the water, lemongrass and the remaining fresh chillies, cooking for 2 minutes more, and again, stirring frequently. Finally, add the chopped shallot or onion, and the basil leaves, along with the lime and fish sauce dressing, give it one final stir and remove from the heat.

Transfer the laab onto one or two plates, sprinkle with fresh mint and add a heavy dusting of ground roasted rice.

Instant-ish geki kara ramen

———

Maligned in the UK for years, instant noodles are actually a superb starting point for a satisfying meal. Many Japanese, Korean and Chinese brands provide decent flavourings. But they are just a base and can definitely be added to.

Crucially, all lack the kind of viscosity of stock found in multi-day-simmered bone broths. Enter the secret, totally inauthentic ingredient: 'nduja. The fatty element of this fully cured but spreadable sausage instantly enriches a noodle stock, both in terms of flavour and mouthfeel; while the fresh chilli peppers (assuming you've got hold of the proper stuff from Calabria) provide an additional, fruity and sweet layer of heat. Honestly, I can't stress how much of a revelation this has been. It's such a handy way to create your own geki kara ('fiercely spicy') ramen.

The rest of the bowl is up to you and your fridge and store cupboard. Definitely add a marinated egg, and something that's pickled and/or crunchy. You could happily stop there, but also consider one or two things from the umami section, one protein and/or one fridge-foraged vegetable.

Pictured on pages 102–103.

Serves 1
–

For the egg
1 egg
1 tbsp light soy sauce
1 tbsp mirin
½ tbsp sesame oil
1 tsp rice vinegar

For the noodles
120g (4¼oz) instant noodles (plus the flavourings from the packet)
35g (1¼oz) 'nduja (or more, to taste)

Bring a milk pan of water to a rolling boil. Gently slip in the egg and leave to simmer vigorously for 6½ minutes (set a timer).

Combine the soy, mirin, sesame oil and rice vinegar in a small container (one that's just big enough to hold a peeled egg, but small enough in volume that much of the marinade will cover the egg – a drinking glass, small mug or dipping bowl is about right).

Once your alarm sounds, remove the egg and cool under a cold-running tap or in a bowl of fridge-cold water. Peel as soon as it's cool enough for you to hold, then transfer to the soy marinade. Leave for as long as you can wait and for at least 10 minutes, turning occasionally.

If any of your optional toppings need to be cooked or reheated (for example the shiitake mushrooms), do that.

When ready to eat, fill a saucepan with 400ml (1¾ cups) water and place on a high heat. Once at a vigorous boil, add the noodles and cook for 2 minutes – which most likely will be less time than the packet says. Jiggle the noodles a little with a fork to help separate them, then transfer from saucepan to bowl while they're still underdone (beyond chalky, but with bite and bounce still evident). Return the saucepan and cooking liquid to the stove, add all the seasonings from the noodle packet, plus the 'nduja, and whisk until that's melted (adding extra once tasted, if you require more heat), then pour over the noodles.

Add the egg (cut in half if you wish), pickles and any other toppings to the noodles. Slurp.

Topping suggestions

1. Pickles and crunch (essential)
Kimchi
Pickled sushi ginger
Quick-pickled daikon, cucumber, radish
   or turnip
Canned bamboo shoots
Pickled chillies

2. Umami (desirable)
Nori sheets or flakes
Sesame seeds
2–3 re-hydrated Shiitake mushrooms
Torn kale, baked (page 140)

3. Protein (optional)
Medium-firm tofu, raw or fried
Pork belly or shoulder, slow-cooked beef
   or chicken leftovers, reheated
Spam
Prawns (shrimp), raw or pre-cooked, heated
   in hot stock
Smoked lardons, fried
Cheese slices (to be draped and left to melt
   over the mound of noodles – trust me)

And/or

4. Vegetables (optional)
Spring onions (scallions), chopped
Broccoli (any varieties), charred or blanched
Corn on the cob or corn from a can
Mushrooms, fried
Sautéd greens: pak choi, pea shoots, kale
   or cavolo nero
Carrot, raw and sliced in strips
Cooked chickpeas (garbanzos)

Sriracha and lemon linguine with chilli pangrattato

Cross-fertilization of cuisines might not be to everyone's taste, but this tangle of classic Italian chilli, lemon and garlic spaghetti with pangrattato, power-splurged by Southeast Asian Sriracha, does work well. Indeed the addition of a pre-made, moreish hot sauce is an incredibly efficient way of layering pasta and breadcrumbs, not just with heat, but a sweet, garlicky, sticky tang that neither fresh nor dried chillies can add on their own. It's an excellent way to quickly quench a heat craving.

As a relatively important aside: your Sriracha could be hotter than mine (I use Flying Goose or Tabasco versions), and indeed our tolerance to chilli may well differ too. So give these quantities a go, but maybe make a note as to whether you need more or less fire the next time.

Serves 2

—

200g (7oz) dried spaghetti
3 tbsp extra virgin olive oil
2 cloves garlic, very finely sliced
15g (½oz) fresh parsley, stalks and leaves
  separated, both very finely chopped
5 tbsp Sriracha
Juice ½ lemon

For the chilli pangrattato
50g (1¾oz) thick sliced bread (ideally something
  springy like sourdough, ciabatta or focaccia)
3 tbsp light olive oil
2 cloves garlic, minced
1 heaped tbsp Sriracha
½ tbsp dried chilli flakes
Heavy pinch flaky sea salt

Make the chilli pangrattato first. Tear and pick the bread into little fingernail-size pieces (including the crusts – don't discard those). Put a small, heavy-bottomed frying pan (skillet) over a medium heat and add the oil. Allow this to heat up a little, then fry the breadcrumbs for 3–4 minutes so they begin to turn golden at the edges. Add the garlic, stir and cook for 20 seconds, then drop in the Sriracha before the garlic browns. Stir and shuffle the pan, cook for an additional 30 seconds, sprinkle over the chilli flakes, stir one more time, sprinkle generously with salt, then transfer to a cool plate until needed. The crumbs should be a rust colour, crisp but also still a little bouncy.

Cook the spaghetti in well-salted, boiling water as per the packet instructions (likely to take around 10 minutes).

Pour the extra virgin olive oil into a wide, heavy-bottomed sauté pan or saucepan and place this over a low–medium heat. Add the garlic slices and let these warm through for 3-4 minutes, to soften, mellow and flavour the oil, but not to fry or colour. Add the parsley stalks and cook for 1 minute more, then add the Sriracha and remove the pan from the heat. Shake the pan to mingle the hot sauce and oil, then after 30 seconds squeeze in the lemon juice.

Around now your spaghetti will be ready. Drain, reserving the cooking water, and transfer the pasta to the saucepan with the Sriracha and co. Return this to the stove and place over a low heat. Add four to five tablespoons of cooking water and toss the pasta through the sauce. Add the chopped parsley leaves, a touch more cooking water, maybe a little bit more water, and mix one last time before decanting onto two plates or into bowls, and scattering over the sticky and spicy breadcrumbs.

Many chilli pepper squid

This is a messy pile of mouth-tingling deliciousness, with pieces of charred squid interspersed with a loose sauce and roast peppers – like a bad Jackson Pollock in 3D form. In one bite you might get a pleasingly pure, acid-licked piece of cephalopod that's been caught only by lemon juice. In the next there's a fiery burst of roast chilli, the tickle of pul biber flakes, lashings of the sweet quick romesco and, perhaps, another jolt of heat from a one-in-ten chance of a fiery Padrón pepper. The fruity and mild to hot characteristics of each of the different peppers jostle for power; I like the Russian roulette nature of it all.

The instructions below assume you are in your kitchen. But it's ideal, too, cooked outside over flames; indeed, barbecue weather could well prompt a craving for something like this.

Serves 4 as a communal starter, or as part of a bigger meal

–

1kg (2lb 4oz) whole squid, cleaned
1 tsp pul biber (Aleppo pepper flakes)
1 lemon, cut into wedges
2 tbsp extra virgin olive oil
1 tsp caster (superfine) sugar
Leaves picked from 20g (¾oz) flat-leaf parsley,
   roughly chopped
3–4 long mild red chillies
130g (4½oz) Padrón peppers
Flaky sea salt

For the romesco sauce
150g (5½oz) jarred roasted red (bell) peppers,
   plus 2 tbsp liquid from the jar
1 tsp caster (superfine) sugar
½ tsp sweet smoked paprika
1 tbsp extra virgin olive oil
1 tsp sherry vinegar or red wine vinegar
40g (1½oz) blanched unsalted almonds
½ tsp flaky sea salt

Serve either on its own, with new potatoes and a green salad, or atop warmed flatbreads.

Put all of the ingredients for the romesco sauce in a blender and pulse until not completely smooth – a few gritty pieces of nuts provide a pleasing textural contrast. Taste and stir in an extra drop of vinegar or an additional pinch of salt if required. Decant and set to one side to be spooned over the squid at the last minute.

If the fishmonger hasn't already cleaned the squid, pull the wings and any grey outer membrane away, discarding the membrane, but keeping the wings. Pull out the quill. Trim the tentacles away then locate the line running up the length of the body and cut along that to open the squid up. Scrape any excess gunge away, then use a table knife to score the inside of the squid in a close cross-hatch. Cut the squid into just two or three large pieces – to fit your griddle and or grill surface. Sprinkle and rub with the pul biber and set to one side on a plate or similar.

Prepare a large mixing bowl with a dressing for the squid and chillies to go in once cooked. Combine the lemon juice from two to three of the wedges with the olive oil, sugar, some salt, and two thirds of the chopped parsley.

Char the red chillies and Padrón peppers on a hot griddle pan or over an outdoor grill, so that they are blackened but still juicy. Quickly cut the red chillies down the middle lengthways and scrape the seeds away. If the blackened skin comes off in your hand, pull that away too. Otherwise don't worry, chop roughly and add these along with the (whole) Padrón peppers to the dressing bowl.

Lay the squid pieces on the still smoking-hot griddle or grill, scored-side down. Press to encourage charring, then after 60 seconds turn the squid pieces over, and with your tongs or a fork prompt the squid to roll into pleasing cylinders. Remove and immediately chop into rings, then add to the dressing bowl and mix.

Let the squid rest for a minute, then decant everything onto a platter. Add the remaining parsley and a few more squeezes of lemon. Eat immediately.

Scotch bonnet and papaya pork collar steaks with a red pepper fruit salad

The mango, papaya and pepper salad that partners this pork collar steak dish should bring a smile and conjure images of the Caribbean. But it's actually the fruity fire of scotch bonnet chilli in the Jamaican jerk-inspired marinade that draws my attention: the fierce capsaicin levels in that chilli should increase the heart rate and cause a dampness to the brow. Use one scotch bonnet if you'd like a little buzz on the tongue and lips, one and a half if you'd like that buzz to continue to the throat and chest, two for a little forehead sweat (and three for a burn). This, matched with the char and smoke of a barbecue or griddle, will hit the spot on any hot day.

As an aside, papaya contains a protease (papain), which is an incredibly effective tenderizer, and so helps traditionally chewy cuts of meat (in this case pork collar, neck or shoulder steaks) become suitable for a relatively quick cook on a griddle pan or barbecue; cooked to a 'medium', they should be tender and juicy, not dissimilar to rib-eye beef steak. That does mean, though, that the meat should marinate for 4–36 hours before eating. The marinade also works well on chicken thighs and drumsticks.

Serves 4

–

4 x 220–250g (7 ¾–9oz) pork collar, neck or
  shoulder steaks, (approximately 4 x 3cm/
  1½ x 1¼in-thick)

For the marinade
½ large ripe papaya (approximately 250g/9oz),
  peeled, deseeded, roughly chopped
1–3 scotch bonnet chillies, deseeded
½ small onion, peeled, roughly chopped
3 cloves garlic
30g (1oz) soft brown sugar
1 tsp allspice (or 10 berries, shelled and ground)
½ tsp ground cloves
¼ nutmeg, freshly grated
Leaves stripped from 4–5 sprigs thyme
Juice ½ lime
2 tbsp neutral cooking oil
1 tsp salt

For the salad
1 small red onion, sliced very finely
½ large ripe papaya (approximately 250g/9oz),
  peeled, deseeded, cut into 1–2cm (½–¾in) dice
1 ripe mango, peeled, pitted, cut into 1–2cm
  (½–¾in) dice
1 red (bell) pepper, deseeded, cut into 1–2cm
  (½–¾in) dice
1 mild red chilli, deseeded, very finely diced
Juice ½ lime
1 tbsp extra virgin olive oil
Leaves picked from 30g (1oz) coriander
  (cilantro)
Flaky sea salt

–

To make the marinade, add the papaya pieces to a food processor or blender, along with the other marinade ingredients, then blend until smooth. (See the intro for scotch bonnet quantities.)

Rub two thirds of the marinade into the pork steaks, then put them, swimming in the marinade, into a container or bag. Cover/seal and refrigerate for 4–36 hours. Refrigerate the remaining (non-rubbed) marinade in a separate container – you will use this to baste the steaks as they cook, and any excess is an enjoyable chilli jam-style condiment.

Shortly before you're ready to eat, make the salad. Put the sliced red onion in a mixing bowl and sprinkle with a generous pinch of salt. Add the diced papaya and mango (and any juices) along with the rest of the salad ingredients to the bowl, and mix well.

Cook the pork steaks on a very hot griddle pan or white-hot barbecue, 2 minutes per side. Brush with the excess marinade and cook each side for 2 minutes more, so the outside is a pleasing combination of bronzed and sticky, and charred and crusty. Allow to rest for 4 minutes before slicing and serve with big heaps of the salad, and perhaps some sweet potatoes roasted in the coals of the barbecue.

Suya and baked plantain with pepper relish

Suya is a Nigerian street food (similar to Ghanaian chichinga), where the meat has been cut and pounded into thin strips, marinated and later skewered in undulating waves then dredged in a peanut (groundnut) spice powder. It's earthy and peppery, and thanks to the cayenne, provides a pleasing tickle to the back of the throat. You might normally find suya served in newspaper, accompanied by tomatoes and onions. Here there's also an option of plantain baked in their jackets, then emboldened with a fiery, scotch bonnet-flecked red pepper sauce based on a pepper soup known as obe ata.

This is ideal when you're in the mood for a hot, dry and convivial day, perhaps with quantities scaled up to suit a group barbecue. You could use slices of goat or mutton leg or rump instead of the beef.

Serves 4
—

For the suya
600–700g (1lb 5oz–1lb 9oz) beef topside roasting joint
3 tbsp groundnut (peanut) or vegetable oil
25g (1oz) fresh ginger, peeled, minced
2 cloves garlic, minced
½ tsp white pepper

For the peanut spice mix
100g (3½oz) blanched peanuts
1 heaped tsp cayenne pepper
½ tsp paprika
1 tsp chicken or vegetable bouillon
½ tsp ground ginger
⅙ nutmeg, freshly grated
Scant ½ tsp ground cloves

For the pepper sauce
250g (9oz) tomatoes, roughly chopped
1 medium–large red (bell) pepper, deseeded, roughly chopped
2 cloves garlic, peeled
½ small white onion, roughly chopped
20g (¾oz) fresh ginger, peeled, roughly chopped

3 tbsp water
½ tsp caster (superfine) sugar
⅓ tsp flaky sea salt
Scant ½ tsp ground cloves
½–1 scotch bonnet chilli, deseeded, finely chopped

To serve
3 plantain
½ white onion, finely sliced
250g (9oz) tomatoes, in chunks
1 cucumber, cut into 5mm (¼in) discs
Groundnut or cold-pressed rapeseed (canola) oil, to drizzle
Flaky sea salt

You'll need four wooden or metal skewers (if using wooden skewers, soak these in cold water for around an hour before required).

Put the beef in the freezer for 30–60 minutes before you cook it as this will make it easier to slice it finely

—

Heat the oven to 200°C/180°C fan/400°F. Spread the peanuts for the spice mix out in one layer on a baking sheet and roast until golden (around 15 minutes), transfer to a cold plate and leave to cool.

After the beef has had its chilling time, prepare the suya. Slice the cold beef as finely as you can, so you have wafer-thin strips that are barely 2mm (1⁄16in) thick and around 5cm (2in) wide. As the piece of beef gets narrower, you will need to lay it flat and cut with the knife parallel to the work surface. (When nearly at the end it will become impossible to cut really finely; use a rolling pin to bash those last pieces to the same thickness as the first.) Combine the oil, ginger, garlic and white pepper in a bowl, add the strips of beef and use your hands to make sure every surface is covered. Leave to marinate in the fridge for an hour or more.

Continued overleaf

Meanwhile, use a blender or food processor to
pulse the (now room temperature) peanuts to
a coarse powder. This will take around ten very
short bursts; don't blend continuously as this
will create peanut butter (nice, but not for now).
Combine the ground peanuts with the rest of the
spice mix ingredients and sprinkle evenly over a
plate or tray.

Make the pepper sauce by putting the chopped
tomatoes, red pepper, garlic, onion, ginger and
water in a blender or food processor and pulsing
until fairly finely chopped (but still with a little
texture). Transfer to a small saucepan, add the
sugar, salt, cloves and scotch bonnet (half for just
a little forehead sweat, one if you want it really
hot), then heat and vigorously simmer for 10
minutes to reduce and intensify both colour and
flavour. Most of the water should cook away, but
it should still be more loose than stiff. Set to one
side (to serve at room temperature or warmer).

Heat the oven to 200°C/180°C fan/400°F and
cook the plantain in their skins for 25–30
minutes, until soft and the skins just begin to
open and the flesh pokes through. Remove and
set to one side (this should fit neatly with the
meat-cooking process).

Thread the beef onto the skewers, dredge them
in the peanut spice mix and line them up ready
to cook (sprinkling any remaining peanut spice
on top). Griddle, barbecue or cook under the grill
(broiler) as you prefer, for around 6–10 minutes
until the meat is nicely browned, and the edges
and prominent bumps char and caramelize.

Prepare the sides by combining in a bowl the
onion, tomatoes and cucumber. Add a drizzle of
groundnut or rapeseed oil and a generous pinch
of salt, then refrigerate until you're ready to serve.

Remove the soft plantains from their skins and
cut into thick pieces, spooning the pepper sauce
over them. Serve alongside the piping hot suya
skewers and the fridge-cold onion, tomato and
cucumber, to help take the edge off the heat.

Three-bean tin-can chilli

Chipotle peppers are smoked jalapeño chillies. They're warming, rather than 'hot hot', and the smokiness lends a rounded flavour to any dish. You can buy them fairly easily in basic dried form. However, what I think you *should* do, instead (or in addition to), is to seek out cans of whole chipotle in adobo sauce (online at souschef.co.uk, for example), where those chillies sit in a sweetly-spiced, vinegary paste, which you can then blitz into a purée, essentially making a relatively effort-free supercharged sauce to power a week-night store-cupboard chilli.

The recipe is of course adaptable... but note that of the three beans, it's crucial to include both the red kidney and black. And though the garnish elements – the coriander, sour cream, fresh chilli and lime – might not be 'essential', they are more 'important' than 'optional', as they really help to bring the store-cupboard ingredients to life.

Serves 4
—

1 x 200g (7oz) can chipotle chilli peppers in adobo sauce
2 tbsp neutral cooking oil
1 medium red onion, finely sliced
1 red (bell) pepper, deseeded and diced
30g (1oz) coriander (cilantro), leaves picked, stems finely chopped
3 cloves garlic, finely sliced
2 tsp ground cumin
1 x 400g (14oz) can chopped tomatoes
1 tsp golden caster (superfine) sugar
1 tsp dried oregano
1 x 400g (14oz) can red kidney beans, drained
1 x 400g (14oz) can black beans, drained
1 x 400g (14oz) can haricot (navy) or pinto beans, drained
Flaky sea salt

To serve
Jacket (baked) potatoes or tortillas
150g (5½oz) sour cream, crème fraîche or Greek yoghurt
1 lime, cut into wedges
1–2 mild green chillies, sliced

Bake your jacket potatoes as you would normally, with the time dependent on their size. (Regardless, you will need to put the jacket potatoes in the oven before beginning the chilli. The latter takes around 30 minutes.)

Decant the chipotle peppers and all the adobo sauce into a blender and blitz until you have a silky-smooth purée.

Place a heavy-bottomed saucepan or casserole over a medium heat. Add the cooking oil, sliced onions and a pinch of salt. Cook for 5–6 minutes, stirring occasionally, to the point the onions are relatively soft and beginning to sweeten, but are not browned.

Add the red pepper, coriander stalks and garlic to the soft onions and cook for a minute. Then add the cumin and stir frequently for the next 30 seconds. Pour in the chopped tomatoes and three-quarters of the chipotle sauce, refill the tomato can with water and pour that in too, and add the sugar, oregano and a hefty pinch of salt.

Increase the temperature and let the tomato sauce bubble away energetically for 5 minutes, then add all of the beans and simmer at a more leisurely pace for 10–15 minutes more. Remove from the heat and then leave for 5 minutes (it'll taste better once cooled a little).

Try a spoonful and add the remainder of the chipotle sauce if your heat sensors require it, salt if necessary, plus half the picked coriander leaves. Serve alongside a jacket potato or tortilla, and garnish with the sour cream, crème fraîche or Greek yoghurt, the lime wedges, remaining coriander and sliced green chillies to taste.

Rainbow root som tam and perfect pork chops

The key draw here is the feisty salad, which is based on Laotian/northern Thai som tam, with green papaya replaced by colourful root vegetables, each of which provides an earthy-sweet tone. In the spirit of the original, this dish is pungent and crunchy, sour, salty and – crucially – hot and sweaty, with bird's eye chillies bringing that kind of delayed fire that, weirdly, can only be quenched by eating more, at speed.

The cooking method for the pork is specifically for fat-heavy chops that derive from slow-grown, rare-breed pigs (leaner commercial pork cooks differently, and is also not great on taste or welfare basis). Cook them as below, then slice and share them as you might a prized beef steak. The resulting crisp-edged yet succulent meat is the perfect foil for this salad. Some rice and a glass of very cold water, beer (or maybe milk...) are the only other things you will need.

Serves 4
–

2 x 350g (12oz) large, fatty, rare-breed pork chops, 2.5–3cm (1–1¼in) thick

For the salad
3 cloves garlic, peeled
10g (¼oz) dried shrimps
3 tbsp roasted peanuts
6 bird's eye chillies, finely chopped
2 limes, 1 cut into wedges, the other juiced
2 tbsp golden caster (superfine) sugar or palm sugar
2 tbsp fish sauce
1 tsp pomegranate molasses
12 cherry tomatoes, halved
12 fine green beans, topped, cut into 3cm (1¼in) lengths
1 large carrot, peeled, cut into very fine matchsticks
400g (14oz) golden and candied beetroot (beets), peeled, cut into very fine matchsticks (you could also use kohlrabi, turnip or courgettes/zucchini)
Flaky sea salt

Serve with sticky rice (page 74) or jasmine rice.

To make the salad, put the garlic, shrimps, half the peanuts and half the chillies in a pestle and mortar with a pinch of flaky salt, and pound to a paste. Add the lime wedges and bash and bruise them. Transfer everything to a mixing bowl, then measure in the sugar, lime juice, fish sauce and pomegranate molasses. Stir until the sugar has dissolved. Add the tomatoes, green beans, carrot, beetroot and remaining peanuts and chillies to the dressing bowl. Mix well and leave to macerate.

To prepare the pork chops, use a sharp knife to cut the rind and about 1cm (½in) of fat away from each chop, leaving 1–2cm (½–¾in) of fat attached. Score the rind with a craft knife or something similarly sharp, sprinkle over a generous pinch of salt, and place in a small baking tin, skin side up. Heat the oven to 240°C/220°C fan/475°F. Then roast for 15–20 minutes until golden, puffed and crunchy.

Stand the chops upright, fatty-edge down, on a cold, heavy-bottomed frying pan (skillet). Place over the lowest heat and let the fat gently render. Because they're thick, they should stand by themselves. Turn your extraction on and open the windows. After 5 minutes the pan should be slick with fat, but the meat still uncooked.

Keep cooking very gently for 15–20 minutes, continuing to ensure that the fatty edge (not the meaty sides) is in contact with the pan. Rather than stand over the chops with tongs, you can rest a spoon in the pan with its handle on the edge, and balance the chops on that.

Begin to cook the meat only once that fat is super-soft and golden – a metal skewer should slide through as if nothing was there (by now it should be above 85°C/185°F). At that point, tip the rendered fat into a jar (save for cooking something else), increase the heat to medium–high, and fry the chops for 1–2 minutes on each side. They will quickly become golden. (They're done when the thickest part is 52–54°C/125–129°F.) Rest on a warm plate for 4 minutes before cutting away from the bone and slicing. Serve with the salad and rice.

Quail gumbo

This gumbo recipe is in a creek-and-swamp Cajun (rather than metropolitan Creole) style, so involves smoked ham and fowl, a hefty punch of throat-tickling cayenne, white and black pepper, and is without the sweetness of tomatoes and shrimp. It's rich because of the dark 'roux' and is thickened and made wholesome by the okra from which the dish derives its name (ki ngombo in a west African dialect). I suppose quail might be seen as a bit of a fiddle (you could swap for pheasant breasts), but it also feels perfectly appropriate to be picking out portions with your fingers – whether thick soup or thin stew, gumbo is soul food that is warming in both form and spice.

Legendary New Orleans chef Leah Chase famously rebuked Barack Obama for adding hot sauce to his gumbo without tasting it first. The 'without tasting it first' part is key though, and a good number of Louisianans are accustomed to adding Tabasco or Crystal to theirs. Indeed, those hot sauces are ultimately the reason I'm offering this recipe to you – the condiment 'hot sauce' is such an impulsive addition for many, that I though it important to suggest a well-suited vessel in this book.

It's best to prep everything before you begin so that, once the meat is browned, you can manage two pans at the same time.

Serves 4–6

—

1 heaped tsp cayenne pepper
½ tsp ground white peppercorns
½ tsp ground black peppercorns
2 tsp paprika
1 tsp ground allspice
2 tbsp dried oregano
4 quails (or 4 pheasant breasts, skin on)
200g (7oz) cooked smoked ham hock, in 2cm (¾in) dice (page 34) or the same weight of chunky, smoked lardons
115ml (scant ½ cup) vegetable oil
150g (5½oz) chilli-laced sausage, cut into 1cm (½in) discs
1 large green (bell) pepper, diced
1 medium onion, finely diced
2 large celery sticks, finely diced
70g (2½oz) plain (all-purpose) flour
1 litre (4⅓ cups) medium-intensity (i.e. not fully reduced) ham or chicken stock
500ml (2 cups) water
3 bay leaves
200g (7oz) okra, cut into 5mm (¼in) discs
1 tsp golden caster (superfine) sugar
2 tsp Tabasco or Crystal hot sauce (plus extra, to taste)
Juice ¼ lemon
Flaky sea salt

Serve with rice – any, though a wild or brown rice mix works well – cooked according to the packet instructions (or your preferred method).

Combine the dry spices plus one tablespoon of the oregano in a bowl and set to one side.

Place the quails breast-side down on a baking sheet, use a pair of sturdy scissors to cut out the back bones, then turn each bird over and press down on their breast bones to splay them. Use a heavy knife to then split each quail in two down the middle. Rub these portions (or pheasant breast if using) with one tablespoon of the spice mix.

Rub the ham hock (or lardons) with another tablespoon of the spice mix.

Measure two tablespoons of the vegetable oil into a large frying pan (skillet) and place over a medium–high heat. Add the quail (or pheasant breasts) skin-side down and brown for 3–4 minutes. Turn over and brown the cut side for a minute more. Then transfer to a plate or bowl and set to one side (chopping the pheasant breasts into 4 pieces if using).

Keep the pan on the heat and immediately add the sausage and ham hock to the hot oil and let them colour for 3–4 minutes before transferring to a container. Add a splash of water to deglaze the pan and pour the juices over the pork. Wipe the pan clean and place it back over a low–medium heat. Add one tablespoon of the oil, along with the green pepper, onion and celery, and sauté gently for 10 minutes until softened.

Meanwhile measure the remaining oil into a high-sided, heavy-bottomed saucepan or casserole and place over a medium-high heat. Add the flour and using a wooden spoon or spatula stir and scrape regularly for 15 minutes or more, until the mix (a roux) is slack, smells toasty and is the colour of dark chocolate. At this point tip the (by now softened) vegetable mix into the roux and stir in the stock ladle by ladle, ensuring the liquid is fully incorporated each time before adding any more. Add the 500ml (2 cups) of water, the ham and sausage, the bay leaves and the remaining

oregano and spice mix. Simmer for 25 minutes, then add the quail (or pheasant), okra, sugar and a teaspoon of flaky sea salt, and simmer for 20 minutes more.

When ready to eat, taste and add more salt if required, plus two teaspoons of hot sauce and a squeeze of lemon juice. Serve as a hefty soup or stew next to or over rice, with the hot sauce bottle nearby for others to add to taste.

Gong bao prawns

The classic gong bao dish (named after a former governor of Sichuan province, Ding Baozhen) is made with chicken. But the flavours, including the heat of chilli and numbing 'ma la' qualities of Sichuan peppercorns, suit prawns too. I've suggested this quick dish is made lip-tingling through Sichuan chilli oil, rather than peppercorns, as good versions of the latter are hard to come by. By contrast there are a number of decent oils available, and you can use that oil frequently in your cooking, whether spooned over a fried egg or on the haggis wontons (page 98).

This is a good-size meal for two but is arguably better spread across more people as part of a larger meal, with other Sichuanese classics such as smacked cucumber, fish-fragrant aubergine, wood ear mushroom salad and mapo tofu. You'll either be familiar with these already, or otherwise, if the ma la sensation here pleases you, seek out the other dishes and cook up a feast next time the urge arrives (try @red.house.spice on Instagram and the writer Fuchsia Dunlop for recipes).

Serves 2 as a main or 4–6 as part of a larger meal

—

40g (1½oz) blanched peanuts
300g (10½oz) raw prawns (shrimp), peeled and deveined
2 tbsp neutral cooking oil
6 dried red chillies, halved and deseeded or 1 tsp dried chilli flakes
20g (¾oz) fresh ginger, peeled, sliced into thin matchsticks
4 spring onions (scallions), finely chopped, whites and greens separated
3 cloves garlic, finely sliced
2 tbsp Sichuan chilli oil
Leaves and thin stems picked from 8–10 sprigs coriander (cilantro)

For the marinade
½ tbsp Shaoxing wine
½ tsp ground white pepper
½ tsp cornflour (cornstarch)
⅓ tsp flaky sea salt

For the sauce
2 tbsp light soy sauce
1 tsp cornflour (cornstarch)
1 tbsp Chinkiang black rice vinegar
1 tbsp Shaoxing wine
3 tbsp water
1 tbsp golden caster (superfine) sugar

Serve with plain rice.

—

Cook the rice according to the packet instructions (or to your preferred method).

Heat the oven to 200°C/180°C fan/400°F. Spread the peanuts out in one layer on a baking sheet and roast until golden (around 15 minutes), transfer to a cold plate and leave to cool.

Combine the marinade ingredients in a bowl, add the prawns, mix and leave to marinate while you prepare the remaining ingredients.

For the sauce, in a small bowl stir the soy sauce into the cornflour to make a paste, then whisk in the remaining liquids and sugar.

Place a wok over a high heat and add the cooking oil. When it's hot, add the dried chillies, ginger and the white parts of the spring onions and fry for 60 seconds or so until fragrant.

Add most but not all of the green parts of the spring onions and the garlic, fry for 30 seconds then push to one side of the wok and add the prawns and any residual marinade, which will ideally fit in one layer. Cook for 60 seconds or so, stirring occasionally, until they begin to turn pink and start to tighten. Add the sauce, mix everything together and let it bubble and thicken a little for around 90 seconds. Throw in the peanuts and remove from the heat.

Give your chilli oil a good stir to dredge up the bits from the bottom and add two tablespoons (including sediment) to the wok, stirring until it's well mixed. Serve over plain rice, with the remaining spring onion greens and the coriander as a garnish.

Rabbit cacciatore

There are meals that stay with you. One that continually returns to my mind is a rabbit cacciatore ('hunters' stew') cooked for me by the masterful Rome-based food writer Rachel Roddy. I remember gnawing at the pieces of meat on their respective bones, intermittently swapping fork and spoon for fingers. I remember nibbling away at petite, sweet-bitter olives with little flesh beyond pit but so much flavour. And I'm sure I remember a hint of chilli nibbling back at my gums and warming my upper chest as I ate. Looking back at Rachel's recipes I wonder whether the heat is a case of my memory gradually rewriting the actual scene, as hers tend to include the barest hint of dried chilli. Still, when I'm after warming notes rather than blow-your-socks-off heat, the dish my memory serves up is the first thing I think of. I took comfort that something akin to this can be called a cacciatore when chatting about it with two Calabrian-born market traders who confirmed their grandmothers' stews tended to be punchy, spiked by the dried versions of their region's fruity and pleasingly warm chilli pepper, and a hint of oregano too.

The stew/braise works deliciously throughout the year, with mashed potato through the cold months and salad leaves or steamed but still-crunchy greens in spring and summertime.

Serves 4

–

1 rabbit, about 1.3–1.5kg (3–3lb 5oz)
3 tbsp plain (all-purpose) flour
6 tbsp olive oil
4 cloves garlic, finely sliced
1 large tomato, roughly chopped
350ml (1½ cup) white wine
1–2 tbsp dried red chilli flakes (Calabrian, if possible)
1 sprig rosemary
1–2 tbsp dried oregano
4 tbsp petite olives (such as Taggiasca, Leccino, Niçoise or Picholine), pits in
1 tbsp red wine vinegar
Flaky sea salt and ground black pepper

Serve with mashed potato and green veggies.

Heat the oven to 170°C/150°C fan/325°F.

Cut the rabbit (or ask a butcher to) into twelve pieces: two shoulders, six pieces from the saddle and ribs, two thighs and two drumsticks.

In a bowl, mix the flour with a teaspoon of both salt and pepper, and roll the rabbit pieces in it.

Warm four to five tablespoons of olive oil in a large lidded casserole, or similar, set over a medium–high heat and fry the floured rabbit pieces in this until golden-tinged and crusted (adding more oil if needed) then remove from the pan. This will take 10–15 minutes and you may need to use two pans or do in batches.

Wipe the casserole clean if the flour has burnt, add a little more oil and briefly sauté the garlic and tomato. Return the rabbit, arranging it to fit in one layer or close to that. Add the wine so that most if not all of the meat is submerged, topping up with water if more than 1cm (½in) is uncovered. Add one tablespoon of chilli flakes, the rosemary, one tablespoon of oregano, one teaspoon of flaky salt and lots of ground black pepper. Cook in the oven with the lid ajar for 60–80 minutes until the thigh meat is tender enough for a spoon to press easily into it (wild rabbit will take much longer than farmed).

At this point, taste the sauce and season with more salt, black pepper, chilli flakes or oregano as required. Add the olives and vinegar, baste any meat that is uncovered and cook for 10–15 minutes more. Serve with mashed potato, perhaps on this occasion loosened and enriched with extra virgin olive oil rather than butter, and some green vegetables nearby.

'Nduja spatchcock chicken

This is a great way to find yourself with a plateful of succulent, crisp-skinned, self-hot-saucing chicken. There's very little to it, though you do need a source of proper Calabrian 'nduja – which is basically 50 per cent pork fat and 50 per cent fruity chilli peppers – in part for the taste, though also because it squishes and spreads so easily between the flesh and skin of a pre-roasted chicken. It's also really truly best if you can buy a slow-grown, free-range chicken: the meat is juicier and more flavoursome, and the skin thicker and better for crisping up (and less likely to tear as you manoeuvre it).

Pictured on pages 124–125.

Serves 4

–

1 chicken, between 1.4–2kg (3lb 2oz–4lb 8oz)
60g (2¼oz) Calabrian 'nduja, at room
  temperature
1 tbsp neutral cooking oil
2 tsp flaky sea salt
4 tbsp water

Serve with fries, green salad and aioli (page 44).

Heat the oven to 230°C/210°C fan/450°F.

Spatchcock the chicken by using sturdy scissors to cut the spine out. Turn the bird over and set it on a baking sheet (not a high-sided roasting tin), pressing firmly down on the breast bone to flatten it. Also remove the wishbone as this makes it much easier to portion once cooked (you could ask a butcher to do all of this if you prefer).

Use one or two fingers to separate the skin from the flesh of the breasts. Also jiggle around at the base of the thighs until you find a gap, and separate the skin from the flesh there too. Divide the 'nduja between the various pockets, pushing the cured meat up as far as you can under the skin with your fingers, then pressing down on top of the skin to squelch and spread it around. Rub a little cooking oil over the skin, then sprinkle the couple of teaspoons of salt on top of that.

Slide the baking sheet into the oven towards the top. Roast for 45 minutes without interruption (40 minutes if the chicken is closer to 1.4kg/3lb 2oz, or 50 minutes if 1.8–2kg/4lb–4lb 8oz).

At the end of the cooking period, the chicken's skin should be golden and crisp. Remove from the oven, transfer to a board or warm dish to rest for 10 minutes, then pour the water into the baking sheet and whisk it around the roasting gubbins to deglaze it, creating a sauce that retains all the delicious oils, heat and flavour.

After resting, pull the legs away from the chicken and separate the thighs from the drumsticks. Cut the breasts off the carcass too, split them in half across their width and arrange everything on a warmed platter. Reheat the pan of deglazed juices for a minute then pour over the top of the chicken pieces, along with any additional resting juices. Ensure everyone gets a good helping of spicy, devil-red juices from the bottom of the pan.

Mango with chilli, lime and salt

This won't be a new flavour combination for many, particularly if you've been to Mexico, bought fresh mango from the street... and then shaken Tajín (a seasoning of salt, chilli flakes and dehydrated lime) over the top. As much as anything, then, it's simply a nudge to embellish some tropical fruit with a salted-chilli tickle, in order that you completely sate a need for a buzzy, capsaicin fix; the same treatment works with pineapple and papaya.

You can find Tajín in the UK now. But I've also conducted a fairly wide range of tests on different fresh, flaked and powdered chillies as an alternative. While finely diced fresh chilli is enjoyable, for me the greatest success comes via relatively mild but fruity chilli flakes – pul biber (Aleppo pepper flakes), Calabrian chilli and Korean gochugaru all work well, as they each add a flavoursome hint of heat without turning the occasion into a 'who can handle the most' competition.

It goes without saying (yet I'll write it anyway), that the success of this sweet treat increases directly in proportion to proximity to mango season and ripeness of the fruit.

Serves 4

—

2 ripe mangoes
1 lime, zest finely grated and juiced
½ tsp flaky sea salt
1 tsp dried, mild chilli flakes, ideally pul biber
  (Aleppo pepper flakes), Calabrian or gochugaru
100g (3½oz) thick Greek yoghurt

Cut the mango into segments and cut the skin away from the flesh.

Squeeze half the lime juice over the fruit. Add a few crystals of salt over each piece, and then a liberal scattering of chilli flakes.

Stir the lime zest and remaining juice into the yoghurt, and serve with the mango.

Orange and scotch bonnet paletas

———

Chilli peppers are about flavour as well as heat. Scotch bonnets, for example, have a distinctive and quite intoxicating fruity scent that pairs incredibly well with mango (see the recipe on page 111) and also orange. It just so happens that they also pack an almighty yet addictive punch. Wow. (Wash hands and don't touch anything sensitive for a while.)

So this idea for orange and scotch bonnet paletas – of the agua fresca style – is one for people who enjoy flavour pairings, but also the strangely enjoyable sensation of warming your tongue and tummy, despite the fact you're sucking on ice.

If it is blood orange season, use those.

Makes 6–8 paletas (depending on the size of your moulds)

—

100ml (scant ½ cup) water
75g (2½oz) granulated sugar
2 scotch bonnet chillies, halved and deseeded
5 large oranges: 4 juiced, 1 peeled and chopped into thumbnail-size segments
Juice 1 lime

You'll need enough paleta/ice lolly moulds to hold around 650ml (2¾ cups) liquid.

Pour the water into a milk pan or small saucepan and bring almost to the boil. Add the sugar, stir until fully dissolved, then remove from the heat and pop in the scotch bonnet halves. Leave to cool for 20–30 minutes, depending on your chilli tolerance.

Strain the orange and lime juice through a fine sieve (strainer), discard the bits and measure the weight of the juice. Top it up with water to 500ml (2 cups) if not already at that (or drink the excess).

Once they've had their 20–30 minutes of infusion, remove the scotch bonnets and combine the syrup with the citrus juice. Discard the chillies or (better) use them in a jerk marinade.

Distribute the orange pieces between your moulds and top up with the chilli-syrup-spiked juice. Freeze for at least 5 hours.

If you are a chilli fiend you might very, very finely chop a quarter–half a scotch bonnet and add that to the moulds before filling with juice. I accept no responsibility for the fallout, though.

spiced and curried

I'd kill for something spicy right now. You know the feeling, right? When you want something, err, spicy. That one, inadequate adjective we have to cover not just tens of dried and fresh seeds, leaves and roots, but also infinite combinations of them, which are utilized in rubs, seasonings, marinades and stews, or dusted over salads, or combined with tomato and/or coconut in stock bases, and which are equally adept at enhancing meat, fish, vegetables, dairy, pulses, breads, cakes and fruits.

'Spiced' means things that are fragrant, perfumed, intoxicating, heady, musty, sweet, aromatic and delicious. Sometimes spiced suggests 'hot'. Often it does not. It is cumin, coriander and ginger (in all its forms); black pepper, sansho pepper, cinnamon and anise; caraway, cloves, cardamom, saffron, and nutmeg too. It is 'exotic' and 'forrin'... except it's very much over here: our advantageous mix of diaspora populations having donated their cuisines to modern Britain's eclectic palate; and also as a seasoning that has been evident for centuries in very British buns, puddings and place names. Spiced is never boring or plain.

'Curried' is problematic. It stands alone in these section titles as a cooking technique, rather than an element of flavour. It's also a historic British term steeped in colonialism that has been, and is still, used to describe all types of 'Indian food' as a homogeneous thing. Which is obviously wrong: Indian dishes (as elsewhere) have their own individually descriptive names; and not everything Indian or of Indian inspiration is curried. Still, for all its faults, 'curry' remains a useful term for certain gravy-based dishes from around the world that utilize spice and evoke a certain emotive flavour – hence using it here.

So, sorry, Spiced and Curried is a broad church. But I'm pretty sure you know what I mean, and most will identify with the urge for it. The good thing about a broad church is it means there are many ways to get your fix.

You'll see that the recipes I suggest include snacks: the sweet-spiced peppercorn cashews, quick breakfasts like masala eggs, slow stews and indeed curries, whether of Cape Malay, Sri Lankan or no particular region in style. There are fast grills and quick fries, too, such as paneer tikka and garlic pepper butter prawns. Sometimes all that is needed is the addition of a spice mix or some curry leaves as a seasoning. At other times the component parts must braise or bubble away for hours until they permeate and riff off each other. The results are always dynamic.

One thing that unifies the recipes is that all are cooked 'from scratch'. That shouldn't be any more daunting than knocking up an Italian-ish ragù without a factory-produced passata, a red wine-soaked beef stew or a Sunday roast. If we want to taste something as it should, we need to pay deference towards original method. Few (or no?) processes here are laborious – just a matter of toasting and grinding spices to order, browning onions until they're truly brown, pounding pastes or blending broths to emulsify them. If time is required, most of that will be hands-free.

Though potential spices are numerous, I don't employ too many across these recipes, nor any unnecessarily. Indeed, I've made a conscious effort to ensure all cupboard ingredients (whether common or 'unusual') are used more than once across the book. So whether you repeat the same recipe or try another, you should get through the ground turmeric, fennel seeds and indeed 'medium curry powder' before they fade to a coloured dust. As with fresh chillies, ingredients like lemongrass, dried shrimps, makrut lime leaves, curry leaves and fresh turmeric freeze well (to be used from frozen, not defrosted).

The dominant influence in this section is definitely 'Indian' cuisine, though as already intimated, that in itself is a huge concept into which this chapter simply magpies a handful of good things. Further, just as Mughlai cuisine (the medieval mix of Indian and Persian ingredients and techniques) has spread, evolved and splintered across the Indian subcontinent and subsequently around the world, spiced and curried cravings extend to other countries and styles too. Some are touched on here, hopefully sating certain sub-cravings. But not all.

To paraphrase Madhur Jaffrey in her *Ultimate Curry Bible*, I love Thai, Malay and Burmese curries with an 'unholy passion'. And yet there's no green curry, rendang or mohinga here. The mackerel, tamarind and turmeric curry and in some ways a Hong Kong-style curried brisket noodles hit a similar spot. But ultimately many versions exist elsewhere, and I didn't feel comfortable implying I'm expert enough to offer lesser-known dishes or others with a 'twist' that are truly mine. Similarly, I know from my eating out that a need for spiced and curried can be satisfied through the food of places like Nigeria, Kenya, Uganda, Guyana and Trinidad. I need to learn more about these before putting anything on paper. Maybe versions will feature in *Still Craving*, to be published in the year of I don't know when... My point being: this is a starting point. For more inspiration and recipes from cooks of authority, look at the Further Reading list (page 246).

And so to some thoughts as to when and why we crave spiced and curried. As with chilli and heat, I personally find that cravings arrive in all seasons. Which does not mean the weather is not relevant. In fact, there are certain things that absolutely scream to be cooked and eaten when, for example, the weather is damp and grey: a twist on a Japanese katsu curry, for example. Mood is also a big driver. That fear of an impending new working week means kale and coconut dal fits neatly into many a Sunday evening. Intense and slightly sour Goan pork shoulder vindaloo with accompanying okra fry seems, on the other hand, to suit days and nights in which cheer is already abundant; the meal maintains the vibe. And again, as with chilli, I also think that spiced foods serve for many as a reminder of upbringing and so bring comfort or a necessary reversion to default. Basically, this is truly a flavour craving that comes at us from all angles, at all times and for myriad reasons – typically specific to the person subject to it.

Of all the chapters, when collating a set of recipes this one could have gone on and on. Unavoidably, so much is not here. But there are enough extremely cookable dishes to stem this particular craving for at least a while.

Sweet-spiced peppercorn cashews

There are two sides to these nuts.

On one, they're a sweet-spiced quick fix that you can keep to hand to garnish other dishes (like the Sri Lankan-style squash curry on page 146) or a side of rice; or to pass around as drinking snacks in the preliminaries of a feast.

On the other, they're dangerously moreish and, if you're anything like me, most of the tray will be eaten before the cashews have cooled, leading to a short period of high blood pressure and self-loathing.

Still, very tasty, whichever way you look at it.

Makes a communal snack-bowl's worth/ one person's mindless gorge

—

300g (10½oz) raw cashew nuts
4 tsp whole peppercorns
1 tbsp ground cumin
1 tsp chilli powder
1 tsp ground turmeric
½ tsp ground cardamom
40g (1½oz) salted butter
2 tsp flaky sea salt
4 tsp golden caster (superfine) sugar

Heat the oven to 200°C/180°C fan/400°F.

Line a baking sheet with baking paper, spread the cashews over it so they fit in one layer, then toast towards the top of the oven for 6 or 7 minutes. Shuffle after 5 minutes and remove before any turn beyond golden to brown.

Meanwhile, grind the whole peppercorns in a pestle and mortar to a coarse grit. Add the other spices and mix.

Melt the butter at a gentle pace in a medium-size saucepan. Remove from the heat and add the spices, stir into a paste, then pour the now part-toasted cashews in. Mix thoroughly, then return the cashews back to the lined baking sheet, ensuring all of the flavourful butter has been scraped from the pan over the nuts.

Toast for 6–10 minutes, checking and shuffling the tray every 3 minutes to ensure an even bronzing, and remove from the oven before any are even close to looking burnt (they'll darken further as the tray cools).

Sprinkle the salt and sugar over the top while still warm and mix thoroughly. Then walk away until the cashews have completely cooled. Store in a sealed container at room temperature. Good for a month or so (but are unlikely to last that long).

Masala eggs

Masala eggs are a very quick way to sate a craving for spice. The mix of turmeric and the sweetness of garam masala provides an aromatic hit, rather than a chilli shock, which makes these appealing whether the craving has struck first thing in the morning, for lunch or a late-night snack. I was going to add a recipe for spiced tomato sauce but, to be honest, I keep enjoying this with a squirt of Heinz ketchup, and don't feel now that a homemade version would improve nor fit the speed of the dish.

On which note, these eggs are neither slowly coddled nor a firm and bouncy scramble; rather, a deliberate cross between a loose omelette and creamy 'baveuse' eggs. If you're cooking for more than two people, do this in batches, as in large quantities it's harder to achieve the recommended consistency (also the butter and spice quantities don't quite scale).

If you can find small, enriched, soft white buns (like Indian pav), then great. If not, well-toasted sourdough or English muffins are still good.

Serves 2

—

2 x soft white buns, or English muffins or slices
   of sourdough
30g (1oz) butter
1½ tsp garam masala
½ tsp ground turmeric
¼ tsp ground black pepper
6 large eggs, beaten
½ tsp flaky sea salt
1 mild green chilli, finely sliced

Ensure your buns are warming or if using bread or muffins, put them on to toast. Also, at some point just prior to the eggs being ready, ensure they are generously buttered.

Put a heavy-bottomed, medium-size saucepan or frying pan (skillet) on a medium–high heat. Add the butter and, once half of it has melted, add the spices. Swirl around the pan, stir the spices in and let the butter melt fully and then foam for 60 seconds. The pan should be really hot by now (though the butter not yet browning).

Add the eggs plus the salt and immediately reduce the temperature to a low–medium heat. Let the eggs be shocked by the heat of the pan for 15 seconds, then use a silicone spatula or wooden spoon to turn and regularly fold (rather than frantically scramble) for 45–60 seconds, until half of the eggs are firm, half loose. Turn out into a warm bowl, or onto two plates.

Serve immediately. With sliced green chillies, to taste. Plus ketchup.

Coronation cauliflower

A little retro and kind of naff, yes, but you can't successfully argue against coronation chicken's performance as a sandwich filler. Which also means it's an excellent way of fixing a mid-day craving.

You can, however, compellingly nitpick and tweak. For example, to my mind the least important element of coronation chicken is the chicken: its bland chew is replaceable, and you could swap in salad potatoes, roast aubergines (eggplants) or courgettes (zucchini) as a carrier of curry powder and fruit preserve-laden mayo. Roast cauliflower is top dog, though – a little bit frazzled, a touch nutty, but ultimately soft and yielding.

Bite and crunch comes by way of celery, crisp lettuce, crusty bread and roast nuts, and there's coriander for herbal fragrance. Don't omit any of these elements – you need all of them for the complete sandwich experience.

Makes enough filling for 4 baguettes/ sandwiches

–

1 medium–large cauliflower (white part weighing around 800g–1kg/1lb 12oz–2lb 4oz)
2 tbsp cold-pressed rapeseed (canola) oil
4 tsp medium curry powder
40g (1½oz) Hellmann's mayonnaise
50g (1¾oz) Greek yoghurt
1 tbsp aubergine (eggplant) pickle or mango chutney
4 celery sticks, cut into 1cm (½in) pieces
Squeeze lemon juice (if you have it)
Flaky sea salt and ground black pepper

To fill the sandwich
Crusty baguettes or focaccia
1–2 baby gem lettuces, leaves separated
Handful spiced cashew nuts (page 136) or blanched cashews or peanuts, roasted
Leaves picked from 15g (½oz) coriander (cilantro)

Heat the oven to 220°C/200°C fan/425°F.

Cut the greens from the cauliflower, discard only the gnarliest and chop the remainder into 2–3cm (¾–1¼in) pieces. Set to one side. Break the cauliflower into florets, cutting the largest third of them in half. Cut the core and stalk into 1cm (½in)-thick slices, then quarters. Measure the oil and half the curry powder into a mixing bowl, add the florets, core and stalk, mix well then tip onto a baking sheet (or two, if they don't fit in one layer) and slide into the hot oven. After 30 minutes shuffle the baking sheet(s), add the chopped greens, mix and return the tray to the oven for 10–15 minutes more, when the cauliflower should be charred but still succulent. Sprinkle with a good pinch of flaky salt then leave to cool completely.

In a large mixing bowl combine the remaining curry powder with the mayonnaise, yoghurt, aubergine pickle or mango chutney, celery, a squeeze of lemon juice (if using), half a teaspoon of salt and a good grind or two of black pepper. Stir the (now cooled) cauliflower and greens through this dressing. Taste and check the seasoning, adding more salt, black pepper, lemon juice, pickle or curry powder if required.

To build a sandwich, use a spoonful or two of excess dressing as a butter/mayonnaise on the bottom layer of bread or baguette. Line with 3–4 gem lettuce leaves, spoon the coronation cauliflower on top of that, and top with cashews (or roast peanuts), then a generous scattering of coriander leaves.

Kale and coconut dal

There's something about an evening in autumn or winter that cries out for a bowl of dal.*

Of course, there are plenty of excellent recipes around for when such a need arises. I include one here mostly for completeness; but also to say that using chana dal (or split peas) instead of red lentil or mung dal leads to an enjoyably chunky texture, which I think is particularly well suited to those times we're really craving both comfort and spice.

Much of the flavour comes from browned onions, so please do stir and wait for as long as is suggested – it's not that arduous and is worth it. Also, garnishes are not optional: crisp kale adds crunch, yoghurt a cool interlude between spoonfuls, green chillies a fruity spice. And if you have aubergine pickle to hand, add that too.

* The rain, the cold, the work the next day.

Serves 4
–

300g (10½oz) chana dal or yellow split peas
500g (1lb 2oz) onions, finely sliced
3 tbsp vegetable oil
3 green cardamom pods
250g (9oz) curly kale
2 tbsp cold-pressed rapeseed (canola) oil
4 cloves garlic, minced
25g (1oz) fresh ginger, peeled and minced
2 tsp ground cumin
2 tsp garam masala
1 tsp ground turmeric
½ tsp dried chilli flakes
250g (9oz) tomatoes, roughly chopped
100ml (scant ½ cup) water
6 tbsp desiccated (dried shredded) coconut, plus extra to garnish
100g (3½oz) plain yoghurt
2 mild green chillies, finely sliced
Flaky sea salt

Serve alongside naan, chapati, paratha or plain rice, plus a handful of coriander (cilantro) leaves and aubergine (eggplant) pickle if you have them.

Soak the chana dal in just-boiled water for 15 minutes.

Get the onions cooking in a heavy-bottomed saucepan over a medium heat, with the vegetable oil and a good pinch of salt. Stir occasionally, then after 10 minutes place a lid on top, turn the heat to low and cook for at least 30 minutes, until golden and fairly intense in smell and flavour.

Once the lid is on the onions, drain the chana dal then transfer to a separate saucepan along with 1.5 litres (6½ cups) of cold water and the cardamom. Bring to the boil then reduce to a lively simmer for 45 minutes, skimming the foam that appears over the first 10 minutes or so.

While the onions and chana dal are cooking, collate and measure the other ingredients. Heat the oven to 180°C/160°C fan/350°F. Wash and dry the kale, then tear into roughly 3–4cm (1¼–1½in) pieces. Spread two thirds of it in one layer over a baking sheet (or two, if necessary), drizzle with the rapeseed oil, tumble, and then bake for 5–10 minutes until crisp but not browned. Salt generously and leave to cool.

Once the onions are golden, stir in the garlic and ginger and cook gently for 5 minutes, before adding the dry spices and chilli flakes (if the mix sticks, add two to three tablespoons of water). Now add the tomatoes and water. Cook over a medium–high heat for 10 minutes to reduce.

Once the chana dal has been cooking for 45 minutes, add the onion and tomato mix along with the coconut, then simmer for a final 15 minutes, stirring regularly to check the bottom isn't catching. After that time, add water to achieve a consistency you enjoy (I prefer it closer to a loose soup rather than stiff porridge), then throw in the remaining fresh kale and remove the saucepan from the heat. Leave to cool for 5 minutes, check the seasoning (it'll need lots of salt, and maybe an additional teaspoon of garam masala) and perhaps add a splash more water.

Serve each bowlful with a tablespoon of coconut, a heap of crispy kale, yoghurt and sliced chillies.

Garlic pepper butter prawns

There are a few things going on here, but the 'garlic', 'pepper' and 'butter' in the title are at the core of it, taking the lead of memorable prawn and crab dishes eaten in Mumbai.

Use the largest king prawns you can find – shelled but still raw. The freezer section of Asian supermarkets is a good source. If they've not already been deveined and scored, there's a little bit of work to prepare them but it's not really that time consuming and is definitely worth it.

Excellent as a light meal with flatbreads or rice (to soak up the butter sauce). But arguably better as part of a feast alongside a collection of other dishes – the paneer and its coriander and mint chutney (page 144), a dal (page 140), rice, breads and pickles.

Serves 2 as a light meal, 4–6 as part of a feast
–

200g (7oz) raw large king prawns
4 cloves garlic, minced
½ tsp ground turmeric
1½ tbsp vegetable oil
1 tsp brown mustard seeds
25g (1oz) salted butter in cubes
1½ tbsp whole peppercorns, crushed to a coarse grit
½ tsp dried chilli flakes
½ lime, cut in 2 wedges
Leaves picked from 15g (½oz) coriander (cilantro)

Serve with basmati rice and/or flatbreads.

Use a sharp knife to score the outside curve of each prawn, two thirds of the way through, so there's more surface area to collect the spices. If not already deveined, use the tip of the knife to pull away the black line. Leave the tails on if they're still there.

Pop the prepped prawns in a bowl, along with the garlic, turmeric and half a tablespoon of the oil. Mix thoroughly, then leave in the fridge for 15 minutes or more.

Ensure the rice (or the rest of your feast) is ready before beginning to fry the prawns – they take just 2–3 minutes to cook.

Put a wok on as high a heat as possible. Add the remaining tablespoon of oil then the mustard seeds and, when 20 seconds or so later the oil is smoking hot and the mustard seeds are popping, tip in the prawns along with all of their garlicky marinade.

Fry for 30 seconds without stirring, then add the butter, crushed peppercorns and chilli flakes. Use a spatula or similar to push and toss the prawns and spices in the rapidly melting butter and cook for barely 90 seconds more, transferring the prawns and the buttery sauce to a serving dish as soon as they're pink.

Ensure all the butter and pepper from the wok is scraped over the top of the prawns, add a squeeze of lime from one of the wedges, leaving the second as optional garnish, along with a generous scattering of coriander.

Paneer tikka

Paneer carries other flavours incredibly well and, when caught at the right moment soon after coming out of a hot oven, is soft and something to relish as your teeth sink in. With that in mind, these skewers provide relatively instant gratification: cooked as fast as possible, and stuffed at indecent pace into your mouth. The speed is accompanied by a riot of flavour: sharp, colourful, spiced yoghurt; a fresh herb chutney, plus mildly abrasive raw red onion and acidulous lime. Alongside flatbreads, the cheese and condiments provide a decent meal. They're also excellent as a component within a larger feast – perhaps with a dal (page 140) and garlic pepper butter prawns (page 143).

Serves 4 (or more as part of a feast)
—

100g (3½oz) Greek yoghurt
2 tsp tomato purée (paste)
1 tsp amchur (mango powder)
½ tsp chilli powder
½ tsp ground turmeric
½ tsp coarsely ground black pepper
15g (½oz) fresh ginger, peeled and minced
2 cloves garlic, minced
500g (1lb 2oz) paneer, cut into 3cm (1¼in) cubes
1 green (bell) pepper, deseeded, cut into 3cm (1¼in) cubes
1 red onion, halved, layers pulled apart and cut to match the pepper
4–6 skewers

For the coriander and mint chutney
20g (1oz) coriander (cilantro), leaves and stems
Leaves picked from 15g (½oz) mint
Juice 1 lime
2 medium tomatoes, roughly chopped
1 mild green chilli, deseeded
1 tsp golden caster (superfine) sugar
½ tsp flaky sea salt
1 tbsp vegetable or groundnut (peanut) oil

To serve
1 small red onion, finely sliced
1 lime, sliced into 8 wedges
Naan, chapati or other flatbread and/or plain white rice

Combine the yoghurt, tomato purée, ground spices, ginger and garlic. Smother the paneer in the yoghurt marinade, then assemble the paneer, pepper and onion squares onto the skewers, alternating in this order. Leave for anywhere between 20 minutes and 24 hours (cover and refrigerate if leaving for longer than an hour).

Put all the ingredients for the chutney in a blender and blitz until smooth. This is best when freshly made (the colours and flavours of the herbs dull after a couple of hours – they're fine, just not as zingy).

Heat the oven to 240°C/220°C fan/475°F. Line a baking sheet with baking paper and arrange the skewers on top. Cook for 8–10 minutes so that the paneer squares are charred at the edges and the peppers and onion are just beginning to soften, while the marinade and centre of the cheese are still relaxed and slack, not dry and tight. Serve with the chutney, sliced onion and lime, plus flatbreads and/or rice.

Sri Lankan-style squash curry

In the Sri Lankan-style vegetable curries I've eaten, the sweetness of coconut, cinnamon, cardamom and anise stands out. I've tried to replicate that, not least because their brightness is light and uplifting and suits a particular mood.

This is best made with a winter squash such as onion, acorn or hubbard, or delica pumpkin (all, confusingly, at their peak in autumn); their sweetness is complex and paired with a nuttiness that prevents the dish becoming sickly.

Serves 4

—

1 large or 2 medium-size winter squash (onion, acorn or hubbard) or delica pumpkin (approximately 1.5kg/3lb 5oz)
2 tbsp cold-pressed rapeseed (canola) oil
2 heaped tsp ground cinnamon
2 tbsp coconut oil
1 red onion, diced
30g (1oz) fresh ginger, peeled and minced
30g (1oz) coriander (cilantro), leaves picked, stems finely chopped
4 cloves garlic, minced
2 small mild green chillies, deseeded, diced
2 tsp ground cumin
2 tsp ground turmeric
½ tsp chilli powder
2 cinnamon sticks
5 cardamom pods
1 star anise
4 cloves
2 heaped tbsp tomato purée (paste)
300ml (1¼ cups + 1 tbsp) cold water
1 x 400g (14oz) can coconut milk (50% coconut solids)
Maple syrup
40g (1½oz) cashew nuts (plain or see page 136), roughly chopped
1 lime, quartered
Flaky sea salt and ground black pepper

Serve with basmati rice and/or chapati or roti-style flatbreads.

Heat the oven to 220°C/200°C fan/425°F.

Cut the squash (or delica pumpkin) in half. Leave the skin on, scoop out and discard the seeds, and cut into 2–3cm (¾–1¼in)-thick slices. Place these on two baking sheets – you need space around each piece so they roast, not bake.

Drizzle about two tablespoons of rapeseed oil and sprinkle a heaped teaspoon of cinnamon over each tray. Jumble the squash (or pumpkin) around so they're all well oiled and spiced, then roast in the hot oven for 30 minutes. Remove the baking sheets after that time.

While the squash (or pumpkin) is cooking, put the coconut oil in a large casserole or sauté pan over a medium heat. As it melts add the onion and a pinch of salt and cook for 7 or 8 minutes so it's soft and sweet and just beginning to colour. Add the ginger, coriander stems and garlic and cook for 2 minutes more, stirring regularly, then add all of the spices. Add a few tablespoons of water if things are sticking, and cook for 1 minute more before adding the tomato purée. Cook the paste for another minute, continually stirring to ensure nothing burns before adding the cold water.

By now the squash (or pumpkin) will most likely have had its 30 minutes and will be out of the oven, so transfer a third of it to the casserole or pan. Use a potato masher to mash into a purée – they'll be very soft (save for the skins which won't mash but that's fine, leave them in). Add the coconut milk and stir so that paste, squash (or pumpkin) and coconut are as one, then simmer for 10–15 minutes (partly so the sauce reduces and thickens a little, but mostly to let the flavours get to know each other).

Cook your rice according to the packet instructions (or to your preferred method).

Amalgamate the remaining roast squash (or pumpkin) onto one baking sheet. Drizzle a little maple syrup over each wedge – just a little, it's not a pudding – then return to the oven, turn the temperature down to 190°C/170°C fan/375°F and cook for the last 10 minutes of the sauce puttering away.

Finally (if not using the sweet-spiced cashews from page 136), toast the chopped cashew nuts in a small, dry frying pan until fragrant and beginning to bronze. Add a pinch of salt and far more black pepper than you think is natural and remove from the heat.

Serve so there's around two ladles of sauce in each bowl/plate, topped with squash (or pumpkin) wedges, a scattering of cashew nuts, as well as the reserved coriander leaves and a wedge of lime per person (encourage everyone to squeeze it over the curry before eating).

Fish fillet katsu curry

———

To me a katsu curry sits alongside dal in the category of comfort curry. Think: rainy sofa day.

The act of deep-frying breaded pork or chicken at home, however, doesn't necessarily correlate with slumping mood, so I've tweaked the Japanese classic to provide a fish-based, oven-baked alternative. Those twists mean this is not technically 'katsu' (because the fish is neither a cutlet nor fried); however, the golden and crisp panko crumb evokes the original, and the flaky white fish within goes remarkably well with a carrot-spiked curry sauce. So, it's still worth making.

Serves 4

–

For the fish
70g (2½oz) panko breadcrumbs
3 tbsp vegetable or sunflower oil
2 tbsp plain (all-purpose) flour
1 egg, beaten
1 tbsp milk
4 x fillets pollack, cod or haddock (around 140g/5oz), skin removed

For the sauce
50g (1¾oz) salted butter
1 medium onion, diced
2 celery sticks, diced
30g (1oz) fresh ginger, peeled and sliced
2 cloves garlic, minced
4 tsp medium curry powder
1 tbsp tomato purée (paste)
500g (1lb 2oz) carrots, peeled and cut into 3–4cm cylinders
500ml (2 cups) vegetable stock
Juice ½ lemon
Flaky sea salt

To accompany
Plain or short-grain rice
Shredded white cabbage (raw) or boiled broccoli, kale or peas
½ lemon, cut into wedges

Firstly, bake the panko crumbs. Heat the oven to 200°C/180°C fan/400°F. Drizzle three tablespoons of neutral oil onto a baking sheet. Sprinkle the panko on top and shuffle to mix. Bake at the top of the oven for 6–12 minutes, until the crumbs are the golden colour you'd expect on a frozen fishfinger. Check after 6 minutes, shuffle to mix, then check and shuffle every 2 minutes thereafter. Leave to cool – store in an airtight container if not using straight away.

To make the sauce, put 30g (1oz) of the butter into a saucepan over a medium heat. Let this melt, then add the onion, a pinch of salt, the celery and ginger and sauté for 4–5 minutes to soften. Add the garlic and cook for 1 minute before adding the curry powder. Stir continuously, and after 30 seconds add the tomato purée. Cook for 30 seconds more before adding the carrots, and vegetable stock. Bring to the boil, then simmer for 15–20 minutes until the carrots are tender.

Remove a couple of pieces of carrot per person and set aside, then blitz the sauce in a blender until silky smooth. Add the remaining 20g (¾oz) of butter and quite a lot of salt, pulse some more, then return the sauce to the pan, along with the set-aside carrots. Taste, add the lemon juice, taste again and add extra salt if you think it needs it (it probably does). Keep warm.

While the sauce is simmering, find three small plates and heat the oven to 220°C/200°C fan/ 425°F. Measure the flour onto one plate, the beaten egg and milk onto another, and the (now cool-ish) panko crumbs onto the last one. Line a baking sheet with baking paper. Roll each fish fillet in flour, then in milky egg, and finally the crumbs. Set on the baking sheet and bake at the top of the oven for 15 minutes.

Meanwhile, cook your rice according to packet instructions (or to your preferred method) and shred the white cabbage or cook your greens.

Use a small bowl to shape a mound of rice onto a plate, pour the sauce to one side, ensuring everyone has a couple of carrots. Then add the fish, cabbage or greens and a wedge of lemon.

Curry leaf mussels and fries

Curry leaves tempering in hot oil is a top-five kitchen smell; my tastebuds become fully activated upon catching a whiff. Indeed, such is their instantly satisfying effect, it's worth buying a packet or two if ever you see them – like chillies they store well in the freezer (and can be used straight from frozen).

Mussels in a creamy sauce carry the aroma particularly well. As it happens, they cook almost as quickly as the leaves, so this works well as a rapid response to a craving for spice. You could obviously drag bread through that sauce, but on this occasion I think a side of salty French fries works best (frozen fries for oven baking are perfect).

Serves 4 as a main course

—

1.5kg (6½ cups) mussels
2 tbsp vegetable oil
1 medium onion or shallot, finely sliced
30g (1oz) fresh ginger, peeled and sliced into fine matchsticks
1 tsp yellow mustard seeds
25–30 curry leaves (2 full sprigs)
2 cloves garlic, finely sliced
1 tsp ground turmeric
2 tsp ground cumin
½ tsp chilli powder
1 heaped tbsp tomato purée (paste)
100ml (scant ½ cup) cold water
300ml (1¼ cups + 1 tbsp) double (heavy) cream
Pinch flaky sea salt

Oven-baked French fries, to serve.

Purge (clean) the mussels by leaving them to soak in cold water for 20 minutes, lifting them out from the bowl after 10 minutes, discarding the dirty, gritty water and refilling it with cold water (and the mussels). Repeat this action 5 minutes later, and then again. Keep the bowl in the fridge during this time, save for the last soak, when you should pull out any straggly beards from the mussels (easier while they're still under water). Discard any mussels that remain open when tapped. This can be done in advance, though you must store the mussels in the fridge until needed.

Cook your fries – I find they usually need a few minutes longer than the packet suggests.

When the fries are nearly done, choose a wide saucepan or wok with a lid that will fit the mussels in no more than three layers. Place this on a medium heat and add the vegetable oil. Let this warm for 30 seconds before adding the onions, ginger, a pinch of salt, the mustard seeds and curry leaves. Cook for 2 minutes, stirring from time to time to prevent the onions or leaves burning. Add the garlic and, 30 seconds later, the spices. Cook these for a minute, stirring frequently, then add the tomato purée.

After 1 minute more, increase the heat to high then add the water, cream and mussels. Stir the contents thoroughly, place the lid on top and cook for 3 minutes, shaking once or twice. If the mussels have not fully opened after that time, use a spoon to scoop them from the bottom of the pan to the top (so as to swap open with closed) remove from the heat but put the lid back on top for a further minute, leaving the remaining mussels to steam open. Discard any that refuse to open.

Ladle into bowls, ensuring everyone has a fair share of the glossy, fragrant and rust-coloured sauce, with piles of well-salted fries nearby.

Lamb and pea keema with minted kachumber

The Mughal dish keema matar translates to mince (keema) and peas (matar). Probably because of the mince element, to me this has the feel of and indeed has become a midweek family meal in the same vein as a spag bol or chile con carne. Which is not to trivialize it. More to encourage anyone who might be stand-offish about making a 'curry' (in the loose sense) from scratch: this is not a project dish.

Chop the kachumber ingredients as finely as you can; like a salsa, albeit one served in the quantities of a side salad, so as to bolster and bring freshness to the meal. The dish is not very hot, so you might consider offering an additional chopped fresh green chilli as an optional garnish.

Serves 4
—

2 tbsp vegetable oil
2 medium onions, finely sliced
1½ tbsp cumin seeds
1 tsp coriander seeds
1 heaped tsp ground turmeric
1 tsp chilli powder
40g (1½oz) fresh ginger, peeled and finely grated
4 cloves garlic, minced
1 mild green chilli, finely chopped (plus 1 more as optional garnish)
400g (14oz) tomatoes, roughly chopped
450ml (2 cups) water
500g (1lb 2oz) lamb mince (ground lamb)
1 cinnamon stick
3 cloves
2 cardamom pods
1 tbsp tomato purée (paste)
150g (5½oz) frozen peas
Flaky sea salt

For the minted kachumber
200g (7oz) tomatoes
150g (5½oz) cucumber, peeled
1 small banana shallot
1 small clove garlic, minced
Leaves picked from 20g (¾oz) mint, finely chopped
Juice ½ lemon

2 tbsp cold-pressed rapeseed (canola) oil
Large pinch flaky sea salt

Serve with basmati rice.
—

Put a wide saucepan or sauté pan with a lid on a medium heat. Add the vegetable oil, a pinch of salt and the onions and cook for 5 minutes, stirring occasionally so that they just begin to bronze. Reduce the heat to very low, cover and cook for 25 minutes more so you have a sweet-smelling, sticky, golden mass of onions. Stir regularly to ensure they are browning but not burning.

Toast the cumin and coriander seeds in a dry pan, grind to a powder and mix with the turmeric and chilli powder.

When the onions are ready, add the ginger, garlic and green chilli. Stir into the onions and continue to cook for 1–2 minutes more (add a tablespoon of water if it's sticking), then turn the heat up to medium, add the tomatoes, a touch more salt and 150ml (scant ⅔ cup) of the water. Simmer for 10 minutes with the lid now slightly ajar.

The tomatoes and onions should cook down to a loose paste in this time. Now add the lamb (no need to brown it), three-quarters of the ground spice mix, the whole spices and another pinch of salt. Prod the mince to break it up, add the tomato purée and the remaining 300ml (1¼ cups + 1 tbsp) of water, stir then cook at a fast simmer for 30 minutes, again with the lid ajar.

Meanwhile, prepare the kachumber by chopping the tomatoes, peeled cucumber and shallot very finely, then combine with the other ingredients in a mixing bowl. Cook your rice according to the packet instructions (or to your preferred method).

Once the mince has been cooking for half an hour, and your rice and kachumber are ready, add the frozen peas and the last of the spice mix, stir, return to an energetic simmer for 5 minutes, then serve, with chopped green chilli to taste.

Mackerel, tamarind and turmeric curry

I have tied myself in knots trying to settle on the origins of this dish. In truth it's a bit southern Thai in the fried aromatic root and coconut-paste base, a bit Keralan through the fenugreek, mustard and coriander seeds, a bit other places between those two spots, and a bit British in me wanting to focus on a fish that's so often available here, while also using up some celery from my fridge drawer.

The bottom line is that it's easy to make and markedly different from the other dishes in this section. The sauce is thin in texture but not flavour, the mackerel pervasive but not domineering. There's a slight tang and a little tingle of chilli on the lips, and the fresh turmeric, lime leaves and coconut are transportive. Don't hold back if there are fewer than four of you; next-day leftovers are remarkably good.

Serves 4
—

30g (1oz) tamarind pulp (from a block)
40g (1½oz) fresh ginger, peeled and
   roughly chopped
30g (1oz), fresh turmeric, peeled and
   roughly chopped
3 cloves garlic, roughly chopped
2 banana shallots, roughly chopped
2 mild green chillies, deseeded and
   roughly chopped
3 tbsp coconut oil
1 tsp brown mustard seeds
½ tsp fenugreek seeds
1 x 400g (14oz) can light coconut milk
   (20–30% coconut solids)
1 tsp red chilli powder
2 tsp coriander seeds, toasted and ground
   to a powder or 1 tsp ground coriander
1 tsp golden caster (superfine) sugar
4 celery sticks, cut into 3–4cm (1¼–1½in) batons
5 makrut lime leaves (fresh or frozen)
2 mackerel (1–1.5kg/2lb 4oz–3lb 5oz), gutted
   and cut through the bone into 2–3cm
   (¾–1¼in) steaks (include heads and tails)
Flaky sea salt

Serve with plain rice.

Put the tamarind in a small container and cover with 120ml (½ cup) of just-boiled water. Leave for a minute before agitating with a fork, stirring until the paste has dissolved into the water. Set to one side until required, then strain through a sieve (strainer), discarding seeds and woody bits.

Pound the ginger, turmeric, garlic, shallots and green chilli into a rough paste using a pestle and mortar. Do this one by one in the order they are written, each time with a pinch of flaky salt as an abrasive, then combine at the end. You can use a small food processor or speed blender to blitz all at the same time, but it doesn't take long to do this by hand, and the bruising rather than chopping somehow makes it taste better (also, the turmeric will stain your processor).

Place a wok, wide sauté pan or casserole over a medium heat. Add the coconut oil along with the mustard and fenugreek seeds. When the mustard seeds are popping add the paste and any thickened cream from the coconut milk can. Fry on a moderate heat without colouring for 5 minutes or so until the paste and oils split. Add the remaining spices and sugar, and continue to fry for a couple of minutes, stirring frequently, adding a few tablespoons of water if sticking.

Now add the rest of the coconut milk can, six tablespoons of the tamarind water, the celery and lime leaves. Let this bubble away and mingle for 5 minutes before adding the mackerel. Cook for 10–15 minutes, try a spoonful of the sauce and add more salt and/or tamarind water to taste. The sauce should be thin and plentiful, with the fish seemingly swimming in it. Serve in bowls over rice.

Spiced tomatoes with baked cod and turmeric yoghurt

Given they form the base of so many curried dishes, we know that tomatoes are a fine match for spice – I think probably because they are sweet and acidic, and the best of them are boldly flavoured. They shouldn't, though, be limited to a background role: a curry of *just* tomatoes is a very fine thing indeed. This is nearly that, but after a few tests I decided to include baked cod, though I do think the fish plays second fiddle.

Enjoy the golden, spiced yoghurt in two stages: initially as a cool and bright contrast to the curried tomatoes, fish and plain rice, and then, about halfway into eating, stirred through the rest of the curry to make the sauce smooth and creamy.

Serves 4–6

–

2–3 tbsp vegetable oil
2 onions, finely chopped
1 tbsp cumin seeds
1 tbsp coriander seeds
2 tsp fennel seeds
2 tsp black mustard seeds
10 cloves
½ tsp white peppercorns
3 green cardamom pods
1 tsp ground turmeric
Around 25 curry leaves (usually 2 sprigs)
3 bay leaves
2 cloves garlic, finely sliced
1–2 tbsp water
1.2kg (2lb 10oz) cherry tomatoes
1 tbsp caster (superfine) sugar
30g (1oz) butter, sliced
4–6 x 120g (4¼oz) fillets cod, ideally skin on
Flaky sea salt

For the turmeric yoghurt
2 tbsp cold-pressed rapeseed (canola) oil
1 clove garlic, minced
1 tsp ground turmeric
6 tbsp Greek yoghurt
Pinch flaky sea salt

Serve with brown rice and finely sliced mild green chilli (optional) as a garnish.

Heat the oven to 170°C/150°C fan/325°F. Put a casserole, or similar, over a medium heat. Add two tablespoons of oil, the onions and a big pinch of salt. Cook gently for 15–20 minutes, stirring occasionally, until soft and lightly golden – we're not aiming for fully browned in this instance.

Meanwhile, measure all the dry spices, except the turmeric, into a dry pan and toast over a low heat for 3–4 minutes until fragrant. Decant into a spice grinder or pestle and mortar and reduce to a powder, then stir in the turmeric.

Add the curry leaves, bay leaves and garlic to the onion and cook for 2 minutes more, then add 2 heaped tablespoons of the ground spices and a tablespoon or two of water. (You will have some spice powder left over – potentially to be added later, but otherwise reserve for a generic 'curry powder' moment. The mix works well, for example, in the curry leaf mussels on page 150).

Add two thirds of the tomatoes to the pan and mix with the onions. Sprinkle with the sugar, dot with the butter and place in the oven (without a lid) for 1 hour 20 minutes. Give it a shuffle after 30 minutes to ensure the onions and tomatoes are mingling, then 20 minutes later add the remaining tomatoes and carefully mix. Return to the oven for the final (pre-fish) 30 minutes.

Stir another tablespoon of the ground spices into the tomatoes, then sit the fish skin-side up, pushing them 1–2cm (½–¾in) below the surface so that they part-poach, part-bake. Return to the oven, still uncovered, for 12–14 minutes so the fish is just cooked – flaking but still succulent.

While the curry is cooking, make the turmeric yoghurt. Heat the rapeseed oil, add the garlic and cook gently for 1–2 minutes without burning. Remove from the heat, add the turmeric, stir and allow to cool. Just before eating, add to the yoghurt with a pinch of salt and stir vigorously until bright yellow.

Peel the skin from the fish and serve with ladles of tomatoes alongside brown rice and turmeric yoghurt, with fresh green chilli scattered to taste.

Curried brisket noodles

There's a superb café called Kau Kee in Central, Hong Kong, famed, in particular, for its brisket and beef-tendon noodle soups: one with a broth that's just about as beefy as you can get, the other curried. The queues are long and service is short, yet it'll be the first place I return to next time I'm there (and the time after that). Beyond simmering beef and bones for hours and hours, I've no idea what the secret to their curried brisket is. Does anyone? But I have it in mind when cooking this dish, with its curry-powder base, the deep, savoury notes of beef in both stock and flaking brisket, plus a hint of sweetness from coconut, cinnamon and anise. It's something I head for when I find myself after a bowl of food that's warming in every sense of the word.

Serves 4

–

750g (1lb 7oz) brisket, with plenty of fat
3 tbsp neutral cooking oil
1 banana shallot, finely sliced
40g (1½oz) fresh ginger, peeled and minced
4 cloves garlic, minced
2 star anise
1 cinnamon stick
2 tbsp medium curry powder
1 tsp ground turmeric
1 tsp Kashmiri chilli powder
1 tbsp golden caster (superfine) sugar
1 x 400g (14oz) can coconut milk
   (ideally 50% coconut solids and cold)
2 tomatoes, halved
1 litre (4⅓ cups) cold water
2 tbsp light soy sauce
2 spring onions (scallions), finely chopped,
   whites and greens separated
2–3 bulbs pak choi (bok choy), separated
200g (7oz) flat egg noodles (e-fu)
Flaky sea salt

Cut the brisket into chunks about 2cm (¾in) wide x 3cm (1¼in) long. Include most if not all the fat – for viscosity, flavour and texture.

Once portioned, place the brisket pieces in a casserole or heavy-bottomed saucepan, cover with cold water, bring to the boil for 2 minutes, skim the impurities then drain through a colander. Clean the pan and set the meat to one side.

Return the saucepan to the stove over a medium heat. Add the oil, shallots, ginger and a pinch of salt and sauté for 3 minutes without colouring, stirring occasionally. Add the garlic and cook for 1 minute more, before measuring in both whole and powdered spices. There should still be quite bit of oil but add another tablespoon if it needs it, cooking for 1–2 minutes more until aromatic. Add the sugar and the solids from a cold, unshaken can of coconut milk. Fry for 2 minutes, stirring continually, then return the beef to the pan, along with the tomatoes, the remaining liquid from the can of coconut milk, the water and the soy sauce. Simmer for 2 hours with the lid off, by which time the brisket and fat should be soft and succulent.

At this point, remove the brisket from the liquid using a slotted spoon. Then either with a stick blender, or by decanting into a stand blender, blitz the sauce until emulsified and smooth and more viscous than before. Return both liquid and meat to the saucepan, add the white spring onions and simmer for 5 minutes more, warming the pak choi through in the sauce. Season as you see fit – add more soy sauce for salt, possibly a little more curry or chilli powder too.

Cook your noodles according to the packet instructions. Once al dente, drain through a colander and return to their now dry saucepan. Add three to four ladles of sauce, and slosh around so the noodles are coated. Divide between four bowls, then add the brisket, pak choi and plenty of sauce to each. Garnish with the spring onion greens.

Cape Malay hogget curry

The roots of Cape Malay cooking extend to those enslaved people of Malaysia, India, what is now known as Indonesia, and Sri Lanka (then, Ceylon) who were brought to South Africa by Europeans in the colonial era. Eventually freed but concentrated in the Bo-Kaap quarter of Cape Town, a distinctive cuisine evolved as an aromatic and fragrant fusion of immigrant culinary traditions and indigenous ingredients. Cape Malay curries are not particularly hot; rather they're characterized by the use of sweet, dried spices (ginger, star anise, cardamom and so on) and often fruit, too.

Cape Malay meals often include a vinegary onion and tomato 'sambal', and I think this one cuts through the dish nicely. If you can't find hogget then use lamb, mutton or goat.

Serves 4–6

—

150g (5½oz) dried apricots
1 rooibos tea bag (or equivalent loose leaf)
400ml (1¾ cups) just-boiled water
4 tbsp vegetable or sunflower oil
300g (10½oz) onions, finely sliced
1kg (2lb 4oz) hogget shoulder (or lamb or mutton), diced
3 cloves garlic, roughly chopped
2 mild green chillies, deseeded and chopped
1 tbsp cumin seeds
1 tbsp coriander seeds
1 tsp fenugreek seeds
8 black peppercorns
½ tsp Kashmiri chilli powder
2 tsp ground turmeric
2 tsp ground ginger
4 green cardamom pods
1 star anise
1 cinnamon stick, snapped in half
⅛ nutmeg, freshly grated
1 x 400g (14oz) can chopped tomatoes
500g (1lb 2oz) waxy potatoes, peeled and chunked
Flaky sea salt

Serve with saffron-infused basmati rice and a tomato, apricot and onion sambal (see opposite).

Put the apricots in a jug or small mixing bowl. Add the tea bag and the just-boiled water and leave to steep for a total of 30 minutes, removing the bag after about 8 minutes. Reserve two soaked apricots for the sambal.

Place a large lidded casserole, or similar, on a low–medium heat. Add two tablespoons of the oil, the onions and a big pinch of salt. Sauté for 7–8 minutes until softening and taking on a little colour. Then put a lid on top and cook for around 20 minutes more, stirring occasionally, by which time they will be golden (but not dark brown).

While the onions are cooking, brown the meat in a separate, large frying pan (skillet) set over a high heat. Add another tablespoon of cooking oil and fry the meat without too much interruption. This will take 7–10 minutes if there's enough space in the pan (you may need to do in two batches). Don't cook for much longer.

While the onions are still cooking, pound the garlic and chilli to a paste in a pestle and mortar. Toast the cumin, coriander, fenugreek and peppercorns in a dry pan for a few minutes until they become aromatic, then grind to a powder.

Once the onions are golden, add the remaining tablespoon of oil, plus the garlic and chilli paste. Cook gently with the lid off for 1 minute, stirring to prevent too much sticking or browning. Then add the chilli powder, ground turmeric and ginger, the cardamom pods, star anise and cinnamon and the nutmeg. Mix well, cook for 5 minutes more, adding two to three tablespoons of water if the mix is dry and catching.

Now add the hogget, any cooking juices, the apricots, tea and the canned tomatoes. Refill the can with water and add that too, plus one teaspoon of flaky salt. Simmer with the lid on top for 1 hour. Add the chunked potatoes, ensure they are submerged and simmer for 30–45 minutes further until both meat and potatoes are tender. Add extra salt to taste (it probably will need it) and stir in another 200–400ml (scant 1 cup–1¾ cups) of water if the curry is dry (it's best if there's a ladle or so of sauce per portion).

Saffron basmati rice

Makes 6 portions

—

360g (12¾oz) rice
900ml (4 cups) water
1 tsp flaky sea salt
10–12 saffron threads

—

Combine the rice, water, salt and saffron in a medium–large saucepan. Place over a medium heat and bring to a steady simmer, stirring a couple of times early on to prevent any rice sticking at the base of the pan. Cook for about 10 minutes more, until the rice is dry on top and very nearly dry at the base (with 1–2mm/ 1/16in of water remaining). Remove the saucepan from the heat, place a lid or clean dish towel on top and leave to steam for 5 minutes. Fluff up with a fork before serving.

Tomato, apricot and onion sambal

1 small white onion, very finely diced
1 large tomato, very finely diced
2 reconstituted dried apricots (see left), finely diced
1 green chilli, deseeded, very finely diced
½ tsp flaky sea salt
1 tsp caster (superfine) sugar
4 tbsp white wine vinegar

—

Combine the onion, tomato, apricots, chilli, salt and sugar. Leave for 10 minutes before adding the vinegar and a splash of water to loosen if required. Set to one side.

Pork shoulder vindaloo and okra fry

As is often written, a punishing British curry house 'vindaloo' bears little resemblance to the Portuguese-Goan 'vinha d'alhos' from which its name derives. This recipe is more akin to the original dish, combining both wine vinegar and port or red wine, with a decent hit of garlic. There's a blaze of smoky-red thanks to paprika, and while the crisp shallot and coriander garnishes are optional, they are very much worth adding if you have them. Serve with rice and do also cook the okra fry too (without the vegetable element, it's otherwise a fairly small meal for 4).

Serves 4

—

For the rub
2 tsp paprika
1 tsp ground turmeric
1 tsp cayenne pepper
1 clove garlic, minced
2 tbsp red wine vinegar

600g (1lb 5oz) pork shoulder, in chunky dice
   (or large cubes of pork belly)
1 tbsp cumin seeds
1½ tbsp coriander seeds
2 tsp garam masala
2 tsp paprika
1 tsp ground turmeric
1 tsp cayenne pepper
2½ tbsp neutral cooking oil
1 tsp brown mustard seeds
300g (10½oz) onion, finely sliced
40g (1½oz) fresh ginger, peeled and grated
6 cloves garlic, minced
3 medium–large tomatoes, roughly chopped
100ml (scant ½ cup) port or red wine
300ml (1¼ cups + 1 tbsp) water
1–2 tsp golden caster (superfine) sugar
1–3 tsp red wine vinegar
2–3 tbsp crispy shallots plus fresh coriander
   (cilantro), to garnish
Flaky sea salt

Serve with the okra fry (opposite) and plain rice.

Combine the rub ingredients in a bowl to make a paste. Add the pork and mix thoroughly, then cover or transfer the meat and its marinade to a sealable bag. Refrigerate for 2–24 hours, turning the meat occasionally to ensure it's marinating evenly.

When ready to cook, gently toast the cumin and coriander seeds in a dry pan for 2–3 minutes before grinding them to a powder, then combine with the garam masala, paprika, turmeric and cayenne pepper.

Place a heavy-bottomed lidded saucepan or casserole over a medium heat, add two tablespoons of cooking oil and the mustard seeds. When the mustard seeds start popping, add the onions and a pinch of salt and cook for 20 minutes, stirring regularly, until the onions are just beginning to turn golden. Add a touch more oil plus the ginger and garlic and cook for 2 minutes more. Mix in the dry spice powder, adding two to three tablespoons of water if the pan is dry and the onions are catching. Cook for a minute, then add the pork, all its marinade and the tomatoes.

Allow the meat to colour a little over 2–3 minutes of cooking, then deglaze the pan with the port or wine, followed by the water, one teaspoon of vinegar, one teaspoon of sugar, and half a teaspoon of salt. Cover the pan and simmer gently for around 90 minutes, until the pork is tender and wobbly, and not yet dry and flaky. Taste the sauce and season accordingly; a half teaspoon of salt and one to two teaspoons of additional vinegar will provide extra spark, consider another teaspoon of sugar too.

Garnish with the crispy shallots and a handful of coriander. Serve with okra fry (see opposite) and plain rice.

Okra fry

25g (1oz) tamarind pulp (from a block)
1 tbsp neutral cooking oil
1 small red onion, finely diced
20g (¾oz) fresh ginger, peeled and grated
2 cloves garlic, minced
1 mild green chilli, finely diced
250g (9oz) okra
½ tsp ground turmeric
1 tsp golden caster (superfine) sugar
1 tsp flaky sea salt
4 tbsp water

Pour three tablespoons of just-boiled water over the tamarind. Disturb with a fork until the pulp has dissolved and pass through a sieve (strainer), saving the water and discarding any stones and vegetal bits in the sieve.

Place a large frying pan or wok over a medium heat. Add the cooking oil and, before it's had a chance to get too hot, the onion, ginger, garlic, chilli and okra. Sauté for 90 seconds, then add the turmeric, sugar and salt. Reduce the heat to low, add the tamarind water and four tablespoons or so of tap water, stir, cover and cook gently for 4 minutes. Shuffle once or twice and remove from the heat just as the colour of the okra begins to mellow, but is still verdant and with a little bite.

Ricotta fritters with coconut and makrut lime chocolate sauce

This is a twist on Italian bombolini (ricotta doughnuts), using flavours from elsewhere to add an aromatic punch – coconut, makrut lime leaves, lime zest and cinnamon. Even if you're not accustomed to deep-frying they make for an easy and memorable finish to a meal.

The sauce requires coconut cream, which is typically listed as including around 70–80% coconut solids (so not 'milk', 'light milk', 'creamed coconut' or 'water'). The quantity made will be more than you need, but in this instance I think it's better to have too much than too little; use any excess as you would Nutella (e.g. on pancakes), or reheat then dilute to make a spiced-coconut hot chocolate.

Serves 4

–

2 large eggs
Finely grated zest 1 lime
120g (4¼oz) caster (superfine) sugar
250g (9oz) strained ricotta
80g (2¾oz) plain (all-purpose) flour
2 tsp baking powder
½ tsp flaky sea salt
2 tsp ground cinnamon

For the sauce
300ml (1¼ cups + 1 tbsp) coconut cream
   (ideally 80% coconut solids)
12 fresh makrut lime leaves
100g (3½oz) dark chocolate (70% cocoa solids),
   broken into small pieces
4 tsp golden caster (superfine) sugar
½ tsp flaky sea salt, plus more to garnish

–

Put the eggs in a mixing bowl and quickly beat them with a whisk, then whisk in the lime zest and two thirds of the sugar. Using a large spoon or spatula, stir in the ricotta (it should look like lumpy wallpaper paste).

In a separate bowl combine the flour, baking powder and salt. Fold this into the ricotta mix, again using the spoon or spatula. Cover and refrigerate the batter until required (anywhere between 1 and 12 hours is fine). If the mixture splits over that time just beat it together again.

Meanwhile put the coconut cream and makrut lime leaves in a small saucepan over a low–medium heat until the cream reaches a moderate simmer (try to avoid it boiling). Reduce the heat to as low as possible for 5 minutes, then remove from the heat and leave to infuse for an hour.

Return the saucepan to a low–medium heat. When a few small bubbles appear, pick out the lime leaves and add the chocolate and sugar. Wait for 30 seconds then encourage the chocolate to melt into the cream, stirring until you have a smooth and silky sauce. Add the salt, stir again and leave somewhere warm until required. You can do this in advance – refrigerate then gently reheat shortly before you need it, serving the sauce slightly above room temperature for optimum viscosity.

When ready to eat, combine the cinnamon and the remaining sugar in a bowl or small roasting tray. Line a second bowl or tray with a paper towel.

Set a deep-fat fryer to 160°C/350°F (if you don't have a deep-fat fryer, fill a saucepan 5–7cm/2–2¾in deep with a neutral cooking oil and heat to the same temperature), then drop 1 dessertspoonful (about the size of a walnut) of batter into the saucepan. Fry for 3½–4 minutes, ensuring both sides are golden. Cut the fritter in half to check the inside is cooked (it should be soft but still cooked all the way through, not molten), then adjust the cooking time accordingly. Fry the remaining mix in two to three batches to fit your fryer or pan.

Transfer each batch of fritters to the paper-lined bowl or tray to absorb most of the oil, then roll them in the cinnamon sugar.

Serve as soon as the final batch has been dusted, with the sauce either in little dipping pots, in puddles on a plate, or with it drizzled lavishly over the fritters, plus a few flakes of salt.

Turmeric and saffron poached pears with spiced crumble

These golden poached pears are regal and fragrant (having been infused with both the colour and scent of saffron, turmeric and ginger), yet delicate and sweet, too. The spiced crumble (essentially a granola) adds more spice – fennel, cardamom, cinnamon – but it seems to season gracefully, rather than overwhelm. So this is a heady dessert to finish a meal in similar soothing and restorative style to a herbal tincture.

Crème fraîche is the best way to tie the fruit and crumble together thanks to its luxurious texture and slight sharpness. Alternatively whip double cream without icing sugar so it's thick but not sweet. Greek yoghurt is fine too... but makes this more like a breakfast (although that's not a bad idea if you've leftovers; indeed, there's lots of crumble, so jar that up for use over a week or so).

Serves 4

–

For the spiced crumble (makes more than is needed)
100g (3½oz) rolled porridge oats (oatmeal)
50g (1¾oz) bran, rye, wheat or spelt flakes
50g (1¾oz) jumbo (wholegrain) oats
50g (1¾oz) sunflower kernels
65g (1¼oz) pumpkin seeds
25g (1oz) linseed or sesame seeds
3 tbsp fennel seeds
2 tsp ground cardamom
1 tsp ground cinnamon
5 tbsp runny honey
100ml (scant ½ cup) cold-pressed rapeseed (canola) oil
1 heaped tsp flaky sea salt

For the pears
1 lemon, zest peeled in strips and juiced
150g (5½oz) golden caster (superfine) sugar
Big pinch saffron (about 24 threads)
10g (¼oz) ginger, peeled and sliced
25g (1oz) fresh turmeric, roughly chopped
700ml (3 cups) just-boiled water
4 conference pears, peeled
Crème fraîche, to serve

Heat the oven to 170°C/150°C fan/325°F.

To make the crumble, combine the dry ingredients, apart from the salt, in a large bowl. Measure in the honey and oil and mix well. Line a large baking sheet with baking paper and spread the oats and co. over this to no more than 1cm (½in) deep – use a second sheet if necessary. Bake for around 30 minutes, checking on the sheet(s) after 20 minutes and moving the (likely) browner outer parts to the middle to ensure an even bake. Remove when well bronzed (but not burnt) and scrunch the salt over the top. Mix and fluff with a fork, then leave to cool completely. Store in an airtight container at room temperature until required.

Put the lemon zest and juice, sugar, saffron, ginger and turmeric in a saucepan in which the pears will fit snugly in one layer. Pour over the just-boiled water and stir to ensure the sugar has dissolved. Pop the pears in the pan and cover with crumpled baking paper to keep them submerged, and then place over a medium heat, carefully bringing the water to a very low-key simmer, with just a few bubbles appearing round the edge. Keep it like this for 15 minutes, never letting the water boil, then remove from the heat, place a lid on top and set to one side.

Twenty minutes later, use a slotted spoon to transfer the pears to a container. Pick out the ginger, turmeric and zest (to avoid bitterness), then place the saucepan onto a high heat and boil for 10–15 minutes, reducing the poaching liquid by half to create a glossy, fragrant syrup. Pour this over the pears. You could serve the pears like this, but the colours and flavours will penetrate further if left, covered and refrigerated, for 12 hours or more.

Serve at room temperature, with a couple of spoons of syrup, a dollop of dairy, and a fistful of the spiced crumble per pear.

rich and
savoury

You might think that the marriage of 'rich' and 'savoury' in this section heading should have been with a more caveated 'and/or'. The pull and effect of, for example, the inherently rich and salty, jet-black cuttlefish rice being quite different from the far more gently savoury pork belly with butter beans. One is a punch, the other a restful soak involving bath salts, scented candles and classical music.

But the two do cross over in enough ways to house them together: salt, bitter and umami overlap as the relevant modalities of taste; the key colour in virtually all the recipes is brown; and the moments when a craving calls tend to be pretty similar too. Whether rich, savoury or both are required, this flavour profile is the sensible one your parents wanted you to marry; the career choice that would have provided security; the talking to – whether abrupt or gentle – required to get things back on track. This is the car that you should have bought and the post-party-season mindfulness retreat that you hope will steady you. Rich and savoury is where chicken soup and beige food fit in.

To be clear, this flavour profile is not boring, and nor are you boring or bored if you crave it. Though brown food is not peacock-pretty and the word evokes 'dull', in flavour it is intense, concentrated and long lasting. It involves the meaty moreishness of umami in miso, dashi, mushrooms and Parmesan. It's the taste and smell of the Maillard reaction at work on toasted bread, nuts and seeds, and at the edge of meats and onions as they braise, roast and fry.

Think of rice, pulses and grains, nuts and seeds, mushrooms, onions, root vegetables and brassicas. Often these things sit quietly behind some showy sauce, fragrant spice or flashy centrepiece ingredient, their primary role being as a base – to provide generic flavour to the dish and the stodge to fill you up. That's not really the case here, when in fact it's precisely these lesser ingredients that you're after above all others (consciously or otherwise). For example, the brown-edged onions and tender borlotti beans are the real point of the sausage dish. Similarly, the nutty, earthy and indeed grounding buckwheat noodles and the steadying sesame dipping sauce they're paired with are not a side dish but the focus. Chickpeas and tahini blitzed into a silky hummus and topped with roasted cauliflower and brown butter-toasted seeds are not a bland accompaniment but a near transformational moment.

As an aside, rich and/or savoury foods can edge towards being a little one-note or overpowering. As such, some balancing components are necessary to maintain interest or respite. So the aforementioned inky rice is paired with a romesco sauce, the pork belly and beans a kind-of tapenade; there's Chinese-style ginger and spring onion paste with the chicken barley, and the cod cheeks and red wine lentils are boosted by a piquant green sauce and crisp capers. Still, these are brief interruptions, the overall effect is dependably wholesome.

Rich and savoury cooking tends to involve a lot of slow-braising, poaching, baking and steeping. It's the opposite of the fresh and fragrant chapter, where you might remember the relevant ingredients are cooked quickly, if at all. On the contrary, here the desired results are achieved only once the components have blipped away slowly in a casserole or low oven, with the derivative warmth and scent of the food infiltrating our kitchens and probably minds too. This time we are sated by green leaves that have been knowingly 'overcooked' so that they squidge rather than snap. Root vegetables are more flavoursome because they are soft and golden-edged. Meat can be cut with a spoon. It's about saucepans set over a low heat with pulses peering out from under water, like alligator eyes, and finished dishes in which the ingredients sit in puddles of broth. Bowls, spoons and often sofas suit both the food and the moment.

This is not the autumn chapter of a seasonal ingredient-focused cookbook. And yet there are certain ingredients and styles of dish that would fit well under that header: mushrooms, kale, swede and squash, lasagne, ragù and broths. One reason, of course, is that we are inclined towards food that feels like a cuddle when the season turns from the colourful and balmy to rapidly shortening, cold wet days. But I'm also certain that there will be times when rich and savoury is required when the weather is actually perfectly pleasing. Maybe you need to recalibrate after some days or weeks of excess. Perhaps your palate requires something quiet and calming, having been battered by more attention-seeking flavours for a while. I once read that our first interaction with umami is through our mother's breast milk. Need we go any further to suggest why an urge for something savoury and calming occurs at times when a safe base is required?

There are, by the way, a handful of sweet-ish things at the end of this section. Which might seem counterintuitive to the theme. However, two of the desserts are pretty savoury and the other very rich. So they should suit those times when a saccharine end to a meal does not feel fitting. All pair particularly well with strong coffee, which also feels appropriate.

Parent and child rice

Oyakodon is a Japanese dish that effectively translates as parent and child rice. I understand that's because both chicken and egg are involved. But the title's apt for personal reasons too because it has become a favourite when it's just my son and me at home, and at least one of us (me) is craving something a touch beyond 'plain', largely store-cupboardy, and relatively quick yet still delicious.

At first glance the cooking stages might seem a bit discombobulating, so as you read it's helpful to remember that it's simply a loose omelette plus broth on rice that, after you've cooked it once, should also become an easy weeknight supper solution for you.

Though everything is prepped together, the final portions are cooked separately – a bit like cooking two omelettes. Obviously if you have two similar-size pans, that works well. But if not, it's very quick and both will still be piping hot when served.

Pictured on pages 172–173.

Serves 2
–

For the rice
200g (7oz) short-grain sushi rice
300ml (1¼ cup + 1 tbsp) cold water
2 tsp sushi vinegar

For the topping
1 x 10g (¼oz) instant dashi sachet
250ml (generous 1 cup) just-boiled water
2 tbsp mirin
2 tbsp light soy sauce
1½ tbsp golden caster (superfine) sugar
2 tbsp neutral cooking oil
2 boneless chicken thighs, skin on (ideally)
½ small onion, finely sliced
4 medium eggs

To cook the rice, first measure it into a saucepan and cover with cold water. Stir for 20 seconds, drain through a sieve, return the rice to the pan and repeat the process six times so the water is much less cloudy. Add 300ml (1¼ cups) of cold water and set on a high heat. As soon as the water boils, stir to ensure the rice is not stuck to the bottom of the pan, then reduce to the lowest heat possible, place a lid on top and simmer for 7–8 minutes. Remove from the heat at the point the water has almost all been absorbed, but the rice is still loose. Stir in the sushi vinegar and place a folded dish towel over the top, leaving just a little gap. Leave for 20 minutes for the rice to steam, finish cooking and also dry out a little, stirring three or four times over that period.

As the rice cooks, dissolve the dashi powder for the topping into the just-boiled water. Stir the mirin, soy sauce and sugar into the dashi.

Add a little cooking oil to a small, heavy-based saucepan and place over a medium–high heat. Cook the chicken thighs skin-side down for 6–8 minutes so the skin is bronzed and about two thirds of the flesh cooked through. Remove from the pan and chop into bite-size pieces.

When the rice is ready, tip half the dashi into a small (18–20cm/7–8in) omelette or frying pan (skillet). Add half of both the chicken and onions and simmer over a medium heat for 3–4 minutes until the liquid is reduced by a third and the onions are softening.

Ensure both chicken and onions are evenly distributed. Lightly beat two of the eggs and pour into the pan, prodding and shuffling so it moves through and around the chicken and onions. Place a lid on top and steam for 1 minute so the egg is about two-thirds cooked – it should still be a little loose in the middle, as part of the pleasure is in the slipperiness of the egg.

Decant half the rice into a bowl and slide the omelette over the top – the dashi will leave the pan first, seasoning the rice as it falls. Repeat (using the remaining dashi, chicken, onions and eggs) for the second portion.

Soggy greens and anchovies on toast

Contrary to popular opinion, green vegetables aren't always best when cooked to al dente so that they're 'crisp and bright' and 'still with snap and crunch'. In fact, there's something steadying and comforting when they're less green than before, not so sweet and easy to chew. Fine green beans are a good example. See also large leaf spinach, kale and cavolo nero, and broccoli.

Indeed, one person's 'soggy' greens is another's 'Italian-style, garlic-dragged', not least when piled onto well-browned toast and topped with anchovies. Particularly good on a Sunday evening, when the end-of-weekend blues are at their peak (nadir?).

Serves 2
—

150g (5½oz) cavolo nero, leaves stripped
   (stems discarded)
Or
200g (7oz) curly kale, leaves stripped
   (stems discarded)
Or
250g (9oz) Tenderstem or purple sprouting
   broccoli, very woody ends removed, stems
   cut into 3cm (1¼in) pieces, florets intact

2 large slices of bread (sourdough ideally,
   but whatever you have)
2 tbsp extra virgin olive oil
8 salted anchovies in oil
2 cloves garlic, sliced as thinly as you can
Ground black pepper

Bring a large pan of well-salted water to the boil. Add the greens and cook for 4–5 minutes (or 3–4 minutes for the curly kale), so they're very definitely cooked and beyond al dente.

Meanwhile, put your bread on to toast (ensure it's very well browned and a little bit crunchy). Place a heavy-bottomed frying pan (skillet) over a low heat, add the olive oil, plus a dash of oil from the anchovy tin, and the garlic. Warm the garlic for 2 minutes without browning. Drain the greens thoroughly, add to the pan and use some tongs to gently cover them in the garlicky oil.

Season the greens very generously with black pepper, scoop them onto the toast and lay 4 anchovies on top of each slice. (You might find that there's more cooking water in the pan, despite draining. I tend to use tongs to avoid accidentally drenching the toast.)

Note: the addition of a soft-boiled egg wouldn't be a mistake (room temperature egg(s) into boiling water, 6½ minutes, transfer into a bowl of cold or iced water and peel them under there so they stop cooking – if you're quick they'll still be warm enough when you slice into them).

Scrag end, root and miso broth

Broths that emerge from the slow simmer of seemingly unpromising ingredients are so often the most restorative.

This one will not disappoint; in part because the scrag end of lamb is the king of expectation management – the thick and gnarly middle end of a lamb neck promises very little yet over-delivers every time. Flavour is best extracted from it over a long, slow simmer, and this dish pairs brilliantly with the similarly unheralded yet powerful swede and turnip. Spices such as nutmeg and pepper bind the three together, and there's also a subtle hit of umami (via miso) at the end, which provides an additional savoury note.

Serves 4

–

4 tbsp cold-pressed rapeseed (canola) oil,
    plus extra for drizzling
1 medium onion, thinly sliced
3 cloves garlic, thinly sliced
25g (1oz) flat-leaf parsley, leaves picked,
    stalks finely chopped
800g (1lb 12oz) scrag end of lamb,
    on the bone, in 2–3cm (¾–1¼in) chops
150ml (scant ⅔ cup) vermouth or white wine
1.5 litres (6½ cups) cold water
3 bay leaves
600g (1lb 5oz) swede (rutabaga),
    peeled and cut into 2cm (¾in) cubes
300g (10½oz) turnips, peeled and cut
    into 2cm (¾in) cubes
1 large carrot, peeled and cut into 2cm
    (¾in) cubes
80g (3oz) pearl barley
5 or 6 sprigs thyme
3 tbsp barley or dark brown rice miso
⅛ nutmeg, finely grated
Flaky sea salt and ground black pepper

Heat the oven to 170°C/150°C fan/325°F.

Put an ovenproof stock pot, with a lid, over a medium heat. Measure in two tablespoons of the oil, add the onions and a pinch of salt and soften for 5 minutes, stirring occasionally. Add the garlic and parsley stalks and cook for 2 minutes more.

Meanwhile, place a heavy-bottomed frying pan (skillet) over a high heat. Add the remaining two tablespoons of oil, allow that to warm up, then add the lamb, browning the meat for around 3 minutes per side.

When the meat is pleasingly brown and any fat crisp, transfer it to the stock pot, then deglaze the frying pan with the vermouth or wine, allowing it to boil and bubble for 30 seconds before adding that to the pot along with the cold water. Drop the bay leaves in, bring to a rapid simmer, put a lid on top and cook in the oven for 45 minutes.

Once that time is up, add the swede and return to the oven for 30 minutes before adding the turnip, carrot, barley and thyme. Cook for a final half hour, by which time the meat should be ready to push from the bone, the broth flavoursome, the roots tender and the barley plump.

Pick out the lamb chops and put them on a plate or board. Use forks to push, pull and pick off the meat, resulting in a pile of lamb niblets. Discard the bones and return the meat and any juices to the pot. Finally, stir in the miso, a dusting of nutmeg, some black pepper, and the parsley leaves, ensuring the miso dissolves and dissipates.

The broth will still be very hot at this point; you'll find it tastes best once cooled a little. When you do serve, ensure each bowl has two to three ladles of meat, roots and barley, then top the bowls with more of the savoury, moreish broth and a drizzle of cold-pressed rapeseed oil.

Soba noodles with sesame dipping sauce

Soba noodles and a no-cook dipping sauce provide a quick, clean and relatively serene mix of savoury flavours: wholesome soba noodles, verdant broccoli, tahini, soy and sesame.

It might seem strange to serve the noodles with a dip that appears as though it could be a sauce. However, if you combine the two all at once, the result is increasingly stodgy and stiff. Dipping the noodles and broccoli alternately in the paste is far more enjoyable.

Serves 2
–

200g (7oz) soba noodles
175g (6oz) Tenderstem or purple sprouting
   broccoli
2 tsp sesame oil
1 heaped tsp toasted sesame seeds
3 tsp nori and sesame sprinkle (page 31)

For the sesame dip
3 tbsp tahini
1 tbsp light soy
1 tbsp mirin
1 clove garlic, minced
1–2cm (½–¾in) ginger, finely grated
1 tbsp tepid water

Put two medium–large pans of water on to boil. Make sure they're both fairly full; the noodles, in particular, are best cooked in a lot of water so as to prevent the end result being sticky and starchy.

While waiting for the water to boil, and subsequently for the noodles to cook, put the sesame dip ingredients into a bowl and stir to combine, then decant into two dipping bowls. If not already prepared, make a batch of the nori and sesame sprinkle (page 31).

Cook the soba noodles in the first saucepan that comes to the boil according to the packet instructions (most likely simmering for 4–5 minutes until tender). After 60–90 seconds you'll need to turn the temperature down to prevent a foam from boiling over – do that but keep it simmering.

At the point the noodles have been cooking for 2 minutes, put the broccoli into the second pan and cook at an energetic simmer for 3 minutes.

Once cooked, separately drain the noodles and broccoli through a sieve (strainer). Run the noodles under a cold tap for 15–20 seconds; not to totally chill them, but to wash starch away. Return the noodles to their pan and stir through the sesame oil and toasted sesame seeds.

Divide both noodles and broccoli between two bowls or small plates. Scatter the nori sprinkle over the noodles and serve, dunking each chopsticks' worth of noodles or broccoli into the dip as you eat.

Crunchy Jerusalem artichokes with cavolo nero and anchovy crème fraîche

Not a snappy recipe title, though it does exactly what it says on the tin: roast tubers, blanched Italian kale, anchovies and seeds for extra crunch. It's a deeply savoury dish and is something that addresses a desire for straight-up but delicious, earthy flavours.

The minerality of the Jerusalem artichokes was the spark for this recipe. If, however, you can't find them (they're an autumn/winter thing), it's still a satisfyingly savoury eat if you double up on the crunchy potatoes.

Serves 4

—

600g (1lb 5oz) baby new potatoes
600g (1lb 5oz) Jerusalem artichokes
2 tbsp cold-pressed rapeseed (canola) oil
20g (¾oz) salted anchovies in oil,
  roughly chopped
1 clove garlic, minced
30g (1oz) butter
130g (4½oz) full-fat crème fraîche
1 tsp red wine vinegar
40g (1½oz) sunflower kernels
250–300g (9–10½oz) cavolo nero,
  leaves picked (stems discarded)
Flaky sea salt and ground black pepper

Heat the oven to 220°C/200°C fan/425°F.

Scrub clean both the potatoes and artichokes. If your potatoes are longer than 4cm (1½in), cut them in half across the middle (so they're stocky, not long). Keep anything smaller whole. Spread over a baking sheet along with the artichokes (which can, and should, be bigger – keep them whole and unpeeled), drizzle with the oil and tumble around, ensuring everything is glossy. Roast for 40–45 minutes, until the potatoes are bronzed, the artichokes browned and crisp, and both seem soft on the inside. Remove from the oven and season with plenty of sea salt.

Meanwhile, put a small saucepan on a low heat. Add the chopped anchovies and a tablespoon of the oil from their container, as well as the garlic, and gently warm this flavoursome gunk until the anchovies melt and break up. Keep the heat low – the garlic should not brown. After about 4 minutes, add the butter, let that melt (not froth or brown), then add the crème fraîche and remove the pan from the heat. Stir to encourage the crème fraîche and sauce to come together. Finish with the vinegar, then set to one side to cool to room temperature and thicken a little.

Toast the sunflower kernels in a dry pan for a few minutes until bronzed. Decant into a cool container.

When the potatoes and artichokes look like they're nearly done, bring another saucepan of salted water to the boil. Cook the cavolo nero (which should look like ribbons) in the boiling water for about 3 minutes. Drain well, return to the pan and season with lots of black pepper.

It makes sense to present this individually rather than on a sharing platter. So divide the potatoes and artichokes evenly among four plates. Spoon over half the anchovy sauce, then pile the cavolo nero on top followed by the rest of the sauce, and finish with a liberal scattering of the toasted sunflower kernels.

Cod cheeks and brown butter capers on lentils

Intense yet not-overfilling, with kicks coming from all directions – the red wine in the lentils is warming, the green sauce is forceful, as are the salty capers fried in nutty, moreish brown butter.

The obvious match for that base would be something like slow-cooked lamb, venison or pigeon. If you want savoury without heavy, however, try white fish: from hake to skate, pretty much any fits the bill. Do consider cod cheeks, though, if you see them. They're typically a thrifty purchase, yet as enjoyable to eat as most of the more expensive things a fishmonger offers.

The cod cheeks and capers take a total of 5 minutes to cook, so only begin these when the lentils are done. On which note, the lentils can be cooked well before, cooled and reheated later as required. Either way, they should be served loose, each portion paddling in a ladle of cooking liquid.

Serves 4
–

4 tbsp sunflower or vegetable oil
1 small–medium onion, finely diced
2–3 celery sticks, finely diced
2 carrots, peeled and finely diced
2 cloves garlic, minced
300g (10½oz) Puy, dark green or dark brown lentils, washed
250ml (1 cup) red wine (something medium–full and fruity, like a Rioja/merlot/Côtes du Rhône)
500ml (2 cups) water
500g (1lb 2oz) cod cheeks
60g (2¼oz) unsalted butter, cubed
4 tbsp Lilliput capers
Extra virgin olive oil, to garnish
Flaky sea salt and ground black pepper

For the green sauce
Leaves stripped from 25g (1oz) tarragon
Leaves picked from 15g (½oz) flat-leaf parsley
Leaves picked from 10g (¼oz) mint
1 tsp Dijon mustard
1 tsp caster (superfine) sugar
1 tbsp red wine vinegar
2 salted anchovies in oil
150ml (scant ⅔ cup) extra virgin olive oil, plus extra for drizzling

Add two tablespoons of the vegetable oil to a medium saucepan over a medium heat. Sauté the onion and celery for 4 minutes or so until they begin to soften but not colour. Add the carrots and garlic and cook for 1–2 minutes more before adding the lentils, red wine and water. Bring to the boil, then reduce to a simmer for 30 minutes. You may need to top up with more water through the cooking process and/or at the end (if you shake the pan the contents should ripple, rather than seem stiff and turgid). The lentils should be plump and tender. Season very generously with salt and pepper.

While the lentils are cooking, put all of the ingredients for the green sauce in a blender, blitz until silky smooth, then decant.

When ready to eat, place a large heavy-bottomed frying pan (skillet) or wok over a medium–high heat. Wait for 30 seconds, add the remaining two tablespoons of oil and wait for 30 seconds more to ensure both pan and oil are hot. Add the cod cheeks, spread them out so they sit in one layer, then don't touch them for 1 minute so they bronze a little. After that time, turn them over, returning to any that seem stuck (don't force them, they will flip easily with a few more seconds of heat). Cook for 1 minute more, turn them again and add 25g (1oz) of the butter around the pan. Let this bubble and foam between the cod cheeks, then once the cheeks have been cooking for a touch under 4 minutes in total, use a slotted spoon to transfer them from the pan into a bowl.

Add the rest of the butter to the hot pan, and the capers immediately into the rapidly melting butter. Let that butter foam and brown, and the capers split open and crisp up a little for 60–90 seconds.

Meanwhile, spoon two to three ladles of lentils plus another of their cooking liquid into four bowls, liberally dribble and ripple with green sauce plus an additional glug of extra virgin olive oil. Divide the cod cheeks and any resting juices between the bowls and spoon the fried capers and browned butter on top.

Hummus

Britain (and elsewhere?) got hummus completely wrong for decades, relegating it to house-party dip territory, rather than the wholesome, gentle meal that it is in places like Tel Aviv, Bethlehem, Beirut and beyond. Good hummus is creamy, soothing, savoury. It serves as a base for things like hard-boiled eggs, piles of spices, puddles of tahini, raw onions, fava beans, more chickpeas rolled in more tahini, chicken livers and fried onions. It is a moment as much as a meal. Once you get that, you return to it often.

It's good to soak and simmer chickpeas yourself, but cooked chickpeas from a can are fine too, and suggested here to make this a quick cook. Some insist the chickpeas should be skinned by rubbing them between dish towels once cooked; with a half-decent blender, I'm not sure it's an essential step. But you do need warm cooking water to ensure an aerated, silky texture.

Pictured on pages 182–183.

Serves 4

—

For the hummus base
2 x 400g (14oz) cans chickpeas (garbanzos)
2 cloves garlic, roughly chopped
150g (5½oz) tahini
Juice ½ lemon (possibly more, to taste)
2–3 tsp flaky sea salt

To serve
60–90g (2¼–3¼oz) tahini
Crisp roast chickpeas (see opposite)
4 x softhardie boiled eggs (see opposite)
Extra virgin olive oil
Flaky sea salt
Handful flat-leaf parsley, chopped
Flatbreads (such as pita)

Plus: roast cauliflower, seeds and paprika
browned butter (optional – see opposite)

Empty the cans of chickpeas, including the liquid, into a saucepan. Fill one of the cans with water and add that in, plus the garlic. Place over a medium heat, bring to a steady simmer and cook for 5 minutes. Strain the contents through a sieve (strainer), reserving the cooking liquid. Measure 100g (scant ½ cup) of that liquid and set to one side.

While still warm, transfer the chickpeas, garlic and cooking liquid to a blender. Add the tahini, two tablespoons of lemon juice and two teaspoons of salt. Pulse, then blend for at least a minute until completely silky smooth. Add a tablespoon or three more of warm water if you think it needs it. Taste and add additional lemon and/or salt too, if needed.

If not using immediately, decant into Tupperware and cover to prevent a skin forming. It refrigerates well for up to 3 days.

To serve, drop 1–2 heavy dollops of warm hummus in a bowl and use the back of a spoon to create a well in the middle. Fill it with tahini, crisp chickpeas, softhardie boiled eggs, some olive oil, salt and a pile of parsley. You can embellish further, whether with relatively traditional additions like chicken livers and onions, or less traditional roast cauliflower with seeds and paprika butter (opposite). Regardless, scoop everything up with warm pita or other flatbread.

Crisp roast chickpeas

1 x 400g (14oz) can chickpeas (garbanzos),
   drained
1 tbsp olive oil
Flaky sea salt

—

Heat the oven to 220°C/200°C fan/425°F

Spread the drained chickpeas over a small
baking tray. Add the oil, roll the chickpeas in that
until glossy and cook at the top of the oven for
30 minutes until golden (they become crunchier
as they cool). Season immediately with lots of
flaky salt then set to one side.

Softhardie boiled eggs

4 x medium eggs, at room temperature

—

Bring a small–medium saucepan of water to
a rolling boil. Lower the eggs in with a spoon
and cook at an energetic simmer for 7 minutes.
Immediately transfer to iced water or leave
under a cold-running tap until cool enough to
peel. Cut in half at the last minute.

Roast cauliflower, seeds and paprika browned butter

2 medium or 1 large cauliflower (1.5kg/3lb 5oz)
   with plenty of green leaves
5 tbsp cold-pressed rapeseed (canola) oil
2 tsp cumin seeds
50g (1¾oz) salted butter
4 tbsp mixed seeds (sunflower kernels/pumpkin
   seeds/sesame or linseeds/flaxseeds)
1 tsp paprika

—

Heat the oven to 200°C/180°C fan/400°F.

Cut the greens from the cauliflower and set to
one side. Break the cauliflower apart and cut the
biggest florets in half. Use the core and stalk too,
cutting them into 2cm (1in) chunks. Measure
four tablespoons of oil into a large bowl, add the
cauliflower, mix well then tip onto a baking sheet
(or two, if necessary) and slide into the hot oven.

Meanwhile, toast the cumin seeds in a dry frying
pan for 2–3 minutes until aromatic. Use a pestle
and mortar to bash the seeds open, but not quite
to a fine powder. Set aside. Cut the really chunky
cauliflower greens in half so no stem is longer
than about 6cm (2½in). Put these in a mixing
bowl (you can use the one the cauliflower was
in), add the remaining tablespoon of oil and toss
so the greens are glossy.

After 25 minutes, give the cauliflower a shuffle
and sprinkle the cumin over the top. Return to the
oven for 10 minutes, after which the cauliflower
should be golden but still quite soggy. Turn the
florets so that different parts face up/down and
then intersperse with the greens. Roast for 10–15
minutes more, until both cauliflower and greens
are charred yet succulent. Season with a lot of
salt and add to the hummus bowls.

To finish, place a frying pan over a high heat and
add the butter. As it melts and begins to froth,
add the mixed seeds to the pan and swirl around.
When the butter is golden and smells nutty, add
the paprika, stir and immediately spoon over the
cauliflower.

Orecchiette with pork, fennel and milk ragù

Like many, the dish I've cooked most in my life is a 'spaghetti Bolognese', the catch-all term for a Britalian-ish beef mince and tomato sauce, seasoned with whichever store-cupboard things are to hand, and served on whatever pasta's in stock.

Increasingly frequently, though, I've turned that vague, mid-week mince habit away from beef and tomato, towards a more prescriptive pork and fennel combination, gently simmered in milk until ridiculously satisfying. Whereas I'm ambivalent as to which pasta a 'spag bol' sauce goes with, this is very definitely best with orecchiette. Though there's milk and a dusting of Parmesan at the end, you'll agree on eating that this satisfyingly beige dish sits in the savoury rather than cheesy category.

Serves 4

—

2 tbsp vegetable oil
400g (14oz) pork mince (ground pork)
20g (¾oz) salted butter
1 large fennel bulb, finely diced, fronds reserved
2 celery sticks, finely diced
2 cloves garlic, minced
1 tbsp fennel seeds
150ml (scant ⅔ cup) dry white wine or vermouth
400ml (1¾ cups) whole milk
1 Parmesan rind
Leaves stripped from 6 or so sprigs thyme
3–4 gratings nutmeg
400g (14oz) dried orecchiette
Freshly grated Parmesan, to garnish
Flaky sea salt and ground black pepper

Pour the oil into a heavy-bottomed lidded saucepan or casserole placed over a medium–high heat. Add the pork mince, fry to colour for 5 or 6 minutes, decant and set aside.

Put the pan back on the stove, with the heat slightly lower than before. Add the butter to the oil and juices still in the pan, then sauté the diced fennel and celery for around 8 minutes so they're glistening and beginning to soften (but not brown – reduce the heat further if necessary). Add the garlic and fennel seeds, stir and cook for 1 minute more, before returning the pork to the pan.

Turn the heat up, wait for 30 seconds then push a portion of meat to one side to reveal the base of the pan and pour the wine or vermouth in. Allow this to boil and bubble for 1 minute before reducing the heat to medium and adding the milk, Parmesan rind, thyme and nutmeg. Place a lid on top, slightly ajar, and simmer very gently for 1 hour. The milk might curdle slightly – that's fine, just stir from time to time to ensure it's not sticking to the bottom, and to encourage the sauce to come together.

Once the time is up, check the seasoning, adding salt, pepper, more nutmeg and/or thyme to taste.

Put a large saucepan of salted water on to boil and cook your pasta according to the packet instructions. At this point remove the ragù from the stove to cool while the pasta cooks (it tastes best when not piping hot).

Once the pasta is cooked to al dente, drain through a colander, reserving a few ladles of cooking water. Return the pasta to the saucepan, add three or four ladles of ragù to it, plus a ladle of reserved cooking water and stir constantly for 20–30 seconds to ensure a loose and creamy glaze to the pasta. Add a splash more cooking water if needed.

Serve, spooning the remaining ragù over each portion of pasta, plus a little dusting of Parmesan and fennel fronds.

Borlotti, browned onions and sausages

This is perfect for the kind of day when hunkering down on the sofa (or bed) is pretty much the extent of what you want to do.

Picture that scene, then imagine your kitchen being filled with the warm notes of buttery onions, beans and sage as they putter away on the stove. Then add the smell of sausages as they caramelize and colour in their own juices... It's brown food. It's nourishing. It's food in which you'll want to wallow.

Serves 4

–

200g (7oz) dried borlotti beans (or the same quantity of fresh, podded beans)
4 medium onions (follow peeling instructions in method)
40g (1½oz) salted butter
1 bulb garlic, halved across its width
3 bay leaves
4 sprigs sage
8 fat sausages
Flaky sea salt and ground black pepper

Serve with a jar of English mustard, and a pot of blanched cavolo nero, curly kale, Tenderstem or purple sprouting broccoli.

–

If dried, soak the borlotti in cold water for 8 hours, then drain. (You can also pour boiling water over dried borlotti and soak for just 1 hour if you need to speed things up.)

Cut the onions in half from tip to root, then peel them, leaving the root section as intact as possible (so that the onion layers stay together while they cook).

Choose a heavy-bottomed lidded casserole or saucepan large enough to fit the onion halves in one layer. Place over a medium heat, add the butter and, once that's melted, the onions cut-side down. Cook for 8–10 minutes without turning so that they are well browned. Add the garlic halves, giving the cut faces a minute of butter time, then remove the pan from the heat.

The butter and base of the pan will probably be burnt and acrid now. If so, remove the onions and garlic, wipe the pan clean with a paper towel or wash it. Then return the onions and garlic to the casserole, cut sides facing up, now, and put it back on the stove (still at a medium heat).

Tip the beans around the onions and fill the pan with cold water to the tops of (but not over) the onions. Add the bay leaves and two sprigs of sage, bring to a gentle simmer and place a lid on top, slightly ajar. Let that bubble away gently for a total of around 90 minutes until both the skin and flesh of the beans are soft. You will need to add water after 30 or 40 minutes, again to the tops of the onions but not over. The sage will be a spent force after an hour, so swap the used with the remaining two sprigs and top up the water again. Ideally there'll be four to five ladles' worth of broth once cooked.

Cook the sausages as you wish to, beginning when the beans are around 20 minutes from being ready. I like to roll sausages around in a frying pan at quite a gentle pace as I think that's the best way to end up with well-coloured plump and juicy snags. But roast or grill them if you prefer a hands-free approach.

Squeeze the soft flesh from the garlic halves into the broth and stir that flavour in and around. Season with lots of salt and a furious amount of black pepper and add more water, if necessary, before serving the beans, onions and broth with the sausages, some greens and a smudge of English mustard.

Mushroom, kale and tarragon lasagne

⎯⎯⎯⎯

This lasagne is meatless* yet extremely rich, as it involves an intense mushroom ragù rammed full of savoury and umami notes, punctuated only by a striking, kale and tarragon-powered green sauce. It's knowingly full-on; take a break every so often with bites of a bitter leaf salad (radicchio, Belgian endive, frisée) doused in a mustardy dressing.

Lasagnes are never a quick fix; however, to speed things along I suggest you use a food processor, rather than finely chop a kilo of mushrooms by hand. If it suits your timings, you could make the mushroom ragù and green sauce in advance of assembling. And on this occasion there's also no need to labour over a traditional white sauce, as that element is taken care of by a simple mix of crème fraîche (which must be full-fat) and Parmesan.

* Ignore the anchovies if you would prefer this to be fully vegetarian.

For 6 (leftovers reheat well)

⎯

For the ragù
30g (1oz) dried porcini (or a wild mushroom mix)
1 medium onion, halved
4 cloves garlic
30g (1oz) salted butter
500g (1lb 2oz) chestnut (cremini) mushrooms, cleaned with a damp cloth
500g (1lb 2oz) portobello mushrooms, cleaned with a damp cloth
Leaves stripped from a handful thyme leaves (about 2 tbsp leaves)
1 tsp Worcestershire sauce
1 heaped tsp Marmite
2 salted anchovies, chopped (optional)
1 tbsp tomato purée (paste)
50g (1¾oz) fresh girolles, cleaned with a damp cloth (or an additional 100g/3½oz portobello mushrooms, cut into 2cm/¾in dice)
Flaky sea salt and ground black pepper

For the green sauce
150g (5½oz) curly kale, leaves picked (stems discarded)
1 clove garlic
Leaves stripped from 20g (¾oz) tarragon
30g (1oz) blanched hazelnuts
6 tbsp extra virgin olive oil
2 tbsp water
30g (1oz) Parmesan

To assemble the lasagne
500g (1lb 2oz) full-fat crème fraîche
90g (3¼oz) Parmesan, finely grated
3–4 gratings nutmeg
500g (1lb 2oz) dried lasagne sheets
125g (4½oz) buffalo mozzarella
Ground black pepper

You will need a 3 litre (105fl oz) baking dish for this.

Put the dried mushrooms into a heatproof container. Pour 400ml (1¾ cups) of boiling water over the top and set to one side.

Pulse the onion and garlic in a food processor. Place a large saucepan on a medium heat, add the butter and then the onions and garlic, and soften for 4–5 minutes, stirring occasionally.

Pulse the chestnut and portobello mushrooms briefly in the processor in 250g (9oz) batches – you want a coarse rubble rather than a paste (doing this in batches will be both quicker overall and more controllable than attempting all at once).

Transfer the blitzed mushrooms to the pan with the onions and garlic, along with the thyme, Worcestershire sauce, Marmite and anchovies (if using), and cook for 15 minutes. At this point add the tomato purée, girolles (or portobello mushrooms), as well as the rehydrated mushrooms and their stock. Simmer enthusiastically for 15 minutes, so much of the stock evaporates and the ragù intensifies; if you swipe a wooden spoon or spatula through the middle, it should take a few seconds for the seas to meet again. Remove from the heat. Season very generously with salt and black pepper and leave to cool for 5–10 minutes (or longer).

Make the green sauce by blanching the kale and garlic clove in boiling water for 4 minutes. Drain, run under cold water, drain again and transfer to a (cleaned) processor or blender. Add the tarragon, hazelnuts, extra virgin olive oil and the two tablespoons of water. Blitz to a paste – it won't be silky but the kale should not be stringy. Add the Parmesan and pulse one more time to blend.

To begin the assembly, combine the crème fraîche, 60g (2¼oz) of the Parmesan, lots of black pepper and a little nutmeg.

Heat the oven to 200°C/180°C fan/400°F.

Spoon a third of the mushroom ragù onto the bottom of your dish. Lay four or five sheets of pasta on top, overlapping where necessary. Spread with half the crème fraîche mixture and continue alternating layers of pasta with half the green sauce, another third of the ragù, the rest of the green sauce, the remaining ragù and finally the remaining crème fraîche mixture. Tear the mozzarella over the top, then dust with the last 30g (1oz) of Parmesan.

Bake at the top of your oven for 40–45 minutes, until the undulating top layer is golden, crusty and pulsating. Once cooked, hold your craving for 10 minutes more, as lasagne is always best cut and served having been left to cool a little.

Cuttlefish rice and romesco

There are few places you want to see jet-black puddles of ink, but one is on top of a pan of plump, glistening rice. Often that rice is flecked with squid, but I like the slightly meatier, certainly more flavoursome, definitely uglier cuttlefish*. Which, as it happens, often provides the ink in 'squid' ink pots and packets anyway. The end dish is powerful but comforting, with the cubes and strips of cuttlefish having simmered away to create intoxicating stock while simultaneously (and perhaps surprisingly) becoming tender.

There's a quick but punchy romesco sauce to inject a blast of colour and vivacity (you've seen this before in the many chilli pepper squid dish on page 108). You might also serve this with a shaved fennel salad, or some leaves with a bit of punch – radicchio or chicory – simply dressed with olive oil and sherry vinegar. These will provide a momentary pause, but really it's about the rich, inky, cuttlefish-powered rice.

* Not always in stock, but any fishmonger will be able to get cuttlefish with barely any notice. Ask them to clean them up for you; they're initially quite imposing, but once trimmed and skinned are easily dealt with.

Serves 4
–

1.2–1.5kg (2lb 10oz–3lb 5oz) cuttlefish
  (weight once cleaned 600–700g/
  1lb 5oz–1lb 9oz)
2 medium-large tomatoes, halved
2 onions
1.2 litres (5 cups) cold water
12g (1 large tbsp) cuttlefish (or squid) ink
8–10 saffron threads
200g (7oz) jarred roasted red (bell) peppers
2 tbsp neutral cooking oil
20g (¾oz) butter
2 cloves garlic, minced
300g (10½oz) Calasparra paella rice
175ml (scant ¾ cup) dry white wine or vermouth
1 heaped tsp smoked paprika

For the romesco sauce
150g (5½oz) jarred roasted red (bell) peppers,
  plus 2 tbsp liquid from the jar
1 tsp caster (superfine) sugar
½ tsp sweet smoked paprika
1 tbsp extra virgin olive oil
1 tsp sherry vinegar or red wine vinegar
40g (1oz) blanched unsalted almonds
½ tsp flaky sea salt

To serve
1 lemon, cut into wedges
Extra virgin olive oil
–

There are a few stages here: make a cuttlefish stock; use that stock to cook the rice; make a quick romesco; and quickly cook any remaining cuttlefish to go on top.

A cleaned cuttlefish comprises a large tube, thick tentacles, and wings, possibly attached by skin. We'll use all of it, though the wings can be a bit tough, so they're mostly for stock.

Cut the tentacles at their base and place in a stock pot (or large saucepan). Add the wings. Open up the main body by scoring down the natural joining line (as you would a squid). Cut into three, saving the middle third. Cut the two sides into 1cm (½in) dice and place in the stock pot. Save the remaining (middle) piece to be cooked as a garnish at the end. Use a table knife to score a cross-hatch across the inner side of the flesh, then cut it into thin strips and refrigerate until required.

Add the tomato halves to the stock pot or pan. Peel and halve one of the onions and add that too. Pour in the water, bring to the boil then simmer for 30 minutes. Once that time is up, pick out the wings and the onions (and discard both), then add the ink and saffron to the stock.

Continued overleaf

Cuttlefish rice and romesco, continued...

While the stock is simmering, dice the remaining onion as finely as you can. Dice the red peppers, making them the same size as the onions. Put a tablespoon of the cooking oil and all the butter in a wide sauté pan or a 24–26cm (9½–10½in) paella dish. Place that over a low heat, add the diced onions and soften gently, without colouring, for 5–6 minutes, stirring regularly, before adding the peppers and cooking for 10 minutes more. Add the garlic and cook for a further 2 minutes. By this point, the stock will be ready (or almost ready).

With onions and stock both ready, turn the heat under the sauté or paella pan up a touch and add the rice. Cook for 90 seconds, stirring occasionally to ensure it doesn't burn. Then add the wine and let that reduce almost entirely. Transfer the stock (plus the cuttlefish and tomatoes) into the paella pan, add the paprika and simmer energetically for 15–20 minutes, until the rice is tender. Most of the stock will have been absorbed, but there should still be a few puddles of ink on top.

While the rice is cooking, make the romesco sauce. Put the roast peppers in a blender or food processor, add two tablespoons of the liquid from their jar, along with the rest of the ingredients. Blitz to a silky purée.

Once cooked, remove the rice from the heat and rest for 5 minutes before serving.

Meanwhile, place a frying pan (skillet) over a very high heat, add the remaining tablespoon of cooking oil, let that heat for 30 seconds then throw in the reserved strips of scored cuttlefish. Cook for no longer than 60 seconds then decant to a serving bowl and add a squeeze of lemon. Present these strips on top of the rice – whether that's from the pan for people to help themselves, or in individual portions – along with the lemon wedges, a glug of extra virgin olive oil and a big dollop per person of the romesco sauce.

Miso-braised duck legs, buckwheat and squash

This is a rich and earthy one-pot braise, underpinned by the umami notes of miso and dashi. The Japanese reference point continues through the nori flakes and sesame seeds used to dust the roast butternut squash. I find steamed greens – spinach, chard or spring greens – a necessarily verdant final element. It's fortifying, mostly hands-free food for testing days.

Serves 4

—

4 x duck legs (900g–1kg/2lb–2lb 4oz in total)
2 celery sticks, sliced into 5mm (¼in) crescents
1 x 10g (¼oz) instant dashi sachet
3 tbsp barley or brown rice miso
1 litre (4⅓ cups) just-boiled water
1 small–medium butternut squash
120g (4¼oz) buckwheat groats
4 tbsp nori and sesame sprinkle (page 31)
Flaky sea salt

Serve with steamed spinach, chard or spring greens.

Heat the oven to 170°C/150°C fan/325°F.

Put a heavy-bottomed frying pan (skillet) over a medium heat. While the pan is still cold, add the duck legs, skin-side down. Turn your extraction on and cook for 10–12 minutes, until the skin is golden brown and crisp. Turn over and cook for 2 minutes more to brown the flesh side (also rendering some of the fat on that side of the legs). Decant the rendered fat to a heatproof container to use next time you roast potatoes.

While the legs are browning, find a lidded casserole, or similar, that's big enough to fit the duck legs in one layer, with a little room to spare, and scatter the celery into it. Dissolve the dashi sachet and miso in the just-boiled water. Place the duck legs on top of the celery and pour in the miso dashi. Place in the middle of the oven, covered, for 30 minutes.

At this point, remove the lid and, separately, place the butternut squash on a small baking tray and put in the oven for around 90 minutes, until blistered and shrunken.

Cook the duck, uncovered, for another 60 minutes, then sprinkle the buckwheat into the broth, pulling the duck legs above the groats. Return to the oven, still uncovered, for an additional 20–30 minutes until near-pullable duck legs sit on top of swollen buckwheat, with just a ladle or three of stock remaining, as most will have evaporated or been absorbed.

The squash will be ready now too. Use the tip of a knife to slice it in half lengthways. Scoop out the seeds (and discard), then cut the flesh into large chunks (leaving the skin on), season generously with flaky sea salt and the nori and sesame sprinkle.

Serve the buckwheat, crisp duck and seasoned squash with some steamed greens alongside for balance.

Chicken barley

This began as a recounting of the brilliant Hainanese dish 'chicken rice'. But through the course of researching and testing, it became clear that a 'simple' dish of poached chicken and rice cooked in chicken stock was actually fraught with numerous views about the method – the bird should be dunked into boiling water a precise but rarely agreed number of times, for a precise but rarely agreed number of seconds, before being shocked in ice...

...so now its inclusion here has morphed into a slightly different dish, albeit no less pleasing to eat.

I want, then, to acknowledge the inspiration (in the accompanying sauce too), but have moved from rice to a savoury mix of barley and lentils, added a side of roast cabbage, and changed cooking pace to a soft put-puttering of a simmer 'until it's done'. All of which should settle any urges for beige and plain yet flavourful food.

There are still a few steps, and dishes to wash, but nothing is rushed or tricky – most activity takes place neatly within the final 30 minutes.

Serves 4

—

1 chicken, about 1.6–1.8kg (3lb 8oz–4lb)
1 onion, halved
1 bulb garlic, halved across its width
50g (1¾oz) fresh ginger, unpeeled and sliced
50g (1¾oz) parsley, stalks and leaves separated, leaves very finely chopped
200g (7oz) pearl barley, rinsed
100g (3½oz) brown lentils, rinsed
1 small hispi (pointed) cabbage
1–2 tbsp extra virgin olive oil, plus extra for drizzling
Flaky sea salt and ground black pepper

For the sauce
50g (1¾oz) fresh ginger, peeled and finely minced
50g (1¾oz) spring onions (scallions), very finely chopped
3 tbsp vegetable oil
1 tsp golden caster (superfine) sugar
1 tsp toasted sesame oil
½ tsp flaky sea salt
3 tbsp cooking liquid from the barley and lentils

Remove the wishbone from the chicken – a process that might seem a faff at this stage, but ensures portioning is easier and yield better at the end.

Put the chicken in a large saucepan or stock pot, along with the onion, garlic halves, ginger and parsley stalks. Cover with cold water, allowing the cavity to fill up so the bird sinks and ensuring there's at least 2cm (¾in) of water clear of the top of the meat. Place over a medium–high heat and bring near to (but not quite) a boil, then reduce to a very gentle simmer (just a few tiny bubbles) for 1 hour. You might find the chicken floats up as air traps between skin and flesh. Gently compress those bubbles to keep the meat below the surface.

Remove the bird from the water after an hour and leave it on a warm plate near the stove. Strain the poaching liquor through a sieve (strainer) and pour 1 litre (4⅓ cups) of it into a medium saucepan, add the barley and lentils, bring to an energetic simmer and cook for 25–30 minutes until they're tender – most of the liquid will be soaked up or evaporate, so check the pan doesn't cook dry. Simultaneously, return the remaining poaching liquor and aromatics to the stock pot and put this on a high heat to reduce by about a half, until you've around 600–800ml (generous 2½–3½ cups) left.

At the same time as the barley and lentils start cooking, heat the oven to 220°C/200°C fan/ 425°F. Divide the cabbage into six long wedges by cutting through the base to the tip, so the wedges stay intact. Place on a baking tray and brush with olive oil, then roast at the top of the oven for 20 minutes, until the edges are charred and the cabbage is tender, still succulent and with a little bite. Remove, chop each wedge into three to four pieces so the cabbage is easy to eat, transfer to a serving platter, season with salt and drizzle with more olive oil.

To make the sauce, put the minced ginger in a heatproof bowl, add the spring onions and mix. Heat the three tablespoons of vegetable oil in a small pan for 3 minutes, then very carefully and slowly pour this over the ginger and spring onions – they should sizzle. Add the sugar, sesame oil, flaky salt, and three tablespoons of liquid from the pot of barley. Stir into a loose paste.

When the barley and lentils are 5 minutes from being ready, remove the breasts and legs from the chicken carcass. Cut each breast into four pieces and chop or strip the meat from the thighs and legs. Place on a warm serving dish, season generously with salt, and pour over a ladle or two of the reduced chicken stock.

Stir the chopped parsley leaves and a generous seasoning of salt and pepper though the cooked barley and lentils. Divide between four bowls and wet each with a ladle or so of stock, so that each mouthful will be succulent. Serve the remaining stock as little portions of broth to drink or pour.

Serve the chicken and cabbage on each bowl or on sharing platters, as you prefer. Pass the ginger, garlic and spring onion sauce around for people to add according to taste.

Pork belly, butter beans and deli olives

There's already a beans-plus-pork recipe in this section (page 188), but the pairing is something that really settles me; whether in response to weather, mood or both.

It's not a quick dish, but it is incredibly satisfying and requires very little effort. Even the tapenade utilizes the already-done-for-you marinades of deli-style olives, whether that's a herby citrusy number, sundried tomato-flecked, or anchovy- or pimento-stuffed. Go with whatever you fancy or is to hand.

The beans require soaking in advance, so be sure to do so ahead of time. If you are not four, cook this quantity anyway, as it lasts and reheats well.

Serves 4
–

300g (10½oz) dried butter (lima) beans
1 onion, halved
2 celery sticks, cut into 3–4 segments
1 bulb garlic, halved across its width
1 carrot, peeled and chunked
1 tomato, halved
2 bay leaves
Stalks from 25g (1oz) flat-leaf parsley
  (leaves used in the tapenade)
A few sprigs sage, rosemary or thyme (optional)
1kg (2lb 4oz) rare-breed pork belly (ribless),
  cut into 4 x 3cm (1½ x 1¼in) strips (ask the
  butcher to do this)
Flaky sea salt and ground black pepper

For the tapenade
200g (7oz) marinated, pitted olives, finely
  chopped
Leaves picked from 25g (1oz) flat-leaf parsley,
  finely chopped (stalks used for the beans),
4–5 tbsp extra virgin olive oil
1 tsp sherry vinegar or moscatel vinegar, to taste
½ tsp caster (superfine) sugar, to taste
Flaky sea salt, to taste

Measure the beans into a bowl, cover with cold water to twice their depth and leave for 8–12 hours. Drain.

Place the rehydrated, drained beans in a large lidded casserole, or similar, and cover with cold water by at least 4cm (1½in). Add the onion, celery, garlic, carrot, tomato, bay leaves, parsley stalks and sage, rosemary or thyme, if using. Bring to a near boil then simmer gently for 90 minutes, with the lid ajar. Stir occasionally to check nothing's sticking to the base and top up with boiling water if the liquid levels drop below the top of the beans.

After 90 minutes, add the strips of pork belly, ensure they're submerged (again, topping up the pan with just-boiled water to ensure the beans and belly are well covered), return the lid leaving a little gap, and continue to simmer for a further 90 minutes – by which time the pork should be wobbly and cuttable with a spoon, and the beans tender and creamy. Simmer for 10–15 minutes more if necessary.

While the pot is simmering away, make the tapenade. Add the chopped olives and their marinade into a mixing bowl. Add the parsley leaves and enough olive oil to ensure a near-runny, salsa-like consistency. Taste it. A dash of vinegar and a sprinkle of sugar and/or generous pinch of salt might be needed.

This dish is best when the beans and belly are served paddling in a puddle of light broth – it's not a soup, but still a touch more than one ladle of cooking liquor per person will hit the spot. Add more water if you think it's needed, bearing in mind the serving suggestion. Then season the beans and broth with plenty of salt and pepper.

Ladle the beans and cooking liquor into four bowls, cut the pork belly strips into manageable pieces and divide between the bowls. Spoon plenty of tapenade over the top, plus a good drizzle of oil from its bowl.

Labneh, salted celery, olive oil and seeds

Sometimes you want a meal to end with something that's subsequent to a main course, but is neither a saccharine dessert, nor a plate of intense cheese.

One refreshing alternative is this combination of strained and thickened yoghurt, topped with wholesome toasted seeds, peppery olive oil and the crunch of lightly salted celery. As with all the best desserts, it also works well at breakfast time (alongside a strong coffee).

I really (really) wouldn't judge if you just bought a pot of labneh, though it is easy to make your own – add a one-quarter teaspoon of flaky sea salt to 200g (7oz) Greek yoghurt, line a sieve (strainer) with muslin (cheesecloth), drop the yoghurt into it, tie the corners of the muslin together and leave over a bowl in the fridge to strain for 12–24 hours.

Serves 2 (easily doubles, trebles etc.)

—

1 celery stick
¼ tsp flaky sea salt
20g (¾oz) pumpkin seeds
4 heaped tbsp labneh
A good extra virgin olive oil

Slice the stick of celery very finely across its width into 1–2mm (¹⁄₁₆in) pieces. Transfer the crescents to a bowl and sprinkle the salt flakes on top. Mix and set to one side.

Toast the seeds in a dry pan over a low–medium heat for 4 or 5 minutes, keeping watch so that they split and bronze but don't burn. You could do a batch of these in advance, although in this instance there is a potentially appealing contrast between still-warm seeds, tepid olive oil and fridge-cold celery and labneh.

Spoon the labneh onto two small saucers or bowls, leaving a dent in the dollops to collect oil. Pile the celery next to the labneh, add a drizzle (around two teaspoons per person) of olive oil, and drop the warm seeds over the top and around. Eat with a teaspoon.

Bitter chocolate and halva bread and butter pudding

This is a hybrid of a much-loved pudding from my youth (Delia Smith's chocolate bread and butter pudding) and a guilty pleasure of my adulthood (Claire Ptak's halva chocolate brownies from her bakery, Violet Cakes, in east London). It is not light. But it is dynamite when matched with double cream and/or vanilla ice cream.

Mark it down for a cold day, perhaps a wintertime Sunday lunch with friends. (N.B. you will need to prepare it 24 hours in advance.)

Serves 6–8

—

400–500g (1lb 2oz) white loaf (weight includes crusts), 1–2 days old
50g (1¾oz) unsalted butter, at spreadable temperature
100g (3½oz) dark chocolate (80–90% cocoa solids), in small pieces
150ml (scant ⅔ cup) double (heavy) cream
1 tbsp dark rum
400ml (1¾ cups) whole milk
2 tbsp cocoa powder
20g (¾oz) dark brown soft sugar
2 large eggs, plus 1 yolk
40g (1½oz) golden caster (superfine) sugar
1 tsp flaky sea salt
100g (3½oz) plain or cocoa-marbled halva, in 1cm (½in) dice
80g (2¾oz) tahini

Serve with double (heavy) cream or vanilla ice cream or both.

You will need a 2 litre(70fl oz) gratin or other ovenproof baking dish.

—

Ideally the bread should be a day or two old but if not, before doing anything else, slice the bread and leave to dry for a while. Cut the crusts from the loaf (yielding 300–350g/10½–12oz) of bread and cut that loaf into 1cm (½in) slices. When ready to assemble the dish, spread the slices with butter, then cut from corner to corner, so portioning into triangles.

Put a saucepan of water on to simmer. Find a bowl that sits on top without touching the water. Add the chocolate, cream and rum. When it looks as though much of the chocolate has melted, begin to stir the pan with a spatula to encourage it further, and to create a dark, glossy cream. Remove the pan from the heat but keep the bowl resting on it.

Meanwhile, put the milk, cocoa powder and the dark brown soft sugar in a saucepan and gently bring to a simmer, stirring occasionally to ensure the sugar dissolves. As bubbles begin to appear around the edge, remove from the heat. In a mixing bowl, use a balloon whisk to beat the eggs and the caster sugar until light in colour and volume. Add a ladleful of the warm cocoa milk into the eggs, beat with the whisk to combine, then gradually pour the rest of the milk on top, whisking constantly. Add the chocolate cream and whisk to combine.

Pour the custard to 1cm (½in) deep in your baking dish. Arrange half the bread triangles in one layer of overlapping scales and pour half of the remaining custard over the top, turning the bread brown. Sprinkle with half a teaspoon of salt, then crumble half the halva, dotting it into the natural crevices. Add another layer of bread, then the last of the custard, again colouring as much of the bread as you can. Press down with the back of a spatula or palette knife to further soak the bread, and spoon a little from between the gaps, onto any remaining white dots. Cover and refrigerate for 24 hours (it needs this time for the custard to fully soak into the bread).

To cook, heat the oven to 180°C/160°C fan/350°F. Drizzle the top of the pudding with the tahini, allowing it to form puddles in the Vs between the bread. Dot those puddles with thumbnail-size nuggets of the remaining halva, then sprinkle the remaining half a teaspoon of flaky sea salt from a height. Bake at the top of the oven for 30 minutes. The top will be crunchy but the underneath should still be luscious. Rest for 10 minutes before serving with cream and/or ice cream.

Peanut butter parfait

There is sweetness here, but the overriding sensation is of deeply savoury and occasionally salty peanut butter; which admittedly is not everyone's cup of tea, though I have converted at least a few naysayers thanks to this frozen parfait. If nothing else, the fact it is in essence a silky and pleasingly springy no-churn ice cream should make you consider it as something to make if you've friends coming round. Or to have on hand for late-night freezer raids, whenever the urge for something cold but not too sweet hits.

You need to use a smooth, dark-roast peanut butter that contains no additives other than a tiny percentage of salt. In the UK, the ManiLife and Pip & Nut brands work well, both of which are widely available in supermarkets, independent shops and online.

Serves 8–10

—

3 egg yolks
50g (1¾oz) caster (superfine) sugar
2 sheets (3g/ ⅒oz) fine leaf gelatine
100g (3½oz) smooth, dark roast peanut butter
   (no added oil or sugar)
1 tbsp runny honey
300ml (1¼ cups + 1 tbsp) double (heavy) cream

To garnish
80–100g (2¾–3½oz) blanched peanuts
Flaky sea salt
Handful raspberries or cherries (optional)

You will need a 800ml–1 litre (28–35fl oz) rectangular container for this.

—

This creates around 600ml (20fl oz) parfait (it's rich) and is best frozen in a rectangular container with a capacity of around 800ml (28fl oz). Line that container with with cling film (plastic wrap) or baking paper before you begin.

Transfer the yolks to a medium–large mixing bowl, add the sugar and use a balloon whisk to beat until the sugar is dissolved and the mixture is light and fluffy.

Put the gelatine in a bowl of cold water and leave to 'bloom' for 3–4 minutes.

Combine the peanut butter, honey and half the cream in a small–medium saucepan and place over a low–medium heat to gently warm the mixture (not even a simmer). Squeeze excess water from the bloomed gelatine and use a wooden spoon or spatula to beat it into the mixture. Remove from the heat once the gelatine has fully melted and become incorporated. If it gets too hot the peanut butter mix will split, with oils separating from solids. (Don't panic, just remove from the heat and add more of the remaining cream, a couple of tablespoons at a time, and vigorously beat until the mix is silky and smooth again. It's not the end of the world if you use most of the leftover cream.)

Add three tablespoons or so of the warm mix to the whipped egg yolk and whisk together. Then add the rest at a steady pour, whisking all the time.

Whip the remaining cream to soft peaks (the quantity is easy enough to do by hand rather than in a mixer) and fold that into the peanut custard.

Decant the custard into the prepared container. Cover and freeze for at least 5 hours until firm, removing from the freezer 15 minutes before serving, turning out of the container and peeling away the lining.

At some point before eating the parfait, heat the oven to 200°C/180°C fan/400°F. Spread the peanuts out in one layer on a baking sheet and roast until golden (around 15 minutes), transfer to a cold plate and leave to cool (store in an airtight container if doing this far in advance).

Use a hot knife to slice the parfait into equal portions. Add a tablespoon of chopped peanuts alongside each portion. Sprinkle salt flakes over each slice (more than you think might be required) and crumble any left between finger and thumb onto the nuts. This is particularly good with a dark coffee, ice-cold amaretto or nocino liqueur. You could add a few raspberries or cherries to lift the mood a little.

A quick fix

A few reminders and ideas for rich and/or savoury snacking:

– Sourdough bread, or white baguette sliced on an angle, toasted to a deep golden, then left to cool for 45 seconds longer than you might normally. Slices or curls of butter lain on top (not spread), with 2–3 quality anchovies on top of that.

– Or just a tin of anchovies on their own.

– Pumpkin seeds and/or sunflower kernels, toasted and salted as per the labneh recipe on page 200, but this time with rosemary leaves stripped from one sprig and finely chopped, added while the seeds warm in the pan.

– A bagel or crumpet, toasted until properly bronzed (which probably means two full turns of the toaster). Within nanoseconds of the bagel popping up, spread with a lot of salted butter, then follow that with a thick swoosh of marmite, and then a similar quantity of honey.

Side note: when I was young, my dad ate this combination for breakfast on some weekend mornings. I now know this was his medicine when hungover, or had been woken early, or both. Now I have a son, I fully understand and endorse its healing powers.

– Radishes, halved or quartered, with flaky sea salt and butter nearby for dipping into.

– A bowl of miso soup, made with a sachet of instant dashi powder (as used on pages 174 and 195), and a tablespoon or two of miso.

– A steaming mug of Bovril – an underrated, very convenient and hyper-savoury drink.

– Egg soldiers. Bring a small saucepan of water to a rolling boil. Lower your eggs in (two per person) with a spoon and cook at an energetic simmer for 4 minutes and 45 seconds. Meanwhile, toast bread, butter well and consider a hint of Marmite, before cutting the toast into soldiers, settling the now cooked eggs into eggcups, and lopping off their tops. Have a little mound of flaky sea salt and black pepper nearby to season the egg in between dips.

– A softhardie boiled egg with celery salt. Bring a small saucepan of water to a rolling boil. Lower your egg(s) in with a spoon and cook at an energetic simmer for 7 minutes. Transfer to iced water or leave under a cold-running tap until cool enough to peel. Halve and sprinkle with salt. A blob of ready-made mayo works wonders.

– A jacket (baked) potato, cooked until the skin is crunchy. Halve, add butter, salt, black pepper, mash around, add more butter, more salt, more black pepper, plus whatever your favourite topping is.

– Traditional German soft pretzel with cooked or cured sausage, or cooked or cured ham. Plus mustard.

– Frozen raspberries and a tablespoon of good tahini.

– A pot of peanut butter, a teaspoon, and no regrets.

cheesy and creamy

You know cheesy and creamy already. The adjectives write themselves (salty, tangy, heavy, decadent, rich and, err, creamy). The moments are familiar (wet days, long nights, sad times). And surely everyone other than those who can't or won't eat dairy (but perhaps some of them as well) feels the magnetic pull of a full cheeseboard; the crusty, bronzed gratin with its molten sauce bubbling through; the crunchy skirt of a cheese toastie; and the silken ribbons and bulbous curves of whipped cream.

What more needs to be said?

Probably not much. Although it is worth noting that I've tried to offer a relatively wide variety of recipes. It's not all luscious mac and cheese nor the aforementioned bubbling bake. Well, none of the former and only a few of the latter. Because while the adjectives do write themselves, the potential list of them is pretty long and nuanced. Cheese can be salty and tangy, but also nutty, blue, mellow, buttery and grassy. Cream encompasses sweet and savoury, rich and light, stiff or runny. This flavour profile is somehow both constrained by being so reliant on dairy, and yet also of infinite variety. So the pages that follow contain oozing and ambrosial treats like truffled-cheese slices, baked cheesecakes, and creamed rice. But also more humble and (sort of) everyday suggestions, such as root vegetable gratins, a side of Parmesan-and-butter-enriched white beans, and cheesy polenta with multiple toppings.

The raw ingredients – cheese and cream – make it easy to create tasty food because the cows, cheesemakers and affineurs have done the hard work already. This is evident in the effort versus reward ratio of dishes like a multi-directional three-cheese soup, onions blanched then baked in Comté and cream, a ham and pea pie powered by the British farmhouse cheese Berkswell, and lip-smacking conchiglioni shells which are filled with ricotta and Parmesan and swim in a gorgonzola sauce. The flavours in these dishes are powerful and memorable, yet all we, the cooks, really do is grate or crumble the relevant cheese. On which note, while cheese is a pretty interchangeable component, for top results please do use the varieties I suggest – and the best of them that you can afford. Quality cheeses are complex and layered, and per gram make a much bigger impact than rubbery mass-produced alternatives. They're worth every penny.

The cliché at the top about wanting cheesy and creamy food on wet days, long nights and sad times rings true – basically, comforting, dairy-rich dishes come calling whenever you need your food to be a metaphorical and physical blanket. Weather is particularly relevant here, I think. The odd slice of quiche aside, these dishes mostly fit the bill in colder, wetter months. Indeed, my experience of testing and retesting them over spring and summer suggests few if any will truly hit the spot in a heatwave.

Research into biological reasons for a trip to a fromagerie also links seasonal changes to this flavour profile, as apparently a deficiency in vitamin D can cause people to desire dairy (should SAD lamps come with a mini-cheese box attached or is that simply a fridge?). Such cravings can apparently also be explained by deficiencies in calcium and fat. Side note to pregnant and breastfeeding mums: to my mind you don't ever need to justify wanting to gorge on any type of food, but be reassured you are absolutely covered on the cheese and pavlova front.

I think there's something of a hedonic hunger thing going on here too. That is to say, a dietitian might suggest the tarragon and crème fraîche chicken (which is sat on a puddle of very creamy bread sauce) is calling to you because all that crème fraîche, whole milk and double cream is actually necessary, as for some reason you need fat and/or calcium-rich calories. Conceivably though, there are many more times that your desire for dairy comes at a time when you don't really need any calories at all; it's simply something you'll derive pleasure from eating. It's entirely possible that such appetite has been triggered by a cheese and/or cream-heavy image (whether on social media or maybe in this book). Outrageous shots involving melting and stretched cheese are among the most successful on Instagram (think mac and cheese, fondue and raclette, a cheeseburger, grilled cheese, cheesecakes and creamy puddings... #Delish). It follows that at least some of those shots will cause scrollers to crave something similar.

Whatever the reason or trigger, I'm certain the pull of cheese and cream is a strong one. Hopefully you'll find something suitable in this section.

Three-cheese, chickpea and kale soup

Yes, there are three cheeses here, but also kale and chickpeas, so we can say that this chapter kicks off with a diet dish, right?

More seriously, while this soup ticks multiple dairy-craving boxes (the tang of Stilton, the gum-receding hit of sharp Cheddar, and the moreish umami of Parmesan), it does so without leaving a lead-weight in the stomach, nor cheese-induced hallucinations up top. Instead, it's hearty, chunky, wholesome and as interesting and satisfying at the last spoonful as it is the first. A deep bowl provides a satisfying and fortifying lunch or supper.

As a side note, given that we want the cheese, vegetables and pulses to the fore, if you use a chicken stock, it's best if it's not intense. For example, 500ml (2 cups) of decent-quality store-bought stock should be diluted to the required quantity.

Serves 4 as a hearty lunch or supper

—   ·

15g (½oz) butter
3 medium leeks, trimmed and sliced
400g (14oz) potatoes, peeled and diced
2 cloves garlic, finely sliced
1 litre (4⅓ cups) not too strong chicken, ham or vegetable stock
250g (9oz) chickpeas (garbanzos) (cooked, drained weight)
1 Parmesan rind
80g (2¾oz) Stilton, crumbled
75g (2½oz) mature/crunchy/farmhouse Cheddar, diced
100g (3½oz) curly kale, leaves picked from stems and roughly chopped
Extra virgin olive oil, to garnish
30g (1oz) Parmesan, finely grated
Flaky sea salt

Some warm crusty bread on the side.

Place a large saucepan or casserole over a medium–high heat. Add the butter, let this melt for 60 seconds, then follow with the leeks, potatoes and a pinch of salt. Cook for 4–5 minutes, so that the leeks soften and begin to mellow, then add the garlic and cook for 1 minute more. Pour in the stock and drop in the chickpeas and Parmesan rind. Bring to the boil, then reduce to a gentle blip-blip-simmer for 20–25 minutes, until the potatoes are soft.

Transfer three ladles of lumpy bits to a bowl (returning any liquid back to the saucepan) and discard the Parmesan rind. Blend what remains in the saucepan using a stick blender or separate blender. When smooth and silky, return everything to the pot, and place that over a very low heat.

Add 30g (1oz) of the Stilton and all of the Cheddar, and stir for a minute or so until the cheese has melted. Add the kale and cook for 4–5 minutes until tender. Check the soup for seasoning – it will need some salt, but not as much as most soups, thanks to the cheese.

As you serve, ensure everyone receives even quantities of lumpy bits and blended soup. Finish with a generous drizzle of extra virgin olive oil, crumble the remaining Stilton over the top, and grate over a significant snowfall of Parmesan.

Comté-baked onions with air-dried beef

This assembly of cheese-and-cream-baked onions, cured meats and cornichons is a nod in the direction of Alpine fondue and raclette. You don't need to have been skiing to enjoy it, though if you are itching for snow this might feel particularly appropriate (or triggering?).

Two to three onion halves and lots of the cheese sauce per person is about right for a light (but also heavy) lunch or supper when matched with pickles and baby potatoes. You could also add a leafy salad dressed with a sharp vinaigrette as an additional side or chaser. Alternatively, these cheesy onions work well as a side dish, in particular alongside roast beef, chicken or lamb.

I think Comté is the best option here, but you could successfully swap in another similarly delicious hard Alpine cheese such as Gruyère, Beaufort or Emmental.

Serves 4

—

6 medium–large onions
8 sprigs thyme
300ml (1¼ cups + 1 tbsp) double (heavy) cream
80g (2¾oz) Comté, finely grated
1 heaped tsp Dijon mustard
Flaky sea salt
100g (3½oz) cured, air-dried beef (bresaola or similar), thinly sliced, to serve
1 x 350g (12oz) jar cornichons and baby onions, to serve
500g (1lb 2oz) baby potatoes, boiled, to serve

Peel the onions without trimming too much off their root or tip (if any). Fill a medium saucepan with water, add a heaped teaspoon of salt and place over a medium–high heat. When the water is boiling add the onions and five or six sprigs of thyme, then simmer for 30–35 minutes until the onions are totally tender – a metal skewer should run through with only a little resistance in the centre. Discard the thyme and cooking water. Slice the onions in half (from root to tip) and place cut-side down in an ovenproof dish that fits the halves in one snug layer.

Heat the oven to 200°C/180°C fan/400°F.

Decant the cream into a small saucepan, add 60g (2¼oz) of the Comté, the mustard and the leaves stripped from the remaining sprigs of thyme. Warm gently over a medium heat for 3–4 minutes to melt the cheese and disperse the mustard. Pour this over the onions (ensuring each is coated) and bake for 15 minutes before basting the onions with the cream sauce, sprinkling with the remaining cheese and returning to the oven for 10–15 minutes until well bronzed and bubbling.

Serve with the suggested trimmings.

Swede, sage and Cheddar gratin

A formidable side that pairs well (in particular) with haggis, most cuts of lamb, beef and chicken. That said, as with any root vegetable gratin, when you pull it out of the oven you'd be forgiven for thinking that it might as well be the centrepiece, with some salad leaves nearby so as to pretend you'd just eaten a fresh and balanced meal.

Point being: it's the kind of side you think of in response to a craving, and then base the rest of the meal around it. I tend to need this when the weather or dark evenings prompt it; and I'll modestly suggest that it's guaranteed to hit the spot.

Do use an English farmhouse or at least extra-mature Cheddar – it needs a forceful punch. Be generous with the seasoning too: you almost can't have too much black pepper, will enjoy more nutmeg in it than you might imagine, and even though the cheese is salty, add extra crystals of salt while you eat and notice the flavours jump out at you.

Serves 4–6 as a side

—

600ml (generous 2½ cups) double (heavy) cream
6 sprigs sage
2 cloves garlic
1 large swede (rutabaga) (around 1kg/2lb 4oz)
¼ nutmeg, freshly grated
1–2 tsp coarse-ground black pepper
80g (2¾oz) British farmhouse Cheddar such as Keen's, Montgomery's, Hafod, Westcombe, grated
Flaky sea salt

You will need a gratin or ovenproof dish around 2 litres (70fl oz) in volume, large enough to hold the sliced swede in three to four layers, ideally leaving 2–3cm (¾–1¼in) clear between the top of the swede and the edge of the dish.

Put the cream and four sprigs of sage in a small, heavy-bottomed saucepan. Flatten the garlic, discard the skins and add the cloves to the pan. Place over a medium heat, bring to a gentle simmer for 5 minutes (don't boil), then remove from the heat and set aside for the sage and garlic to infuse for 20–60 minutes (i.e. for as long as you can wait).

Heat the oven to 180°C/160°C fan/350°F.

Peel the swede and cut it into quarters. Cut each quarter into slices about 2mm (⅟₁₆in) thick. A mandoline is the quickest way to do this if you're comfortable using one. Pick the leaves from the remaining sage sprigs and set them to one side.

Arrange the swede in three to four layers, with a generous dusting of grated nutmeg and black pepper, plus a scattering of cheese between each layer, using about half the cheese in doing so. You don't need to fastidiously overlap the first couple of layers of swede, just make sure they are level. Take a bit more time on the top layer if you wish.

Pour the contents of the cream pan over the gratin – the liquid will finish below the swede, but try to wet all of the top surface as you pour it over. Discard the garlic but arrange the soggy sprigs of sage leaves on top.

Bake in the middle of the oven for a total of 90 minutes. Every 25–30 minutes use a spatula or fish slice to gently push and persuade the top layer of swede down under the bubbling cream. This helps to avoid the top being cremated before the middle is tender. Fifteen minutes before the end, add the picked sage leaves to the top of the gratin, plus a little more black pepper and salt and the remaining grated cheese. Return to the oven for a final 15 minutes, by which time the gratin should be soft within, bubbling around the edges, and pockmarked and crisp on top.

Truffled Brie and potato slice

It's not uncommon to simultaneously desire starchy potatoes, buttery pastry and oozing, melted cheese. Maybe you're having one of those moments right now? Well, this truffle-infused pie (essentially a posh cheese and potato pasty) does indeed answer all three needs in one go. It's excellent with a sharply dressed green salad. Or, as you might with other pies, made into a very British meal involving peas and broccoli. Maybe carrots too. But hold the mash.

Truffle pastes range in power and price. You do get what you pay for, and for this sort of thing there's no need to spend too much. Many supermarkets stock reasonably priced pastes near the pestos and other pasta sauces, as do Italian delicatessens and online. Look for pastes that are mostly mushroom, with about 5 per cent sliced truffle (not truffle oil-infused).

Serves 4–6

—

750g (1lb 10oz) Charlotte potatoes
  (or another waxy variety)
150g (5½oz) full-fat crème fraîche
5 tsp truffle paste
1 egg, beaten
2 tsp whole milk
2 x 320g (¾oz) all-butter puff pastry
  ready-rolled sheets
1 onion, thinly sliced
200g (7oz) Brie, cut into 3–4mm (⅛–¼in) strips
40g (1½oz) strong hard cheese, such as Comté,
  Parmesan or mature Cheddar, finely grated
Flaky sea salt and ground black pepper

—

Put the potatoes in a saucepan and cover with cold water. Add a teaspoon of salt, place over a medium–high heat and bring to the boil. Reduce to an energetic simmer for 15–20 minutes, until the potatoes are just cooked, so you can push a fork into the centre but there's still a little resistance. Drain, leave to cool, then slice into 1cm (½in)-thick discs.

Mix the crème fraîche and truffle paste in a bowl. In a separate bowl beat together the egg and milk.

Line a baking sheet with baking paper and unroll one of the puff pastry sheets onto it (keep the other puff pastry roll in the fridge for now). Use the back of a knife to lightly score a margin of 3cm (1¼in) from the edge of the sheet. Spread half the crème fraîche and truffle evenly within the margins and scatter over half of the onions evenly before arranging the potato discs on top. Season with a few sprinkles of salt and pepper. Add the remaining onions then top with the Brie. Dot the rest of the crème fraîche and truffle mix on top and spread it out as much as you can – this is a bit of a fiddle, but I believe in you (particularly if you have a spatula and palette knife). Finally, sprinkle over the grated cheese.

Paint the pastry margin with a little of the egg wash, then get the second roll of puff pastry out of the fridge. Lay this over the top, stretching it slightly to match up the edges, pressing down on the egg-washed pastry joins. Transfer to the fridge to chill for 30 minutes.

After half an hour, remove from the fridge. Trim the sides to straighten the edges of the pastry then use the tip of the backside of a fork to further push the edges together (as well as neatening the finish). Paint the whole pie with egg wash. Return it to the fridge for 15 minutes, then paint again and return for 15 minutes more.

Heat the oven to 220°C/200°C fan/425°F. Remove the pie from the fridge and, if you wish, score a pattern over the middle of the pastry with the back of a knife. Bake in the middle of the oven for 20 minutes, lower the temperature to 200°C/180°C fan/400°F, and bake for 15 minutes more. Wait for 5 minutes before slicing (best with a bread knife). It's excellent if served straight away, but still good later, whether at room temperature or reheated.

Artichoke, Gruyère and cod bake

The 'no cheese with fish' rule is a pretty sound one. But there are some significant carve-outs, including fish bakes involving cheesy white sauces.

This one manages to be both decadent and not overly heavy. Which is one advantage of using a cream, rather than a full béchamel sauce base; the other advantage being speed – it really doesn't take much effort to turn out a classy and rewarding bake.

Excellent with a herb-laced green salad, bitter leaves, or blanched greens like broccoli, and either baby potatoes or some good bread to mop up the cream.

Serves 4
—

15g (½oz) salted butter
1 small banana shallot, finely diced
1 large clove garlic, thinly sliced
100ml (scant ½ cup) dry white wine or vermouth
300ml (1¼ cups + 1 tbsp) double (heavy) cream
60g (2¼oz) Gruyère, finely grated
300g (10½oz) artichoke hearts
450g (1lb) cod, pin-boned, skinned and cut into
    3–4cm (1¼–1½in) cubes
50g (1¾oz) panko breadcrumbs
Flaky sea salt and ground black pepper

Serve with new potatoes or good bread,
    and either a salad or blanched greens.

You will need a low-sided ovenproof pie or gratin dish with 2 litres (70fl oz) capacity. I tend to use a circular one, 23–24cm (9–9½in) in diameter.

Heat the oven to 200°C/180°C fan/400°F.

Put a milk pan or small saucepan over a medium heat. Melt the butter, then add the sliced shallot and a pinch of salt. Cook gently for 4 or 5 minutes, stirring occasionally, so the shallot softens but does not colour. Add the garlic and cook for a minute more, then increase the heat and wait for 15 seconds before adding the wine or vermouth. Let this boil, bubble and reduce by half, then add the cream, half the Gruyère and a few hefty grinds of black pepper. Cook for 2 or 3 minutes more, until the cheese has melted. Remove from the heat.

Halve or quarter the artichokes, so that they're a similar size to the fish, and arrange both evenly in the cooking dish, so each spoonful will have similar proportions of artichoke and cod. Pour the sauce over the top (scraping every last drop of goodness from the saucepan). Mix the remaining Gruyère with the panko crumbs and sprinkle over the bake.

Cook at the top of the oven for 20 minutes, by which time the crumbs should be bronzed, the cream will be bubbling through, and the cod will be cooked but not at all dry.

British farmhouse cheese and tomato tart

You can't beat a good quiche. This one has a sneaky tomato paste layer between pastry and filling, and also raw onions, both of which provide an edge that I think is helpful. However, it's ultimately about the cheese. Which is of course an ever-changeable flavouring of infinite variety, but it's certainly true to say that you will get more satisfaction from those that are complex and characterful in a way that British artisan and farmhouse cheeses are, and mass-produced alternatives can never be. Such cheeses might seem more expensive, but they pack more flavour, so you need less of them. I enjoy this mix of buttery Ogleshield, a dense, intense and gum-wrecking West Country Cheddar like Montgomery's, and the mellow tickle (and colour) of Sparkenhoe Red Leicester.

Very fine on a hot day with little more than a salad; though you could also make more of a meal of it and serve with buttery baby potatoes and some peas or wilted greens, such as chard or spinach.

Serves 4–6

—

For the pastry case
230g (8oz) plain (all-purpose) flour
½ tsp flaky sea salt
125g (4½oz) cold butter, cubed
1 egg, beaten
1 tbsp apple cider vinegar
1–2 tbsp chilled water

For the filling
300g (10½oz) tomatoes, roughly chopped
1 tbsp olive oil
1 tsp golden caster (superfine) sugar
½ tsp apple cider vinegar
200ml (scant 1 cup) water
90g (3¼oz) Montgomery's Cheddar, coarsely grated
70g (2½oz) Ogleshield, coarsely grated
90g (3¼oz) Sparkenhoe Red Leicester, coarsely grated
300ml (1¼ cups + 1 tbsp) whole milk or 200ml (scant 1 cup) double (heavy) cream and 100ml (scant ½ cup) whole milk

5 large eggs, beaten
1 small onion (no more than 60g/2¼oz), very finely diced
Flaky sea salt and ground black pepper

Use a 24cm (9½in)-diameter, 3–4cm (1¼–1½in) deep-sided, loose-bottomed tart tin or a similarly sized pie dish.

—

Rub the flour, salt and butter together, either with your fingertips or (much quicker) pulsed in a food processor, until the mixture resembles breadcrumbs. Make a well in the middle of those breadcrumbs, add half the beaten egg, the vinegar and one tablespoon of the chilled water, then stir the mixture so it comes together, compressing it into a ball with your hands at the point you become impatient, and then flattening that into a disc about 2–3cm (¾–1¼in) thick (add the second tablespoon of water if it doesn't come together easily). Wrap or keep in a covered bowl and refrigerate for at least 60 minutes.

Roll the cold pastry into a 3mm (⅛in)-thick circle big enough to line the base and sides of your tin with a little overlap. You can do this on a lightly floured surface, but as the pastry is quite short (buttery and flaky), it's easiest if rolled between two sheets of baking paper. Line the tart tin, pushing the pastry into the fluted sides and patching up any holes or tears, then chill in the fridge or freezer for another 30 minutes or more.

Heat the oven to 200°C/180°C fan/400°F.

Line the pastry base with baking paper or foil and fill with baking beans (pie weights) or a dried pulse. Place on a baking sheet and bake in the middle of the oven for 15 minutes. After this time, remove the lining and the beans, brush the pastry with the remaining beaten egg, and bake for an additional 15–20 minutes until well bronzed.

Continued overleaf

Meanwhile, put the chopped tomatoes, olive oil,
sugar, vinegar and water in a small saucepan over
a medium heat. Cook for 20 minutes or so to
reduce the tomatoes to a paste – thick enough
that if you swipe a spoon through it, the two
parted sides take a good few seconds to meet
again, if at all.

Mix together the grated cheeses. Whisk the milk
into the beaten eggs.

Once the pastry case is baked, trim the edges
from the tart shell with a sharp knife and lower
the oven temperature to 160°C/140°C fan/325°F.
Spread the base with the tomato paste, sprinkle
the onions on top to form a layer, then distribute
the cheeses evenly over that. Return the tart
to the baking sheet, pour in half of the milk and
eggs, then slide into the middle shelf of the oven.
With the shelf half out, pour in the remaining milk
and then bake for 40–45 minutes, so the top
is burnished and there's just a hint of wibble in
the centre. Allow to cool for 15 minutes before
removing from the tin and portioning (to eat it
warm), or let it cool completely.

Tarragon chicken with bread sauce

The combination of cream, tarragon and chicken is a gentle embrace. I like to serve it with bread sauce, the creamy and plentiful nature of which turns that gentle embrace into a full-on deep and meaningful hug.

To interrupt the tender moment, send in some roast Brussels sprouts (a desire for this dish does tend to be weather-induced – specifically cold and grey days and nights from mid-autumn to late winter – so there'll likely be sprouts around). Alternatively, kalettes, wilted cabbage, any of the kales or purple sprouting broccoli match well too.

Serves 4
–

For the bread sauce
900ml (4 cups) whole milk
75g (2½oz) butter
12 cloves
2 bay leaves
1 onion, quartered
8 black peppercorns
⅛ nutmeg, freshly grated
1 sprig rosemary
150g (5½oz) soft breadcrumbs
100ml (scant ½ cup) double (heavy) cream
Flaky sea salt

For the chicken
4 whole chicken legs or 8 thighs, bone in, skin on
1 tbsp sunflower oil
3 banana shallots, quartered lengthways
6 cloves garlic, skin on and flattened with a
   heavy knife
200ml (scant 1 cup) dry white wine
200g (7oz) full-fat crème fraîche
15g (½oz) tarragon sprigs
Juice from ¼ lemon
Flaky sea salt and ground black pepper

Serve with green vegetables: Brussels sprouts,
   cabbage, kalettes, kale, purple sprouting
   broccoli or similar.

Ideally you will cook the chicken in an ovenproof sauté pan, in which you can both fry and bake. If you don't have that, begin in a frying pan (skillet), then transfer the shallots and chicken to a roasting tin that fits the chicken snugly in one layer.

–

Start with the bread sauce; you can rush this, but it's best if the milk and aromatics steep for an hour or so. Put the milk, two thirds of the butter, the cloves, bay leaves, onion, peppercorns, nutmeg and rosemary in a medium heavy-bottomed saucepan. Bring almost to the boil, then reduce to a gentle simmer for 10 minutes. Remove from the heat and leave to infuse, ideally for 1 hour or more.

Later on (when the chicken is in the oven) strain the infused milk into a jug (discarding the aromatics), then pour all but 100ml (scant ½ cup) or so of the milk into a clean pan. Bring to a gentle simmer, add the breadcrumbs and stir or whisk until incorporated. Turn the heat right down to the lowest setting and cook for 15 minutes until thickened, stirring occasionally to stop it catching. Add half a teaspoon of flaky salt, the cream and remaining butter and stir until incorporated. It should be the consistency of a loose porridge – add the set-aside milk (and more) if you need to. Taste to check the seasoning and add more salt and/or nutmeg if you wish.

Continued overleaf

Tarragon chicken with bread sauce, continued...

To cook the chicken, 45 minutes before you want to eat heat the oven to 200°C/180°C fan/400°F and sprinkle salt generously over the skin of the legs/thighs. Place a heavy-bottomed, ovenproof sauté pan on a medium–high heat, add the tablespoon of sunflower oil, and, when it's hot, place the chicken in, skin-side down. Cook for 10–12 minutes until the skin is crisp and golden; don't even think about looking or prodding for at least 7 minutes.

Temporarily remove the chicken from the pan. Add the shallots and, a minute later the garlic, then a minute after that pour in the wine. Let the liquid bubble and reduce a little for 1 minute more, before stirring in the crème fraîche and adding half the tarragon sprigs. Distribute everything evenly then return the chicken to the pan, skin-side up this time. The liquid should come about halfway up the chicken and shouldn't cover much (if any) of the crisp skin. Cook in the middle of the oven for 25 minutes.

Strip the leaves from the remaining tarragon sprigs and chop roughly. Then, just before serving, remove the pan from the oven and transfer the chicken to a warm dish. Return the sauté pan to the stove over a medium–high heat, and replace the tarragon sprigs with the chopped tarragon leaves. Boil for 5 minutes until the sauce has reduced by a half, then remove from the heat, add the lemon juice, taste and season with salt, pepper and a tiny bit more lemon if required (it shouldn't be overly lemony, the citrus just lifts things a touch).

Serve the chicken on top of puddles of bread sauce, with the crème fraîche sauce spooned over the top, and loads of green vegetables nearby.

Milk-poached smoked haddock, dill sauce and mash

Poached fish with a milky sauce and creamy mashed potato has the feel of a nostalgic supper, even if poached fish and milky sauces weren't part of your childhood. It's pale beige food at its best (albeit with the essential pop of frozen peas).

Two cooking notes: (1) though calming to eat, there's a little bit of pan juggling – read the method thoroughly before starting out; and (2) the potato purée needs to come from oven-baked, not boiled, potatoes. In part this is to reduce the number of saucepans on your stove, but mostly because the haddock-infused milk will make already saturated boiled potatoes wet and sloppy.

Serves 4

–

1.5kg (3lb 5oz) jacket (baked) potatoes
600g (1lb 5oz) undyed smoked haddock (skin on)
500ml (2 cups) whole milk
3 bay leaves
350g (12oz) frozen peas
30g (1oz) unsalted butter, cubed
Fronds picked from 15g (½oz) dill, finely chopped
4 lemon wedges, to serve
Flaky sea salt and ground black pepper

Heat the oven to 220°C/200°C fan/425°F. Bake the potatoes for 1 hour or so until soft and fluffy on the inside.

When the potatoes are ready, place the haddock skin-side down in a heavy-bottomed, wide lidded saucepan or casserole. Pour in the milk and add half a teaspoon of pepper and the bay leaves. There might be a few bits of fish poking out – don't worry.

Put the pan over a medium–high heat and bring to an energetic simmer, with small bubbles beginning to roll over the fish. At this point remove from the heat, place a lid on top and leave for a total of 10 minutes while the rest of the meal comes together.

At the same time as you heat the milk, put a separate saucepan of water on to boil to cook your peas (and cook them).

After the fish has been off the heat for 5 minutes, remove the (cooked) potatoes from the oven, cut in half, scoop the innards into a mixing bowl and allow the steam to escape for 3 minutes before mashing and adding lots of salt and pepper. Now ladle in 200ml (scant 1 cup) of haddock-infused milk from the fish pan and beat with a wooden spoon or silicon spatula to make a silky purée.

Transfer an additional 100ml (scant ½ cup) of milk from the haddock pan to a small saucepan (leaving a touch of warm milk in the pan along with the haddock and the lid on). Bring the milk to the boil, then add the butter, 1 cube at a time, and use a balloon whisk to emulsify the sauce. Add the dill fronds and remove from the heat.

Peel the skin from the haddock (peeling easily is a good sign the fish is cooked), and serve chunky flakes of the fish next to the purée and peas, ladling the dill sauce over the top, with wedges of lemon to hand.

Chorizo and blue-cheese leeks

This is a gathering of tender, bright green leeks and mouthwatering, flame-coloured chorizo, smothered by a silken blanket of blue-cheese sauce. It is as enjoyably soporific as that sounds.

Unusually, I think this cook-separately-and-assemble approach trumps a one-dish gratin, as you get to enjoy each of three powerful components at their best and still tasting of themselves; whereas if they're left to mingle in the oven, they cancel each other out. Also, good though bubbling and burnished cheesy gratins normally are, this feels smooth and clean(ish).

It's best, I think, with some warmed ciabatta and a handful of peppery rocket or watercress, all of which enjoy being dragged through the dregs of blue-cheese sauce and chorizo juices.

Serves 4–6

—

50g (1¾oz) butter
50g (1¾oz) plain (all-purpose) flour
500ml (2 cups) milk
1 small onion, finely diced
1 clove garlic, minced
1 bay leaf
80g (2¾oz) Stilton, crumbled
⅛ nutmeg, freshly grated
1kg (2lb 4oz) leeks (trimmed weight),
   cut into 3–4cm (1¼–1½in) lengths
1 tbsp neutral cooking oil
300g (10½oz) cooking chorizo,
   cut into 1cm (½in)-thick discs
Leaves stripped from 5 sprigs thyme
Flaky sea salt and ground black pepper
1 ciabatta loaf, served warm
200g (7oz) rocket (arugula), dressed
   with lemon juice and olive oil

Begin by making the cheese sauce. Place a heavy-bottomed saucepan over a medium heat. Add the butter and allow it to melt gently (if it foams, turn the heat down). Add the flour and stir for 2 minutes using a wooden spoon or silicon spatula, so the roux begins to slacken and thin but doesn't colour. Add the milk in four to five stages, stirring until each addition is fully incorporated (and there are no lumps) before adding the next measure. Add the onion, garlic and bay. Cook for 15–20 minutes, stirring frequently, until the sauce is thick and silky and there's no taste of raw flour. At this point remove the sauce from the heat and stir in the Stilton. Season with nutmeg and just a little pinch of salt.

While the cheese sauce is cooking, boil a full kettle. Put the leeks in a large saucepan, cover with the just-boiled water, and place over a medium–high heat, bringing the water to a simmer. Cook for about 8 minutes until tender but not soggy or dull.

Meanwhile, place a heavy-bottomed sauté or frying pan over a medium heat. Add a splash of cooking oil, followed by the chorizo, and cook for about 5 minutes so that the oils render from the sausage and the edges brown a little, but the meat remains succulent. When the chorizo is almost done add most of the thyme leaves and cook for 1 minute more, then turn the heat off and transfer to a serving dish.

The leeks and sauce will both be just about ready by this point. Drain the leeks then add to the chorizo and gently mingle the two. Ladle the cheese sauce over the top, sprinkle with ground black pepper and the remaining thyme leaves, then serve with warmed ciabatta and rocket salad.

Lamb chops with cacio e pepe white beans

So many of these cheesy and creamy recipes are ones that respond well to glum mood and/or glum weather. This one, however, seems to call to me whatever the weather, and whether I'm down or I'm bouncing. It's just a base urge for the slight tang and umami notes of the Pecorino or Parmesan in a buttery sauce. I could psychoanalyse that. Or just accept it's probably, simply, because of the deliciousness.

Given such an urge can come at any time, it's handy that this recipe provides something of a rapid, store-cupboard relief, including pre-cooked beans from a can to suit the speed. Those beans go with lamb in any form (whether roast leg, slow-cooked shoulder, breast, rump or rack) but chops are appropriately quick to cook.

Serve with something like purple sprouting or Tenderstem broccoli, curly kale, or a side salad of bitter or peppery leaves.

Serves 2
–

4 lamb chops or 2 thick Barnsley chops
  (about 400–500g/14oz–1lb 2oz in total)
4 cloves garlic, unpeeled
2 sprigs rosemary
1 x 400g (14oz) can haricot (navy) beans, drained
200ml (scant 1 cup) water
60g (2¼oz) butter, cubed
2 tsp ground black pepper
60g (2¼oz) Pecorino or Parmesan, finely grated
Blanched greens or bitter/peppery-leafed salad,
  to serve

Collate all the ingredients including the greens or salad, as you should cook both chops and beans pretty much simultaneously and neither takes long.

Stand the chops on their fatty edges in a (still cold) frying pan (skillet), large enough that it'll still hold the chops once sat flat. Place on a low–medium heat and gradually warm up so as to cook the fat until it's golden and soft – much of which will seep ('render') out. Resist cooking too quickly or at too high a temperature; it's a gentle process that should take 5 minutes or more.

While this is happening, bash the garlic cloves to flatten them then add to the pan (keeping the skin on to prevent burning), along with the sprigs of rosemary. Let those cook away for a few minutes to release their flavours into the ever increasing pool of lamb fat. Then, once the fatty edges are golden and soft, push the chops onto their flatter sides, turn up the heat and cook for about 90 seconds on each side, basting regularly with the flavoursome oil, until the chops are browned and buzzing with hot oils and juices. (If ready before the beans, remove from the heat and rest on a warm plate for a couple of minutes.)

Also while the lamb chops are standing, add the drained beans to a wide frying pan or saucepan and set over a low–medium heat. Pour in the water and let them warm gently – so the liquid begins to simmer but not boil, and therefore the beans remain intact. Scatter the cubes of butter over and around the beans and allow them to melt, before sprinkling the black pepper over the top. Shake the pan vigorously so the butter and cooking liquid become one, then add the cheese, again waiting for it to melt before shaking and stirring to emulsify everything.

Puddle the beans and their cheesy, peppery sauce in a bowl or onto a plate with a rim, add the lamb and greens and tuck in.

Cavolo nero and ricotta conchiglioni in a Gorgonzola sauce

For the avoidance of doubt, cheese and cream are involved here: in the stuffing mix (x2), in the sauce (x3), on the top at the end (x2). The result is both surprisingly light and unsurprisingly rich.

For everyone's benefit I selflessly tested this multiple times, each time concentrating on portion control, and concluded that seven shells per person is the right amount for a one-course meal, with four extra in the pan for the cook to quietly return to while no one is looking. To bulk the meal, add some retro garlic bread and a rocket (arugula) salad with balsamic glaze.

Serves 4

—

32 (230–250g/8–9oz) conchiglioni
   (large pasta shells)
300g (10½oz) cavolo nero, leaves stripped
   (stems discarded)
Leaves from 7–8 sprigs flat-leaf parsley,
   very finely chopped
400g (14oz) ricotta
40g (1½oz) Parmesan, finely grated
⅛ nutmeg, freshly grated
½ tsp ground black pepper
1 clove garlic, minced
220g (7¾oz) full-fat crème fraîche
150ml (scant ⅔ cup) just-boiled water
150g (5½oz) Gorgonzola piccante
3 tbsp walnuts, chopped/crumbled

You will need an ovenproof dish that fits the shells snugly in one layer once filled (you can check by putting the dried shells in – they should cover about two thirds of the surface area).

—

Put a large pan of salted water over a high heat and bring to a rapid boil. Add the pasta and cook for two thirds of the time recommended on the packet (so probably for 10–11 minutes), until wobbly and pliable yet still a little chalky rather than al dente. Drain through a sieve (strainer) or colander and leave under cold-running water until chilled. Set to one side.

Put the ribbons of cavolo nero along with three tablespoons of water in a saucepan over a medium heat, place a lid on top and let them wilt for 4–5 minutes, until soft and tender. Transfer to a sieve or colander, chill under running water, then squeeze the leaves in your hands to remove as much liquid as possible. The cavolo nero will end as a tightly packed green ball. Chop this very finely, then chop a bit more.

Make sure the parsley leaves are chopped to a dust, then in a bowl use the back of a fork to combine the ricotta, cavolo nero, parsley, 10g (¼oz) of the Parmesan, the nutmeg and black pepper.

Decant the crème fraîche into the ovenproof dish. Add 20g (¾oz) more of the Parmesan and pour in the just-boiled water. Use a whisk or fork to gently swirl the cream, water and cheese until they are one. Crumble in two thirds of the Gorgonzola, and all of the walnuts (ensure both are evenly distributed).

Heat the oven to 200°C/180°C fan/400°F.

Now use a teaspoon to fill the pasta shells, pushing the ricotta mix down a little and smoothing off the top before placing each shell in the ovenproof dish, and repeating until all are filled and arranged. Crumble and add the rest of the Gorgonzola over the top of the shells, then finish with a liberal dusting of Parmesan all over.

Bake towards the top of the oven for 20 minutes, by which time the sauce should be bubbling, the Gorgonzola on top of the shells melted, and a few (but not all) pasta edges burnished.

Serve seven shells per person, spooning plenty of blue-cheesy walnutty sauce over and around them. You can tell everyone there's one filled shell each if they get a second wind. Or smuggle them away for yourself.

Cheesy polenta

I've written before that if you think you don't like polenta, it's probably because you haven't been adding enough cheese and butter. When those items are included in noticeable (but not overwhelming) proportions, polenta becomes a beautifully smooth and sloppy base that suits a variety of toppings; a go-to whenever hug-in-a-bowl food is needed. Meatballs, creamed greens, and braised mushrooms are among my favourite toppings, so I have included a version of each. Finish all with a snow shower of Parmesan – cheese below and cheese on top never fails.

The polenta recipe is for coarse-grained polenta bramata, which must be cooked for around 40 minutes. As if by magic, each of the toppings below can be cooked in the same time (or less), while you occasionally turn back to the polenta to ensure it's not sticking. Quick-cook polenta is widely available and is indeed much quicker. If that is what you have, still lace it with this amount of cheese and butter for four people. You typically need a little more dry weight per person (around 50g/1¾oz), but cook it to the per-person quantities and timings written on the packet.

Serves 4

–

For the polenta
1.2 litres (5 cups) boiling water
160g (5¾oz) polenta bramata (not quick-cook)
40g (1½oz) salted butter, cubed
90g (3¼oz) extra-mature or strong farmhouse Cheddar, grated
Flaky sea salt and ground black pepper

–

Fill a large saucepan with the water, add a teaspoon of salt and bring it to the boil. Pour the polenta into the pan in a steady stream, stirring continuously. Reduce to a simmer and stir as the polenta thickens in the water. After 15 minutes reduce the heat to the lowest possible and cook for 15–25 minutes more, until the polenta is smooth, with grains softened and barely noticeable. You will need to beat the polenta regularly to ensure it doesn't stick. Add a little water from time to time if you think it is required.

When the grains are soft and the polenta quite stiff, add the butter, cheese and a good few grinds of a pepper mill. Beat the polenta vigorously until incorporated, remove from the heat and taste. If you think it needs more cheese, add a pinch of salt, then taste again (and then add more cheese if you still think it needs it – remember, 'noticeable (but not overwhelming)'. Ladle into bowls before it cools and sets.

Sausageballs, thyme and wine

Serves 4

–

400g (14oz) high-pork content (no breadcrumbs) sausages
2 tbsp vegetable or light olive oil
4 celery sticks, finely diced
2 cloves garlic, minced
Leaves stripped from 15g (½oz) thyme
200ml (scant 1 cup) white wine or dry vermouth
5 tbsp double (heavy) cream (or soft cheese)
30g (1oz) Parmesan, finely grated
Ground black pepper

–

Make an incision along the length of each sausage, then pull the casings away (and discard). Roll the meat into balls about the size of a cherry tomato (approximately 15g/½oz each).

Put a high-sided frying pan (skillet) on a high heat and add the oil. Add the sausage balls and cook for 90 seconds without touching them, so they begin to form a crust, then shuffle the pan and fry for another 90 seconds, and then once more. Push the balls closer to each other now and add the celery. Cook for 90 seconds, add the garlic and thyme, and stir. After a further 90 seconds pour in the wine, then let this bubble and reduce before adding the cream (or soft cheese). Simmer for 5 minutes, stir in a third of the Parmesan, add a splash of water if necessary and season to taste (the sausages and cheese will already be salty but add lots of black pepper). Ladle over the polenta and top with a generous scattering of Parmesan.

Creamed cherry tomatoes and chard

Serves 4

–

For the anchovy breadcrumbs
60g (2¼oz) soft breadcrumbs, finely ground
3 tbsp cold-pressed rapeseed (canola) oil
2 cloves garlic, minced
2 anchovies, minced

450–500g (1lb–1lb 2oz) cherry tomatoes
150ml (scant ⅔ cup) water
4 anchovies, chopped, plus 1 tbsp of their oil
2 cloves garlic, finely sliced
400g (14oz) Swiss chard, stalks cut to 1cm (½in) pieces, leaves in 3–4cm (1¼–1½in)-wide strips
4 tbsp double (heavy) cream
20g (¾oz) Parmesan
½ tsp ground black pepper

–

Heat the oven to 220°C/200°C fan/425°F.
On a baking sheet, tumble the breadcrumbs, rapeseed oil, garlic and anchovies until most of the breadcrumbs are glistening. Bake in the top of the oven for 10–15 minutes until golden (and shuffle the crumbs if necessary for even colouring). Remove when golden and set aside.

Tumble the cherry tomatoes into a wide saucepan or sauté pan, add the water and place over a medium–high heat. Bring the water to the boil and shuffle the pan occasionally as it bubbles and froths over the tomatoes. After 5 minutes add the chopped anchovies and their oil, the garlic and the chard stalks. Cook for 2 minutes more, so the garlic and stalks soften and the anchovies melt. Sacrifice about eight of the most affected tomatoes by squashing them with the back of a fork. Leave the remainder, which should still be whole – albeit close to collapse – once the sauce is cooked. Add the cream and chard leaves, stir then simmer for 2 minutes more until the chard has wilted. Fold two thirds of the Parmesan plus the black pepper into the sauce and remove from the heat. Spoon onto the polenta, and sprinkle the breadcrumbs and remaining Parmesan over the top.

Taleggio and rosemary portobello mushrooms

Serves 4

–

12 medium–large portobello mushrooms
60g (2¼oz) salted butter
4 sprigs rosemary
3 cloves garlic, finely sliced
200ml (scant 1 cup) water
120g (4¼oz) Taleggio, in thin slices
20g (¾oz) Parmesan, finely grated
Flaky sea salt and ground black pepper

–

Heat the oven to 170°C/150°C fan/325°F.

Fry the mushrooms in butter for 4–5 minutes, curved-sides down, so as to colour them. You will probably need to do this in two or three batches and will use about 40g (1½oz) of the butter.

When the mushrooms are browned, arrange them in an ovenproof dish in which all snugly fit in one layer, with the open cup-side still facing up. Push the rosemary sprigs in between and/or underneath them. Season the inside of each mushroom with salt and pepper and divide the garlic slices and remaining 20g (¾oz) of butter between them. Pour about 200ml (scant 1 cup) of water into the dish, so it comes 1–2cm (½–¾in) up the sides. Wet and crumple a piece of baking paper a little bigger than the baking dish, unravel, lay it over the mushrooms and tuck in at the sides. Bake in the middle of the oven for 25 minutes, then remove the paper and put about 10g (¼oz) of Taleggio in the cup of each mushroom. Return to the oven for 5–10 minutes' more until the cheese has melted and the mushrooms are still juicy.

Top each portion of polenta with three mushrooms, add a few spoonfuls of braising stock, plus a good dusting of Parmesan.

Berkswell, ham and pea suet pie

Berkswell is an unpasteurized ewe's milk cheese made in the West Midlands, England. It's a little bit grassy, a tad buttery, a touch briny yet with a sweet edge – similar to a young Spanish Manchego or Pecorino Toscano. Which means it's excellent on a cheeseboard near a quince conserve, but also good when melted into a white sauce as a subtle, layered seasoning to match chunks of cooked ham and sweet peas. This pie *could* be topped with store-bought puff pastry but it's much better and not much more effort to make a suet pastry and bake until that's golden and the cheese sauce bubbling. It's a real sofa slump of a pie, best served with boiled or mashed potatoes, plus buttered, leafy brassica.

Serves 4–6

–

For the ham
800g–1kg (1lb 12oz–2lb 4oz) boneless
    gammon or collar ham
1 carrot, roughly chopped
2 celery sticks, roughly chopped
1 onion, halved
1 tomato, halved
Or
500–600g (1lb 2oz–1lb 5oz) pre-cooked
    and flaked ham or ham hock (page 34)

For the pastry
200g (7oz) self-raising flour
100g (3½oz) shredded beef suet
1 tsp flaky sea salt
120ml (½ cup) chilled water
1 egg, beaten

For the filling
90g (3¼oz) butter
1 small onion, diced
70g (2½oz) plain (all-purpose) flour
600ml (generous 2½ cups) whole milk
200ml (scant 1 cup) ham stock
130g (4½oz) Berkswell cheese, coarsely grated
200g (7oz) frozen peas
Flaky sea salt and black pepper

This fits well in a 2 litre (70fl oz) pie dish (or any ovenproof dish with the same volume).

Cook the ham in advance: place it in a large saucepan, cover with water, bring to the boil then discard that water to remove excess salt. Refill the saucepan to 1–2cm (½–¾in) clear of the top of the meat. Add the aromatics and simmer for 40 minutes, skimming any scummy foam away. After 45 minutes, remove from the stove and ignore until both ham and stock are completely cool. Trim any rind and excess fat from the top and discard, then cut a slice or two for your lunch, leaving 500–600g (1lb 2oz–1lb 5oz) for the pie. Shred the meat into 2–3cm (¾–1¼in) chunks. Refrigerate until needed. Boil the ham stock to reduce by half, reserve 200ml (scant 1 cup) for this recipe and save the rest for something like the three-cheese, chickpea and kale soup (page 210).

On the day you want to eat the pie, make the pastry by combining the flour, suet and salt in a bowl. Add the water and use a fork to bring everything together, then press into a ball, adding a little more water if required. Don't knead – the whole process is a 60-second in-bowl task. Cover the bowl and refrigerate for 1 hour.

Melt the butter for the filling in a heavy-bottomed saucepan over a medium heat. Add the onion and a pinch of salt and cook to soften (not colour) for 5 minutes. Stir the flour into the buttery onions for 3 minutes before adding the milk and ham stock in four stages, each time beating until fully incorporated before adding the next amount of liquid. Fold in the cheese, ham and peas, taste and season. Decant into an ovenproof dish.

Dust a surface and a rolling pin with flour. Unwrap the pastry and roll it out to 1cm (½in) thick, and just bigger than the pie dish, then lay it over the top. Leave a rim of pastry around the edge (you can crimp and/or neaten this with a sharp knife). Brush the pastry with half the beaten egg. You can either chill the pie until required or cook immediately in a pre-heated oven at 220°C/200°C fan/425°F for 40–45 minutes. Brush the remaining egg wash over the pastry after 25 minutes in the oven. The pie is cooked when the top is golden all over, crisp and with some cheesy sauce bubbling through.

Honeyed Basque cheesecake

The burnished, Basque-style cheesecake has become something of a food media darling in recent years. Indeed, I wondered if it was too clichéd and of the moment to include a version here. However, this is the only kind of baked cheesecake I enjoy, and I'm certain that when it stops being *A Thing*, it will still be deliciously satisfying in its cream-cheesy, bronze-top-yet-wibbling-middle way. It's also very easy* to make (essentially: mix the ingredients put them in the oven and burn).

So here is 'my' version, which is emboldened with honey to a level that should support rather than dominate the dairy; although it's still worth saying that the more characterful the honey, the better the end result.

Delicious with poached or roasted seasonal fruit like rhubarb, quince, pears and plums, but also excellent on its own.

* You *could* make this by hand and elbow grease, but the recipe assumes you have a stand mixer.

Serves 8

—

Butter, for greasing
600g (1lb 5oz) full-fat soft cheese (without additives or stabilizers – check the ingredients)
120g (4¼oz) golden caster (superfine) sugar
4 large eggs
300ml (1¼ cups + 1 tbsp) double (heavy) cream
2½ tbsp good-quality raw runny honey
Scant ½ tsp flaky sea salt
40g (1½oz) plain (all-purpose) flour, sifted

This recipe requires baking paper and a 20cm (8in) spring-release cake tin. You could squeeze it into a smaller (16cm/6¼in) tin for a deeper, gooeyer result, but make sure the baking paper collar clears the cake tin sides by 5–6cm/2–2½in).

Butter the base and sides of the cake tin, then line with baking paper to leave 4–5cm (1½–2in) of paper above the edges of the tin. The paper doesn't need to be neat, a rippled fluting is fine.

Collate and measure all the ingredients before starting. Heat the oven to 220°C/200°C fan/425°F, and set a rack a touch higher than the middle, ensuring the tin and its high-sided lining will fit.

Load the mixing bowl of a stand mixer with the soft cheese and sugar, and use the paddle attachment at medium speed to beat and cream them together until the sugar is fully incorporated (it'll take about 2 minutes).

Keep the mixer at a medium pace and break the eggs in one by one, adding the next only once the previous egg is fully incorporated. (Tip: crack each egg first into a bowl then tip that into the machine to avoid spending time fishing shells out the cake mix.)

Pause. Scrape the sides down, then return the mixer to medium speed and add the cream, honey and a pinch of salt. Allow the machine to keep beating the mix for 1 minute more, then slow it right down (but don't turn it off) and sprinkle in the sifted flour one tablespoon at a time. Increase the speed to medium again for a final 60 seconds, then pour the custardy batter into the lined tin.

Place the filled cake tin on a baking sheet and slide into the oven for 40 minutes if you'd like a slightly gooey centre; 45 minutes if the priority is a browned top. Whichever you choose, at that moment remove the puffed-up and burnished cheesecake from the oven and leave to completely cool (and sink), before serving at room temperature or below.

This keeps well for 2 days if covered and stored in a cool place or the fridge.

Strawberries and creamed rice

A stove-top rice pudding is a tiny bit more effort than one baked in the oven, but you do end up with a pure-white and deceptively luxurious result, which is a wonderful contrast to warm, soft strawberries and their ruby-red syrup.

This is best made to order, although you could cook it in advance to the point before the cream is added, and chill that quickly (in a thin layer in as wide a container as possible), later reheating with a touch more milk plus the cream, until the consistency is suitably molten and flowing.

Serves 4–6
–

175g (6oz) arborio or carnaroli risotto rice
800ml (3½ cups) whole milk
1 vanilla pod (bean), split with seeds scraped out
3 strips orange zest (via a speed peeler)
Scant ½ tsp flaky sea salt
50g (1¾oz) caster (superfine) sugar
150–200ml (scant ⅔ cup–scant 1 cup) double (heavy) cream

For the strawberry conserve
500g (1lb 2oz) strawberries, hulled and halved
1 heaped tbsp caster (superfine) sugar

Rinse the rice under cold-running water for 30–60 seconds until the water draining through begins to clear, then transfer the grains to a heavy-bottomed saucepan. Add the milk, vanilla pod and seeds, orange zest and salt, set over a medium heat and warm to a simmer, stirring occasionally to ensure the rice is not sticking.

Once simmering, reduce the heat to as low as possible. Place a lid on top, leaving it slightly ajar, and cook for 20–25 minutes, stirring at first occasionally, then over the last 5 minutes relatively frequently as the ratio of liquid to rice reduces. Taste the rice. It should be almost cooked through, but still with a slight bite, and there should be a fair amount of liquid remaining, with the grains almost swimming rather than clagging together. If not, add enough milk to loosen.

Pick out the strips of orange zest and the vanilla pod then stir in the sugar. Leave the rice to sit and swell further for 10 minutes with the lid on – returning a couple of times to give it a quick stir.

In the meantime, put the strawberries in a saucepan with the sugar, turning the fruit over so the sugar coats all surfaces. Heat gently at first until the sugar dissolves, then bring to a simmer and cook for 2 minutes, so the strawberries leach a syrupy liquid and are softening but still bright red and intact. Remove from the heat and set aside for 5 minutes.

Once rested for 10 minutes the rice should be soft and luscious, but a little stiff. Add 150ml (scant ⅔ cup) of cream and stir that through – this should ensure that once decanted the rice flows, rather than stands stiffly. Add a dash more cream if necessary (or if it seems like a lot more is needed, then add extra milk).

Serve in shallow bowls, topped with the strawberry conserve.

A quick fix

A few reminders for closing out a meal/general cheese-related snacking:

– The easiest way to satisfy a craving for cheese is to simply open up your favourite cheese and cut a wedge. You don't need a recipe for that.

– You will also already have a favoured approach to cheese on toast. Carry on.

– That said... my most frequented cheesy moment comes via well-browned sourdough, buttered quickly and excessively while the toast is still hot enough to make the fat dance, topped with cold wedges of the strongest, most crystalline supermarket Cheddar available (try Waitrose Cornish Quartz – thank me later), and then a spread of whichever chilli-based condiment I'm favouring at that point, from kimchi through to a chilli jam.

– No one ever received negative feedback for passing round a baked soft-ripened cheese, such as Camembert or Tunworth. Leave it in the wooden box, then (a) stud with garlic and thyme or rosemary, sprinkle with a little flaky salt and pepper, and drizzle with extra virgin olive oil; (b) slash and add a sharp conserve (try rhubarb or gooseberry); or (c) trim the top off, add a lavish layer of honey and truffles/truffle paste, return the top... and then bake at 200°C/180°C fan/400°F for 15–20 minutes until scoop- and/or dunk-able.

– Vacherin Mont d'Or. Oooof. The season for this insanely rich and creamy cheese from the Jura region of France runs from October through to March. When ripe it should already be fondue-like below that undulating chalky crust, and so is best at room temperature (not warmed), served with a spoon, and with a crusty baguette, roast grapes, apple wedges and/or sorrel or Belgian endive leaves nearby.

– Finally, consider baking triangular slices of hard sheep's cheese such as Berkswell, Pecorino Toscano, Pecorino Sardo, or Manchego, and then drizzling them with honey. Cut two to three 5mm (¼in)-thick slices per person, trim the rind from these, then arrange in a small ovenproof dish (tapas-style dishes are perfect) so they sit in one layer, albeit each slice overlapping with the next. Sprinkle with thyme leaves (stripped from their woody sprigs) and cook at the top of an oven heated to 200°C/180°C fan/400°F for 8–10 minutes until molten. Drizzle with runny honey and sprinkle with crumbled walnuts. Eat with thin crispbreads or crackers.

– Or, to repeat, just cut yourself a wedge from whatever's in the fridge.

Directory of alternative cravings

Flavour profile isn't the only driver for wanting to eat a particular thing. Here are a few other urges that regularly shape what I decide to cook, along with recipes to sate those cravings.

–

Something (mostly) vegetarian

Slow-cooked, minted courgettes with white beans and fresh cheese 28
Celery, fennel and egg salad with rye croutons 40
Honeyed halloumi with apricot fregola 37
Grand aioli 44
Pomegranate and sumac roast courgettes 67
Agrodolce squash platter 68
Sweet and sour vegetable puff tart 70
Three-bean tin-can chilli 115
Kale and coconut dal 140
Paneer tikka 144
Coronation cauliflower 139
Sri Lankan-style squash curry 146
Spiced tomatoes with baked cod and turmeric yoghurt 156
Soggy greens and anchovies on toast 175
Crunchy Jerusalem artichokes with cavolo nero and anchovy crème fraîche 179
Hummus 184
Mushroom, kale and tarragon lasagne 190
Swede, sage and Cheddar gratin 215
Truffled Brie and potato slice 216

–

Something meaty

Ham hock, spring greens and radish salad 34
Cider vinegar-roasted pork belly and apricots 79
Pickled walnut-braised shallots, steak and rocket salad 80
Suya and baked plantain with pepper relish 112
Scotch bonnet and papaya pork collar steaks with a red pepper fruit salad 111
Rainbow root som tam and perfect pork chops 117
Quail gumbo 118
Rabbit cacciatore 122
Curried brisket noodles 158
Cape Malay hogget curry 160
Pork shoulder vindaloo and okra fry 162
Borlotti, browned onions and sausages 188

Pork belly, butter beans and deli olives 198
Miso-braised duck legs, buckwheat and squash 195
Lamb chops with cacio e pepe white beans 228
Berkswell, ham and pea suet pie 234

–

Something fishy

Poached salmon green goddess salad 30
Chopped kale, dill and chickpea salad with smoked trout 32
Bream with whipped tahini and glazed green beans 41
Cantonese-style steamed white fish with pea shoot and garlic asparagus 46
Fermented tomato, pickled celery and salted cod crudo 62
Charred mackerel rice bowls with ginger-pickled rhubarb 71
Thai-style dipping sauces with sticky rice 74
Chipotle tomatoes and sardines on toast 94
Many chilli pepper squid 108
Gong bao prawns 121
Fish fillet katsu curry 148
Mackerel, tamarind and turmeric curry 154
Spiced tomatoes with baked cod and turmeric yoghurt 156
Cod cheeks and brown butter capers on lentils 181
Cuttlefish rice and romesco 192
Artichoke, Gruyère and cod bake 217
Milk-poached smoked haddock, dill sauce and mash 224

–

Something crunchy

Not Caesar salad 26
Celery, fennel and egg salad with rye croutons 40
Grand aioli 44
Fermented and fresh tomato salad with feta 65
Buttermilk chicken with sour watermelon salad 72
Brown-sugar meringues, tamarind and blood orange 82
Rainbow root som tam and perfect pork chops 117
Fish fillet katsu curry 148

Turmeric and saffron poached pears with spiced crumble 166
Crunchy Jerusalem artichokes with cavolo nero and anchovy crème fraîche 179
Berkswell, ham and pea suet pie 234

—

Something soft

Slow-cooked, minted courgettes with white beans and fresh cheese 28
Chicken, sour cream and dill pickle soup 66
Buttermilk pudding with sharp fruits 86
Masala eggs 138
Kale and coconut dal 140
Lamb and pea keema with minted kachumber 153
Spiced tomatoes with baked cod and turmeric yoghurt 156
Parent and child rice 174
Soba noodles with sesame dipping sauce 178
Orecchiette with pork, fennel and milk ragù 186
Hummus 184
Chicken barley 196
Pork belly, butter beans and deli olives 198
Comté-baked onions with air-dried beef 212
Artichoke, Gruyère and cod bake 217
Milk-poached smoked haddock, dill sauce and mash 224
Tarragon chicken with bread sauce 221
Cheesy polenta 232
Honeyed Basque cheesecake 236
Strawberries and creamed rice 239

—

Something for a hot day

Chilled cucumber and melon soup 18
Burrata with burnt peaches and basil 17
Celery, fennel and egg salad with rye croutons 40
Bún chả 25
Slow-cooked, minted courgettes with white beans and fresh cheese 28
Poached salmon green goddess salad 30
Grand aioli 44
Fermented and fresh tomato salad with feta 65
Thai-style dipping sauces with sticky rice 74
Fiery chicken laab with extinguishing salad 100

'Nduja spatchcock chicken 123
Buttermilk chicken with sour watermelon salad 72
British Farmhouse cheese and tomato tart 219
Soba noodles with sesame dipping sauce 178
Mackerel, tamarind and turmeric curry 154
Labneh, salted celery, olive oil and seeds 200
Scotch bonnet and papaya pork collar steaks with a red pepper fruit salad 111
Orange blossom melon with frozen raspberries 50
Papaya, lychee and Thai basil fruit salad with anise syrup 49
Orange and scotch bonnet paletas 128
Mango with chilli, lime and salt 127

—

Something for a cold day

Bún chả 25
Chicken, sour cream and dill pickle soup 66
Cider vinegar-roasted pork belly and apricots 79
Chicken adobo 77
Tteokbokki rice cakes 97
Instant-ish geki kara ramen 104
Three-bean tin-can chilli 115
Quail gumbo 118
Rabbit cacciatore 122
Sri Lankan-style squash curry 146
Fish fillet katsu curry 148
Curried brisket noodles 158
Cape Malay hogget curry 160
Scrag end, root and miso broth 176
Crunchy Jerusalem artichokes with cavolo nero and anchovy crème fraîche 179
Orecchiette with pork, fennel and milk ragù 186
Borlotti, browned onions and sausages 188
Chicken barley 196
Pork belly, butter beans and deli olives 198
Miso-braised duck legs, buckwheat and squash 195
Bitter chocolate and halva bread and butter pudding 203
Three-cheese, chickpea and kale soup 210
Swede, sage and Cheddar gratin 215
Chorizo and blue-cheese leeks 227
Tarragon chicken with bread sauce 221

Something to share

Burrata with burnt peaches and basil 17
Grand aioli 44
Poussin, artichoke and pea traybake 42
Cantonese-style steamed white fish with pea
  shoot and garlic asparagus 46
Papaya, lychee and Thai basil fruit salad with
  anise syrup 49
Agrodolce squash platter 68
Sweet and sour vegetable puff tart 70
Buttermilk chicken with sour watermelon salad
  72
Pickled walnut-braised shallots, steak and rocket
  salad 80
Cherry and apricot slab pie 83
Buttermilk pudding with sharp fruits 86
Brown-sugar meringues, tamarind and blood
  orange 82
Many chilli pepper squid 108
Suya and baked plantain with pepper relish 112
'Nduja spatchcock chicken 123
Orange and scotch bonnet paletas 128
Sweet-spiced peppercorn cashews 136
Curry leaf mussels and fries 150
Ricotta fritters with coconut and makrut lime
  chocolate sauce 164
Mushroom, kale and tarragon lasagne 190
Cuttlefish rice and romesco 192
Bitter chocolate and halva bread and butter
  pudding 203
British Farmhouse cheese and tomato tart 219
Cavolo nero and ricotta conchiglioni in a
  Gorgonzola sauce 231
Berkswell, ham and pea suet pie 234
Honeyed Basque cheesecake 236

–

Something to eat solo

Slow-cooked, minted courgettes with white
  beans and fresh cheese 28
Fridge-drawer pickles 56
Pickled mussels 59
Charred mackerel rice bowls with ginger-pickled
  rhubarb 71
Chipotle tomatoes and sardines on toast 94
Kimchi jeon 96

Tteokbokki rice cakes 97
Instant-ish geki kara ramen 104
Sriracha and lemon linguine with chilli
  pangrattato 107
Haggis wontons with chilli oil 98
Mango with chilli, lime and salt 127
Masala eggs 138
Garlic pepper butter prawns 143
Coronation cauliflower 139
Curried brisket noodles 158
Soggy greens and anchovies on toast 175
Soba noodles with sesame dipping sauce 178
Hummus 184
Peanut butter parfait 204
Lamb chops with cacio e pepe white beans 228

Further reading

If your appetite has been piqued by these flavour profiles, and you want to explore those themes, below are a handful of the books that inspire, educate and guide me. Obviously there's crossover (David Thompson's *Thai Food* could happily sit in Fresh and Fragrant, Chilli and Heat and Spiced and Curried), and there are tens of other places to look; this is just a starting point.

–

Fresh and Fragrant

Sam and Sam Clark, *Moro the Cookbook*, Ebury Press (2003)

Diana Henry, *A Change of Appetite: where delicious meets healthy*, Mitchell Beazley (2014)

Anna Jones, *A Modern Way to Eat*, Fourth Estate (2014), and *A Modern Way to Cook*, Fourth Estate (2015)

Clare Lattin and Tom Hill, *Ducksoup Cookbook: The Wisdom of Simple Cooking*, Square Peg (2016)

Marianna Leivaditaki, *Aegean: Recipes from the Mountains to the Sea*, Kyle Books (2020)

Travis Lett, *Gjelina: California Cooking from Venice Beach*, Chronicle Books (2015)

Gill Meller, *Root Stem Leaf Flower*, Quadrille (2020)

Yotam Ottolenghi and Ixta Belfrage, *Flavour*, Ebury Press (2020)

Claudia Roden, *A New Book of Middle Eastern Food: The Essential Guide to Middle Eastern Cooking*, Penguin (1986)

Alison Roman, *Nothing Fancy*, Hardie Grant (2019)

Nigel Slater, *Greenfeast: Spring, Summer*, Fourth Estate (2019)

Sami Tamimi and Tara Wigley, *Falastin; a cookbook*, Ebury Press (2020)

–

Tart and Sour

Angela Clutton, *The Vinegar Cupboard*, Bloomsbury Absolute (2019)

Mark Diacono, *Sour: the magical element that will transform your cooking*, Quadrille (2019)

Thom Eagle, *Summer's Lease: How to Cook Without Heat*, Quadrille (2020)

Olia Hercules, *Summer Kitchens: Recipes and Reminiscences from Every Corner of Ukraine*, Bloomsbury Publishing (2020)

Catherine Phipps, *Citrus: Recipes That Celebrate the Sour and the Sweet*, Quadrille (2020)

Kay Plunkett-Hogge, *Baan: Recipes and stories from my Thai home*, Pavilion Books (2019)

Phia Sing, *Traditional Recipes of Laos*, Prospect Books (1995)

Rene Redzepi and David Zilber, *The Noma Guide to Fermentation (Foundations of Flavor)*, Artisan Publishers (2018)

–

Chilli and Heat

Zoe Adjonyoh, *Zoe's Ghana Kitchen*, Mitchell Beazley (2017)

Lope Ariyo, *Hibiscus*, Harper Collins (2017)

www.betumi.com

Jordan Bourke and Rejina Pyo, *Our Korean Kitchen*, Weidenfeld & Nicolson (2015)

Fuchsia Dunlop, *The Food of Sichuan*, Bloomsbury Publishing (2019)

Diana Kennedy, *The Essential Cuisines of Mexico*, Clarkson Potter (2000)

Enrique Olveira, *Tu Casa Mi Casa*, Phaidon (2019)

www.redhousespice.com

Andy Ricker, *Pok Pok: Food and Stories from the Streets, Homes, and Roadside Restaurants of Thailand*, Ten Speed Press (2013)

Lee Tiernan, *Black Axe Mangal*, Phaidon (2019)

David Thompson, *Thai Food*, Pavilion Books (2002)

–

Spiced and Curried

MiMi Aye, *Mandalay: Recipes and Tales from a Burmese Kitchen*, Bloomsbury Absolute (2019)

S. H. Fernando Jr, *Rice & Curry: Sri Lankan Home Cooking*, Hippocrene Books (2012)

Madhur Jaffrey, *Madhur Jaffrey's Ultimate Curry Bible*, Ebury Press (2003)

Asma Khan, *Asma's Indian Kitchen: Home-cooked food brought to you by Darjeeling Express*, Pavilion Books (2018)

Yasmin Khan, *The Saffron Tales: Recipes from the Persian Kitchen*, Bloomsbury Publishing (2016)

Supplier directory

Maria Teresa Menezes, *The Essential Goa Cookbook*, Penguin India (2000)

Meera Sodha, *Made in India: 130 Simple, Fresh and Flavourful Recipes from One Indian Family*, Fig Tree (2014), and *Fresh India: 130 Quick, Easy and Delicious Vegetarian Recipes for Every Day*, Fig Tree (2016)

Charmain Solomon, *The Complete Asian Cookbook (new ed.)*, Hardie Grant Books (2016)

Shamil and Kavi Thackrar, *Dishoom*, Bloomsbury Publishing (2019)

Sumayya Usmani, *Summers Under the Tamarind Tree: Recipes and memories from Pakistan*, Francis Lincoln (2016)

—

Rich and Savoury

Reiko Hashimoto, *Hashi: A Japanese Cookery Course*, Absolute Press (2011)

Georgina Hayden, *Stirring Slowly: Recipes to Restore and Revive*, Square Peg (2016)

Ambrose Heath, *Good Savouries*, Foley Press 2010 (1st ed. 1934)

Fergus Henderson, *Nose to Tail Eating: A Kind of British Cooking*, Bloomsbury Publishing (2004)

Simon Hopkinson, *Roast Chicken and Other Stories*, Ebury Press (1999)

Alex Jackson, *Sardine: Simple seasonal Provençal cooking*, Pavilion Books (2019)

Jacob Kenedy, *Bocca: Cookbook*, Bloomsbury Publishing (2011)

Tessa Kiros, *Twelve: A Tuscan Cook Book*, Murdoch Books (2003)

Richard Olney, *Simple French Food*, Grub Street (2003)

Rachel Roddy, *Five Quarters: Recipes and Notes from a Kitchen in Rome*, Headline Home (2015)

Nigel Slater, *Tender: Volume I, A cook and his vegetable patch*, Fourth Estate (2009)

—

Cheesy and Creamy

Nigel Slater, *The Kitchen Diaries (the series)*, Fourth Estate (2005, 2012, 2015)

Gizzi Erskine, *Slow: Food Worth Taking Time Over*, Harper Collins (2018)

Simon Hopkinson, *Week In, Week Out: 52 Seasonal Stories*, Quadrille (2007)

Support your local independent food shops!

If however, you find your options a little limited, then every ingredient named in this book is available online*. I use:

souschef.co.uk — for a wide range of specialist and international spices, herbs, vinegars, oils, grains and condiments.
belazu.com — for oils, vinegars, grains and things like Lilliput capers.
longdan.co.uk and waiyeehong.com — for Asian ingredients.

For fresh ingredients, the following home delivery options are excellent:

natoora.co.uk — for high-quality, super seasonal fruit and vegetables. Also for other deli and store-cupboard items, such as 'nduja.
allgreens.co.uk — for fruit and vegetables.
oddbox.co.uk — for fruit and vegetables.
swaledalefoods.co.uk — for exceptional native-breed meats reared in the Yorkshire Dales (including all the meat used in the shooting of this book).
philipwarrenbutchers.co.uk and warrens.on-the-pass.com — for exceptional native-breed meats reared in Cornwall.
thebutcheryltd.com — London's best butchers, with home delivery in the south and east of the city.
peskyfish.co.uk — an online marketplace connecting fishermen with home cooks.
hendersontohome.com — nationwide delivery of quality fish and shellfish.
wrightbrothers.co.uk — nationwide delivery of quality fish and shellfish.
secretsmokehouse.co.uk — for smoked salmon, trout, kippers, haddock and more.
soleshare.net — a fish box scheme for Londoners.

Apologies that these suppliers are only helpful for UK readers. I can't give personal recommendations for suppliers in other countries, but nothing I use is so specialist that you will not also be able to shop locally or online for it.

Index

INDEX

253

Acknowledgements

Turning 75,000 digital words and a few vague design ideas into an actual book (this actual book) is a team effort involving loads of talented people. I'm really proud of *Crave*, and grateful to everyone involved:

Thank you Zoe Ross at United Agents for tidying the idea and moving it to reality so effectively.

To everyone at Quadrille Hardie Grant: you consistently publish supreme cookbooks; I'm chuffed to be part of the family.

In particular, Harriet Webster, Claire Rochford and Sarah Lavelle for putting this project together with such calm reassurance and expertise; not least making things work through Lockdowns, Tiers, Teams calls and my chronic indecisiveness. Susannah Otter, thank you but also sorry that you succumbed to the curse of the Ed Smith commissioner. And on a subtly related note, huge thanks to Tamsin English for doing such a grand job with the copy edit – it was great to work together on the second half of a book... I'm sorry I tend to write ten words when one or two or none would do.

Thanks also to Emma Marijewycz, Laura Willis and Laura Eldridge for making noise about the book, and Caroline Proud and Diana Kojik for ensuring its presence on shelves.

It was just words and washing-up until the photoshoot stage. We shot *Crave* wearing facemasks, at a social distance, and in scorching summer heat. But also with good humour and great skill. Anna Wilkins, you found the best bowl ever (and many other ace things). Becks Wilkinson, you're an absolute star – you made it happen; I really appreciate it – and Hayley Marshall too. Sam Harris and Matt Hague – what a set of images. You did a grand job, let's do more.

Also for the shoot: Natoora generously provided fruit and vegetables, and Swaledale the incredible meat; while Sous Chef and Belazu arranged store-cupboard and specialist ingredients; Crane Cookware, your pots and pans are a dream; thanks to Lucky & Joy for the loan of your ace restaurant tableware; and @saltbyjames, I still owe you a beer or two for sending a clattering box of good things down the country at such speed.

Finally, Diana, you give so much to us at all hours; we're very lucky. B, this is your second cookbook now – you're still not a massive help, but I love your enthusiasm and appetite and can't wait to cook more and more with you. And Laura, thank you for everything – your endless creativity is inspiring xx.

Publishing Director Sarah Lavelle
Junior Commissioning Editor Harriet Webster
Head of Design and Art Direction Claire Rochford
Photographer Sam A Harris
Photography Assistant Matthew Hague
Food Stylists Ed Smith and Becks Wilkinson
Food Stylist Assistant Hayley Marshall
Prop Stylist Anna Wilkins
Head of Production Stephen Lang
Production Controller Nikolaus Ginelli

Published in 2021 by Quadrille, an imprint
of Hardie Grant Publishing

Quadrille
52–54 Southwark Street
London SE1 1UN
quadrille.com

Cataloguing in Publication Data: a catalogue
record for this book is available from the British
Library.

Reprinted in 2021
10 9 8 7 6 5 4 3 2

ISBN 978 1 78713 579 6
Printed in China

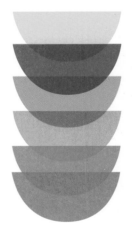